侬 [nE√]

好 [hæv]

nǐ hǎo
你好 – Hello

zài jiàn
再见 – Good bye

xiè xiè
谢谢 – Thanks

bù kè qi
不客气 – You are welcome

shì
是 – Yes

bù shì
不是 – No

láo jià
劳驾 – Excuse me

duì bù qǐ
对不起 – Sorry

míng bai
明白 – Understand

bù míng bai
不明白 – Don't understand

děng yí xià
等一下 – Wait a minute

zài nǎ er
在哪儿 – Where

zěn me qù
怎么去 – How do I get there

gòu le
够了 – Enough

hǎo chī
好吃 – Yummy

hái xíng
还行 – So so

zài lái yí fèn
再来一份 – One more serve

duō shǎo qián
多少钱 – How much

lái wǎn miàn
来碗面 – Give me a bowl of noodle

chī bǎo le
吃饱了 – I am full

tài lěng
太冷 – Too cold

hǎo rè
好热 – Too hot

gān le
干了 – Bottoms up (when drinking)

tīng bù dǒng
听不懂 – I don't understand what you are saying

jiù mìng
救命 – Help me (in emergency)

cè suǒ zài nǎ er
厕所在哪儿? – Where is the bathroom

SUZHOU A CITY ON WATER A PARADISE ON EARTH

苏州 一座漂在水上的城市 一个落在人间的天堂

A work by *iSuzhou Studio*

城市商报《情调苏州》工作室出品

外文出版社
FOREIGN LANGUAGES PRESS

总顾问 Chief Consultant

蔡丽新 Cai Lixin

名誉主编 Honorary Chief Editor

刘文洪 Liu Wenhong

总策划 Executive Directors

陈嵘　黄漪沦 Chen Rong　Huang Yilun

总执行 Operation Director

张俊启 Zhang Junqi

执行运营 Operation Managers

金迪　奚晓平　范小玲 Jin Di　Xi Xiaoping　Fan Xiaoling

执行主编 Chief Editors

黄新绿（澳洲）　夏睿睿 Xinlu Cindy Huang (Australia)　Xia Ruirui

编审 Editors

Steven Bernath (Australia)　Suzanne Hill (Australia)

Michael van Zyl (South Africa)

视觉总监 Art Director

盛诚 Sheng Cheng

版式设计 Graphic Designers

贾茹　王达　陈戌 Jia Ru　Wang Da　Chen Xu

编务 Assistant Editors

付尧　陆禾禾　杨娟 Fu Yao　Lu Hehe　Yang Juan

林沂　姚雨洁　余涛 Lin Yi　Yao Yujie　Yu Tao

联合出品 Jointly produced by

苏州市人民政府新闻办公室 Information Office of Suzhou Municipal Government

苏州日报社 Suzhou Daily Group

上海日报社 Shanghai Daily

Suzhou's beauty awaits you.

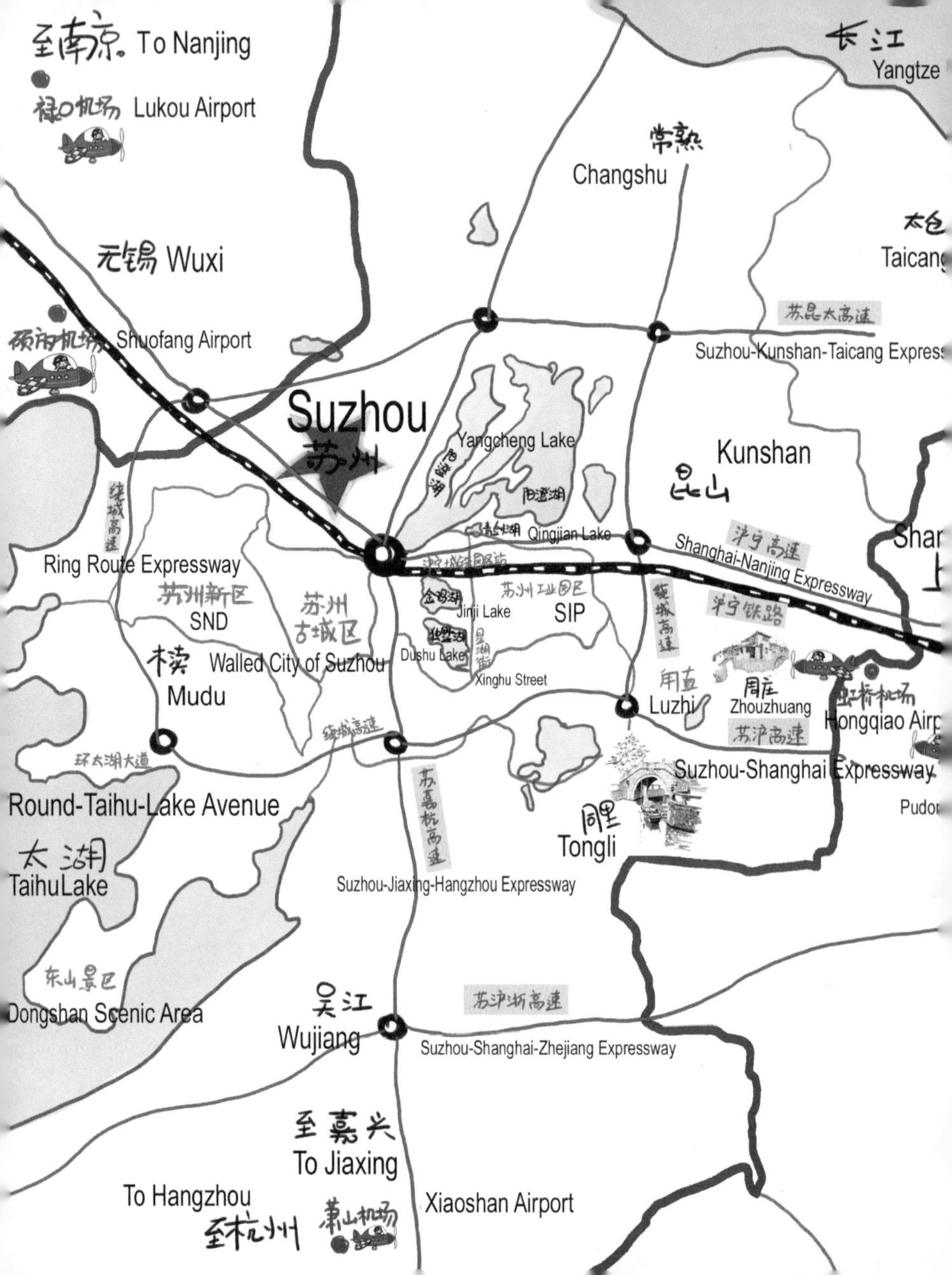

至南京。To Nanjing
禄口机场 Lukou Airport
长江
Yangtze
常熟
Changshu
Taicang
无锡 Wuxi
硕放机场 Shuofang Airport
苏昆太高速
Suzhou
苏州
Yangcheng Lake
阳澄湖
Kunshan
昆山
绕城高速
Ring Route Expressway
Qingjian Lake
沪宁高速
Shanghai-Nanjing Expressway
沪宁铁路
苏州新区
SND
苏州
古城区
Walled City of Suzhou
金鸡湖
Jinji Lake
苏州工业园区
SIP
Dushu Lake
Xinghu Street
木渎
Mudu
甪直
Luzhi
周庄
Zhouzhuang
虹桥机场
苏沪高速
Suzhou-Shanghai Expressway
环太湖大道
Round-Taihu-Lake Avenue
太湖
TaihuLake
苏嘉杭高速
Suzhou-Jiaxing-Hangzhou Expressway
同里
Tongli
东山景区
Dongshan Scenic Area
吴江
Wujiang
苏沪浙高速
Suzhou-Shanghai-Zhejiang Expressway
至嘉兴
To Jiaxing
To Hangzhou
至杭州
萧山机场
Xiaoshan Airport

Experiencing Suzhou

DIFFERENT places on Earth excite our different senses.

For our nose, there is the smell of perfume from Paris and espresso coffee from Italy. For our eyes, there are the colorful reefs and astonishing coastlines from Australia. For our taste buds, there is the delicious Yum Cha from Hong Kong and the rich creamy curry from Thailand.

However, Suzhou does not just excite our five senses, but also our heart.

Do not miss the experience of Suzhou, or you may miss out on your dream.

The Oriental Venice

Only a 30-minute drive from Shanghai, Suzhou is a beautiful and classical city that you won't want to leave. The Beijing-Hangzhou Grand Canal is like the mandolin she plucks gently, and the tears from her distant lover form the Taihu Lake on the southwest of Suzhou. Moistened by these mighty water sources, Suzhou and its 13 million residents are blessed with a pleasant climate and over 8,000 square kilometers of rich and fertile soil.

This is a place that has been flourishing for over 2,500 years.

In the year 514 B.C., the King Wu named his capital after himself, and thus established the original Suzhou. With such a rich history, it is recognized as the third-largest ancient Chinese capital and is now one of the 24 oldest Chinese cities, with a profound and vibrant culture.

With all the modernization happening in the world, the old part of Suzhou still manages to keep its old and ancient town structure, its long-established waterways and its exquisite architectural styles.

This is Suzhou, a wonderland that

was once praised as "The Oriental Venice" by Marco Polo, and described by the French philosopher Baron de Montesquieu as "The Work of Deity".

More than classical gardens

Suzhou needs to be explored with your feet, and felt with your heart.

Yu Qiuyu, a prominent Chinese writer, has precisely described the intricacies of Suzhou: "Here you can sense the times of Wu and Yue, walk on bricks of Qin and Han, see the scenery of Tang, hear the poems of Song, and perhaps even step on your ancestor's footprint on a casual walk."

Suzhou has more historical sights than any other Chinese cities, except Beijing and Xi'an. Take the instance of Suzhou's classical gardens - nine of them have been recorded in the UNESCO World Heritage List.

Hanshan Temple, a sight publicized by a remarkable ancient poem "Mooring by Maple Bridge at Night" ("Feng Qiao Ye Bo" in Chinese), is a place filled with spiritual meanings. On New Year's Eve every year, tens of thousands of people would gather here, not to gasp at fireworks or light displays, but to stand quietly to listen to the sound of the holy bell. Such sound is said to be able to unburden and purify one's mind.

Take a walk on some of the ancient streets, Pingjiang and Shantang, or on the Three Bridges in Zhouzhuang and Tongli, or to the Taihu Lake in the suburbs – Suzhou will never fail to bring you joy and warmth.

The old culture

The most renowned "local product" from Suzhou is probably *zhuang yuan*, referring to prestigious scholars winning the first place in nationwide examinations. During the 1,300 years of running this ancient exam, 3,000 Suzhou scholars made it to the final round and 50 of them won first place. Zhuang Yuan to Suzhou is like Duke to Britain.

Unsurprisingly, not everyone can make it to this elite position. There was this Suzhou guy named Tang Bohu, who was so disheartened by his failure in exams that he indulged himself in poetry, art and travel. Eventually, he turned out to be Suzhou's own "Shakespeare."

Nowadays, his works of art can be easily auctioned for tens of million of yuan. Not bad indeed for someone who failed the exam in the first place.

Suzhou is also one of the origins of Chinese civilization. Six items originated in Suzhou, including Kunqu Opera, Guqin (an ancient stringed instrument), Dragon Boat Festival, all of which have been recorded in the UNESCO list of Intangible Cultural Heritage. In 2004, the 28th Session of the World Heritage Committee was held in Suzhou.

In 2008, World Cultural Forum (Taihu, China), a national organization endeavoring to popularize Chinese culture and encourage cultural exchanges, was also established in Suzhou.

This is Suzhou in a nutshell.

Everyone has a piece of Suzhou in his or her heart. It is a spiritual homeland for all possible dreams. You don't have to stay there all the time, but if you have the desire of being embraced by its beauty and culture, Suzhou is always waiting for you.

Do not miss the experience of Suzhou, or you may miss out on your dream.

My dear friend, are you ready to see Suzhou yet?

The allure

To visit Suzhou is to fall in love.

What is Suzhou?

Local girls are renowned for their femininity. Maybe your future Ms. Right is one of them?

Suzhou caresses one's soul with her peaceful beauty.

Communication here: comfortable and fun

A long history of refinement

Area: 8848 sq. km

Population: 13 million

A city of silk and pearl

Fresh water crabs, they are very yummy!

Suzhou food: artfully constructed and light in taste

A great place to find bargains if you know where to go

It is one of the few places that actually is and looks the same as on TV or in travel books about China.

A glimpse of beauty

Dreaming in Suzhou

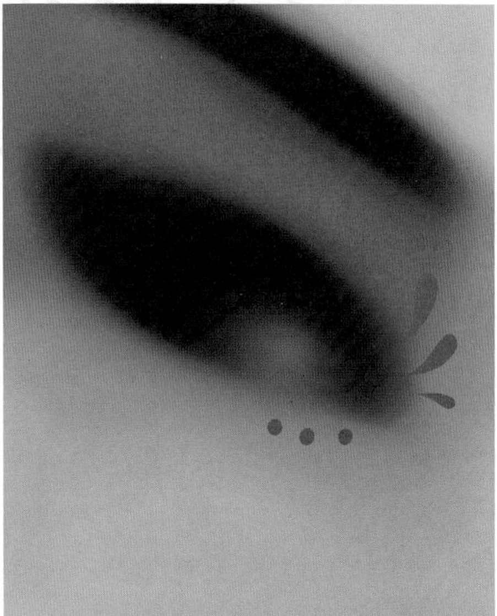

VISITORS to Suzhou are often told of a moving love story, a story that shares the same power and magic as "Romeo and Juliet".

A beauty falls asleep by a peony pavilion and dreams of her lover, a man she has never met. She wakes in despair and has to ask a goddess for help. The beauty finally dies of a broken heart, as she could not find the man of her dreams. Even when she becomes a ghost, she still does not give up the pursuit of her love. Finally the god is moved to help her. To cut a long story short, it is about of the triumph of love.

This story is endowed with a sweet name "Peony Pavilion", the place where they meet in the dream. The beauty is called Du Liniang and her love story has been elaborated for hundreds of years in Kunqu Opera. Kunqu is the folk opera of Suzhou.

The eyes on the cover of the book are those of Liniang, which perceive both the past and future.

This whole book is interpreted in the tone of Kunqu Opera – poetic, romantic, unique and fantastic. It's not an ordinary tourist handbook, but an expression through the eyes of "Petit Bourgeois". With it, you will find the most beautiful sceneries in Suzhou; with it, you will encounter and embrace your lover in a dream.

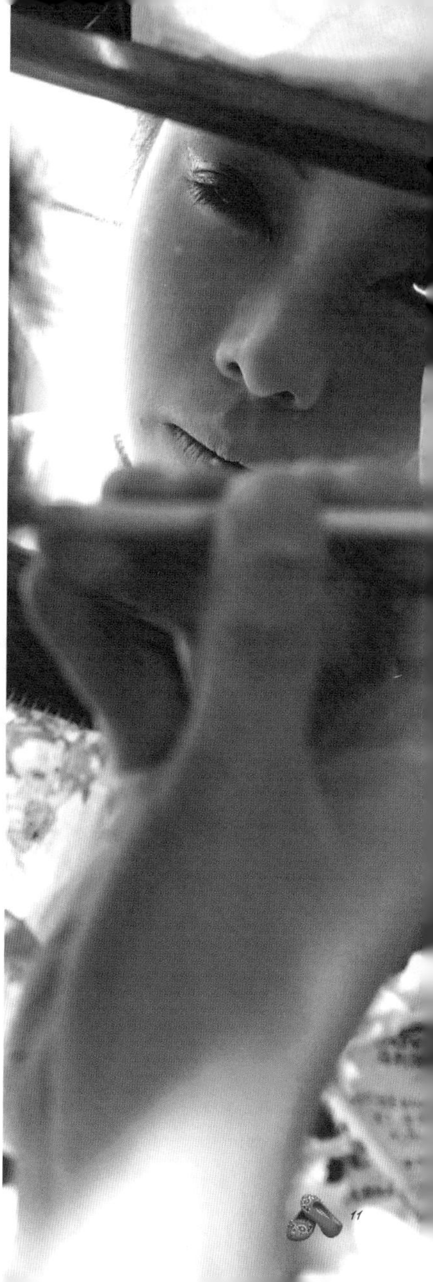

City calender

SUZHOU has many traditional festivals celebrated by specialty foods and an array of colorful events that make it a favorite stop on the tourist map.

Jan.

The Chinese New Year, or Spring Festival, is the first day of the lunar calendar. It falls between late January and mid-February.

Although *jiaozi*, or dumplings, is a traditional Spring Festival food throughout most of China, they are not always part of the holiday fare in Suzhou.

The family reunion dinner on the eve of the Lunar New Year always features soybean sprouts, which symbolize the fulfillment of personal wishes. Meatballs are eaten to symbolize reunion, and egg dumplings in soup portend good fortune. Unpeeled water chestnuts in rice, which add a golden hue, are also tied to the idea of finding gold, or good fortune.

On the first day of the Lunar New Year, the people of Suzhou also often break with the common tradition of visiting relatives and friends. The stay-at-home practice dates back to ancient times, when Suzhou residents believed that going out, using knives or opening cupboards on the first day of the new year would bring bad luck. Even nowadays, rice cakes are cut the day before the New Year and rice balls are bought ahead of time from shops.

Welcoming the God of Wealth at Panmen Gate occurs on the fifth day of the Lunar New Year. Beginning at midnight, firecrackers are lit to welcome the god. As dawn breaks, smaller shops end holiday closures and resume business.

Feb.

The Plum Blossom Festival is held in late February or early March in Xishan Island and Linwu Cave at Taihu Lake, as well as Guangfu Plum Blossom Resort. Linwu Hill is surrounded by thousands of hectares of plum trees, one of the biggest and most diverse plum-growing areas of China. In early spring, the orchards are ablaze with red, green and white blossoms.

The festival began in ancient times in Guangfu Plum Blossom Resort. Plum blossoms in the resort were among the best ones in ancient China. The Emperor Qianlong from the Qing Dynasty (1636-1912) is said to have visited the area for six times.

Mar.

The New Tea Drinking Festival starts in late March, when the first crop of Bi Luo Chun tea grown on Dongting Mountains at Taihu Lake comes into market. Many special tourism activities themed around the tea are held in Wuzhong District.

Apr.

The Qingming Festival, or Pure Brightness Festival, falls on April 4 or 5. It is a day when people pay homage at the tombs of ancestors. It is the custom to eat cakes made from fermented glutinous rice in Suzhou one or two days before the festival.

The International Tourism Festival in Suzhou occurs in late April. The annual opening ceremony features a floral boat parade in the moat from Xumen Gate to Midu Bridge,or Jinji Lake. The floral boat will berth and cruise in the area in the following two weeks.

May

The Gods Temple Fair is a traditional public activity held on the 14th day of the fourth month of the Lunar Calendar, which usually occurs between early May and early June. It is said to be the birthday of Lv Dongbin, one of the Eight Immortals in Chinese legend. Nowadays, an annual fair is held along Nanhao Street in Jinchang District. It features stalls selling food, artwork, goldfish and birds.

June

The Dragon Boat Festival falls on the fifth day of the fifth month of the Lunar Calendar, usually from late May to late June. People traditionally eat *zongzi*, a glutinous rice dumpling wrapped in bamboo or reed leaves, as they watch the dragon boat races. The event is also a tribute to Wu Zixu, the founder of Suzhou. The major venue for the day's activities is the moat outside Xumen Gate. You can buy *zongzi* with different stuffings in shops like Wu Fang Zhai on Guanqian Street.

Sept.

The Mid-Autumn Festival falls on the 15th day of the eighth month of the Chinese Lunar Calendar - usually between late September and early October. Apart from the traditional moon cakes and family get-togethers, taro root and Ji Tou Mi, or foxnut, are commonly part of the festivities. Ji Tou Mi, produced in Suzhou, is a soft, sweet traditional Chinese medicine with high nutrition.

Oct.

The Tiger Hill Temple Fair falls between late September and mid-October at the famous Tiger Hill scenic area in Jinchang District. The fair features a parade highlighting folk culture and performance, a dragon lantern show, a lion dance, singing and acrobatics. Visitors also can taste Suzhou traditional snacks, like plum blossom cakes and crabapple cakes, and see traditional artisans at work making handicrafts such as dough figures, hot syrup paintings and fragrant sachets.

Nov.

The red maples on Tianping Hill provide a burst of autumn color that has drawn visitors for more than 400 years. **The Red Maple Festival** goes on from November to December annually. The striking colors are even more pronounced after the first frost of the season. The seasonal display is often called the "Maple of Five Colors" because of the various shades of crimson. The old saying is: The red maple leaves on Tianping Hill belittle those anywhere else.

Dec.

The Winter Solstice Festival on December 21 or 22 is considered a new year of sorts by the people of Suzhou. Some say it's as important as Spring Festival, though that may be a bit of exaggeration. The December festival began in the Song Dynasty (960-1279). At that time, people hung paintings of the God of Joy to pay respect to their ancestors. Children, attired in new clothes, were required to pay visits to their elders. Wives, by custom, were supposed to have dinner on the eve of the solstice at the homes of their mothers-in-law.

Many of the old customs have ebbed away. Today, the event is marked by drinking winter wine at a family reunion dinner. The menu is filled with as many sumptuous dishes as the fete for Spring Festival.

The Hanshan Temple Bell Ringing Festival is held on December 31 in the Hanshan Temple. Starting from 10 seconds past 11:42pm, the abbot of the 1,000-year-old temple strikes the bell 108 times to farewell the old year. The last gong occurs exactly at midnight. The bell ringing symbolizes gratefulness for past blessings and upbeat hopes for the new year.

I

Blending into the classical gardens 2

The Master-of-Nets Garden(4)
The Humble Administrator's Garden and Lion Forest Garden(7)
The Tiger Hill(12)
The Canglang Pavilion(14)
The Lingering Garden(16)
The Hanshan Temple(18)
The Couple's Garden Retreat(20)
The Mountain Villa with Embracing Beauty (22)
Rock turned into enchantment(24)

II

A city called the "Oriental Venice" 26

It would not be the same without water(28)
Panmen Gate(30)
Xumen Gate(34)
Beijing-Hangzhou Grand Canal(36)
City moat cruise(38)
Baodai Bridge(40)
Wumen Bridge(42)
Old wells tell stories from the deep past(44)
Mudu's Covered Wooden Bridge (46)

III

Let our cuisine enchant your palate 50

Let's go eating (52)
Suzhou snacks(54)
Song He Lou(56)
Old Suzhou(58)
Castle Hotel(62)
Suzhou noodles(64)
Wu Men Ren Jia(66)
Tang Gui Hua(68)
Huang Tian Yuan's Gao(69)
Jinjin Bean Curd(72)
Ya Ba Sheng Jian(74)
Cangshu mutton(76)
Da Fang Gao(78)
Cai Zhi Zhai(80)
Hairy crabs(82)
Crab banquet accessories(84)

Seven signature dishes(88)
Ah Mi Xiang(92)
Tian Mi Mi(93)

IV

A curious encounter with Pingjiang Road 94

A lady of renewable charms (98)
Gang Gang, the celebrity dog(100)
Momi Café(102)
Dingxiang Lane, Xuanqiao Lane(104)
Banyuan Garden(106)
Mingtown Youth Hostel(108)
San Wei Restaurant(110)
Fuxi Chinese Guqin Guild(112)
Sculptor finds himself in his artwork(114)

V

La Rive Gauche in the old city 118

Shangtang Street (122)
Ancient Theatrical Stage (124)
Rong Yang Lou(126)
Zi Sun Tong(128)
Sheng Jia Dai(130)
China's Picasso and his Peachblossom Hut(132)
Suzhou Museum(134)
Soochow University(138)
Confucian Temple(140)
Suzhou Folk Custom Museum(142)
Pan Pacific Hotel(144)
Shangri-la Hotel(146)

VI

Stylish Suzhou 148

Old Bookworm(150)
Suzhou's wet markets(152)
Pet Market(154)
Galleries and sources of fine arts(156)
Shopper's paradise(158)
Restaurant 101(160)
Guihua Park(162)
A sweet place for cycling(164)

VII

Jump off the treadmill of life 166

VIII

Fashion code of Jinji Lake 190

The other side of the double-sided embrodiery (194)
Li Gong Di(196)
SSCAC(198)
Harmony Times Square(200)
RainboWalk(202)
Kempinski Hotel(204)
Moon Harbor(206)
Bei Jiang Restaurant(208)
Renaissance Hotel(210)

IX

The beauty of Taihu Lake, in the melodies 214

Fresh air and fresh food await at Taihu Lake (218)
Ming Yue Wan(220)
Sanshan Island(224)
Luxiang Ancient Village(226)
Diao Hua Lou(228)
Bi Luo Chun(230)
Lake food(232)
Red Bayberry(234)
An Oriental Venice without Gondolas(236)

X

Starry, starry night 238

One night in Suzhou(240)
Block 1912(242)
Pulp Fiction(244)
Harry's Bar(248)
Foot massage(250)
It's SPA time! (252)
Night snacks (253)

XI

An earful of Suzhou 256

Kunqu Opera(258)
Suzhou Pingtan (263)

XII

History unfurls its stories in neighboring towns 266

A water town perfect for a walking tour(268)
Tongli(270)
Zhouzhuang (276)
Luzhi(282)
Qiandeng(284)
Jinxi(286)
Mudu(290)

XIII

From Suzhou, with love 296

Qipao(298)
Pearl(304)
Woodblock Prints(306)
Inkstone(308)
Fan(310)
Suzhou-made Furniture(312)
Olive Nut Carving(314)
Jade(316)

XIV

Live in Suzhou 318

Bringing soft serve to Suzhou streets(320)
Find a little piece of Ireland in China (322)
Kunqu Opera? Yes, I can! (324)
Daniel likes Suzhou!(326)
Itineraries
One-day tours, two-day tours, three-day tours (328)

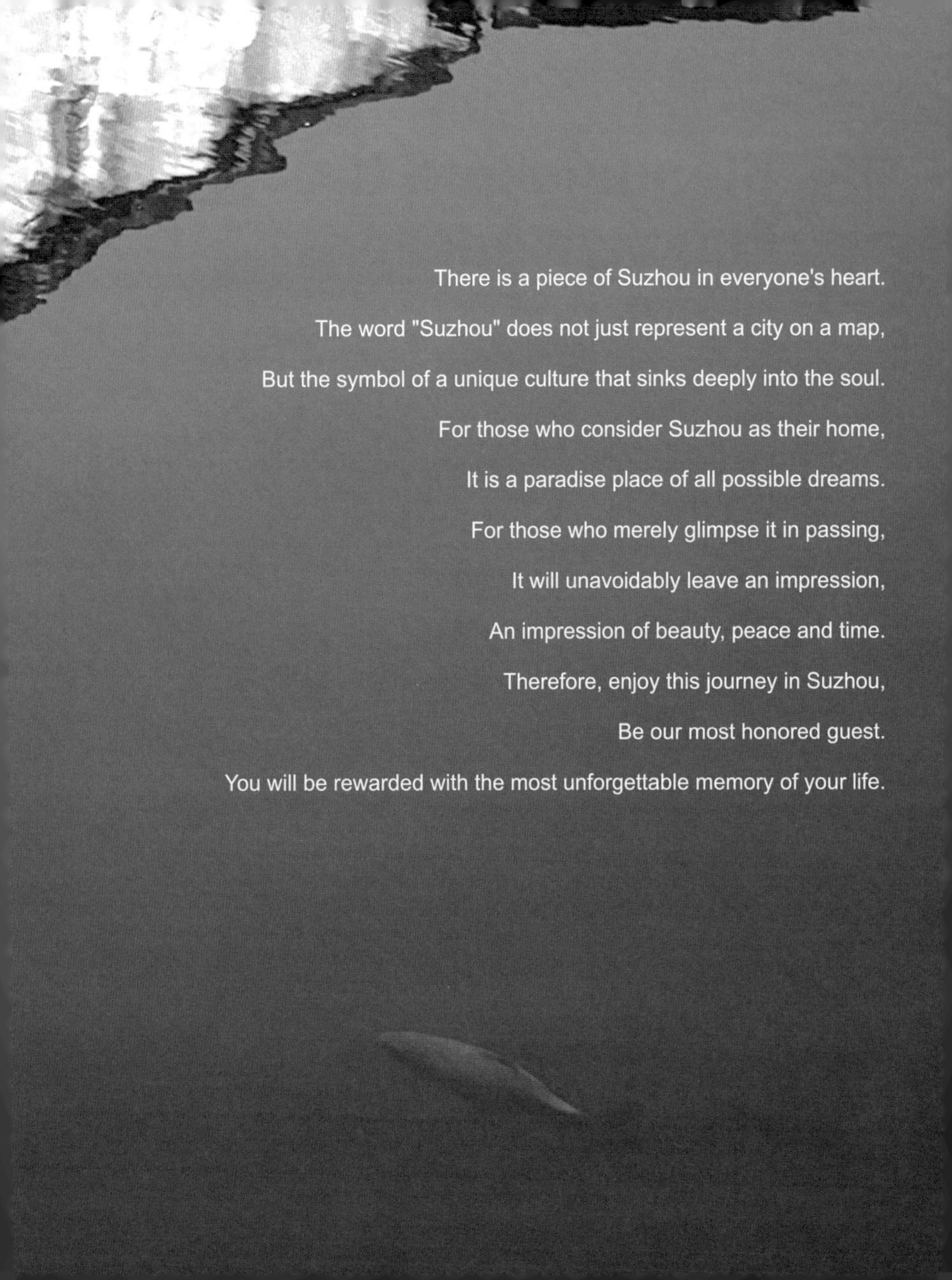

There is a piece of Suzhou in everyone's heart.

The word "Suzhou" does not just represent a city on a map,

But the symbol of a unique culture that sinks deeply into the soul.

For those who consider Suzhou as their home,

It is a paradise place of all possible dreams.

For those who merely glimpse it in passing,

It will unavoidably leave an impression,

An impression of beauty, peace and time.

Therefore, enjoy this journey in Suzhou,

Be our most honored guest.

You will be rewarded with the most unforgettable memory of your life.

Blending into the classical gardens

Without classic gardens,
Suzhou would not be Suzhou.
Without a respite from all the modern buildings,
You would not be able to appreciate raindrops on tree leaves.
Forget everything else!
In Suzhou's classical gardens,
All you need to do is lose yourself.

I

Caught in the net of the master

IT is said that The Master-of-Nets Garden (网师园) is one of the smallest, but the most beautiful gardens in Suzhou. It's in the perfect downtown location of Shiquan Street and walking down the alleyway to the garden is like taking a trip back in time. Walking through the giant doors and into the sedan chair parking area makes you forget that you are in the middle of town.

Some people say once you have seen one garden you have seen them all, but this is totally untrue. The gardens were designed for different seasons and weather. It's true the buildings never change but the gardens take on a different form with each passing season.

Every garden has a place for sitting and enjoying the beauty of each season. I was fortunate enough to have visited the gardens in the winter of 2008.

That year had the worst snow Suzhou had seen in 70 years. I was lucky to have caught the garden in its frozen beauty. Icicles were hanging down from all of the stone carvings above the huge doors. The pond was slightly frozen and there was snow along all of the paths.

You need to see the gardens many times to appreciate their true and complete magnificence. In the winter everything is still and peaceful, the summer is buzzing with tourists and wedding photographers, autumn is full of colorful fruit from the trees and spring is brought to life by all the artists enjoying the comfortable weather.

When people come to visit me, I always take them to this garden. You can drink tea in the teahouse, watch the fish in the pond, play cards, draw the Lotus flowers, study, and practise your photography, which is great when the professionals are in and the models are wearing traditional costumes.

The art gallery displays and sells work by local artists, which is well worth a browse. The friendly staff and local people make you very welcome. It is also a wonderful place to find a quiet spot to meditate, as it is not as busy as some of the other gardens in the city.

(Sharrif Tbealeh)

TIPS

In the evening between March and November you can visit the garden after 7:30pm. You will find its grounds transformed into a living house. Then you can get a feeling of being one of the residents. Walking around the different rooms, you will find people in costume to entertain you. You can listen to some classical Chinese instruments or watch some Suzhou opera (umbrella term for such Suzhou local art forms as Kunqu Opera, Pingtan, etc.). It has all the makings for an unforgettable trip.

Tickets: 30 yuan in busy season (April 16 to October 31)
20 yuan in slow season (November 1 to April 15)

Tickets for the night garden are 100 yuan each (opening time: mid March to late November, 7:30pm-10:00pm)

Add: 11 Kuojiatou Lane

Public transport: Bus No. 2, 47, 55, 202, 204, 529, 931

The Humble Administrator's Garden

This once private garden is now a must-see delicacy of Suzhou. Where large lotus flowers bloom in the summer, the wavy corridor will lead you to many fine pavilions. With distant fragrance coming from everywhere, one afternoon in the garden will be a perfect escape to peace.

这个曾经的私家花园如今是苏州不得不看的精致。在荷花盛开的夏日，弯弯的长廊把你带去精心打造的亭阁。伴随四溢的远香，在园中的一个下午将是完美的脱离尘嚣的宁静。

Two gardens, one great experience

A short walk from the stylishly designed Suzhou Museum is the Humble Administrator's Garden (拙政园). It houses an array of horticultural gems and is a masterpiece in landscaping.

Partitioned up for effect, one is firstly introduced to this hidden world by rounding a large pond that hides a multitude of pathways from sight. The most decorated of these heads northwest, and by following this route one is able to gently meander through floral displays and pagodas, under draping grape vines that in summer are heavily laden with fruit, and arrive at a water-enclosed knoll that acts as a guard post to an interior garden.

In order to enter the

real heart of this site though, one has to firstly pass through a doorway in this initial walled garden. That done, a mixture of blues and greens stretching as far as the eye can see come into view. Waterways, ponds and tree-lined paths constitute the vast interior setting, and in summer the magnificence of this is accentuated by the whites of the lilies and the sun-kissed bamboo that is situated left and right.

The Humble Administrator's Garden is quite simply a stunning proposition. It is also somewhere one can while away the hours and contemplate life in its entire splendor.

As if this were not enough, upon leaving, and but one hundred meters due south lies the Lion Forest Garden (狮子林). This is a very different offering to the aforementioned destination as rocks, not dissimilar to those found in the world heritage sites of Yunnan, take precedence.

Again the garden's central feature is a guarded secret, but this time instead of a preceding garden to navigate one's way through, hallways, rooms and enclosed alleyways act as a taster to what is to come. Doorways

in walls yet again provide the final barrier to cross, but this time the immediate wonders remain hidden.

This is because instead of a quick arrival, you still have to navigate your way through a labyrinth of rocky tunnels and stairwells, albeit with traditionally styled buildings interspersed amongst them. The effort, if it can be termed that, is worth it though, for but a short walk away resides the central water feature. With greenery all around, a waterfall in the background, and a stone ship to the side, albeit not quite as illustrious as the one found at the Summer Palace in Beijing, another magical view meets the eye. With a teahouse located just behind this, and traditional Chinese instruments playing, harmony certainly resides amongst chaos.

Ultimately, central Suzhou should be visited not for the hype that surrounds Guanqian Pedestrian Street , but for the cultural district that is found just north of it where history breathes and nature thrives.

(Gareth Morris)

TIPS

Humble Administrator's Garden:

The garden is suitable for all four seasons. Spring for azalea, summer for lotus, autumn for hibiscus and winter for plums.

Opening hours: 7:30am-5:30pm (the garden closes at 6pm and the ticket window closes at 5:30pm)

Tickets: 70 yuan in busy season
(April 16 to October 31)
50 yuan in slow season
(November 1 to April 15)

PS: We kindly suggest not joining a tour group and not visiting Humble Administrator's Garden during holidays, as it is too crowded. It's better to visit it at 2pm or 3pm on a quiet afternoon, especially when it drizzles and you can appreciate the most beautiful scenes of the garden.

The portable electronic guide machine is available for rent at the entrance. Inside Shuxiang Hall, you can watch a video of the garden and get a tour map in Chinese, English, Japanese, Korean, all for free.

Add: 178 Dongbei Street

Lion Forest Garden:

It's one of the top four greatest gardens in Suzhou and enjoys the long history of 650 years. I.M. Pei, the outstanding architect once played hide and seek there in his childhood.

Opening hours: 8am-5pm

Ticket: 30 yuan in busy season
(April 16 to October 31)
20 yuan in slow season
(November 1 to April 15)

Add: 23 Yuanlin Road

Mystery awaits inside the hill of tigers

THE story of Tiger Hill（虎丘）goes back 2,500 years, when a white tiger lingered for three days around the tomb of the King HeLu after his death in a battle. As one of the most visited historic sites in Suzhou, Tiger Hill was also highly regarded by poets and Emperors throughout the ages.

Rumor has it that, Yu Chang Sword, which is one of ancient China's most famous swords, was buried beneath the Sword Pond in Tiger Hill among 3,000 others. Around the pond, the aura of the thousands of swords rises up, turning the air into shivering chills that can penetrate your skin. It was recorded in historic books that the pond was once drained and people found the tomb's entrance. In 1955, an attempt to drill through and explore the tomb was aborted due to concerns for Tiger Hill Pagoda directly above. The entrance was closed down, and so the mystery of the Emperor's tomb, his treasures and the 3,000 swords live on.

Tiger Hill Pagoda, 1,400 years old, has survived dozens of conflagrations. Originally a wooden structure, the pagoda now has seven levels, is octagonal and entirely made of bricks, weighing some 6,000 tons. If not for the wisdom of experts in ancient architecture, this

pagoda would have collapsed due to its increasing inclination. Tremendous amounts of historical treasures have been retrieved from the pagoda's secret chambers in modern times, including bronze Buddha and celadon vases.

Strolling amongst the kiosks, palaces, pagodas, temples and bridges, hearing the sound of springs flowing down the rocks, you will surely feel an aesthetic rush. This is the true art of Tiger Hill, unique as it is, though portrayed by numerous poets and artists, it can never be fully revealed to you without you experiencing it for yourself.

(Zhang Mengyuan)

TIPS

Tickets: 40 yuan (June 1 to August 31, December 1 to February 28/29)

60 yuan (March 1 to May 31, September 1 to November 30)

Add: Jinchang District, Tiger Hill Scenic Area

Opening hours: 7am-5:30pm

Public transport: Direct buses No. 8, 32, 146 and 949; Tour Bus No. 1 and 2

Temple Fair: From late September to mid October. Folk art performances such as dragon and lion dances and acrobatics are offered. Local products and handicrafts, including dough figurines and sachets are exhibited or sold.

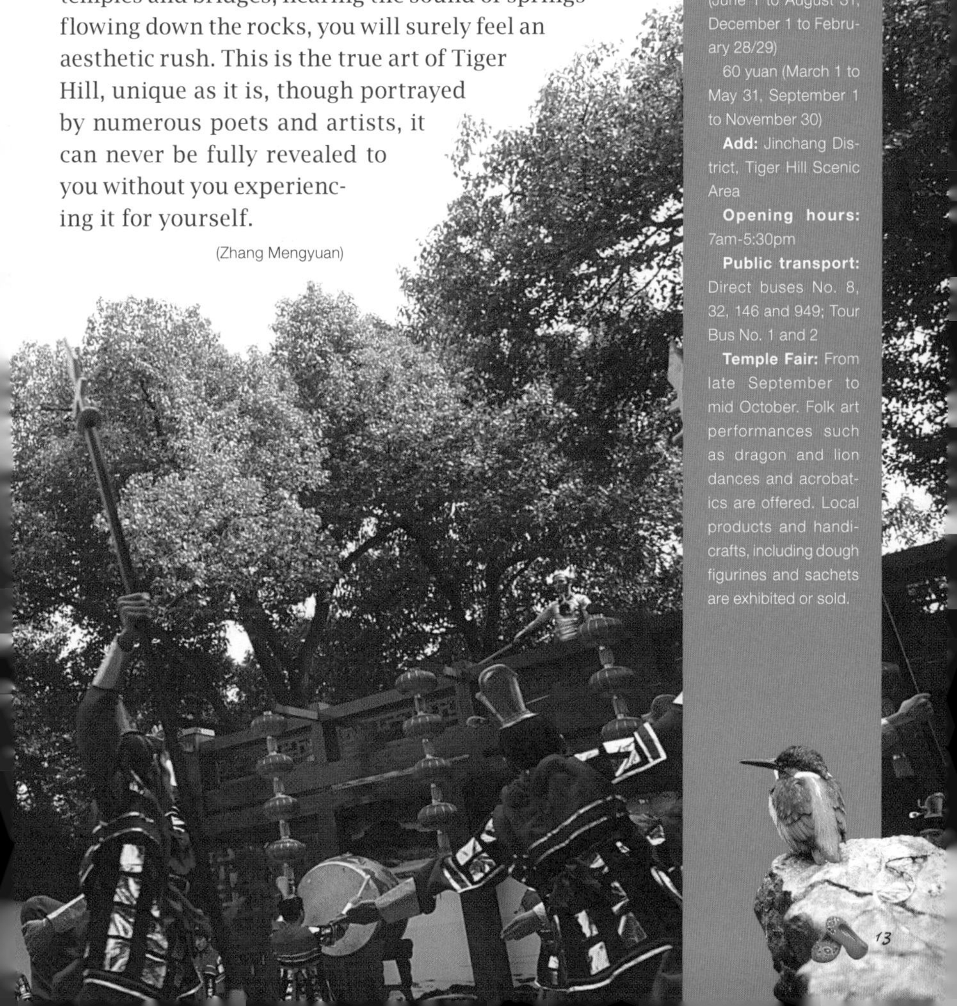

Discreet charm of city's oldest garden

CANGLANG Pavilion（沧浪亭）is one of Suzhou's most famous sights, but it is hardly visited by the many tourists flocking every day to experience the ancient city's charms. One of the reasons is its discreet location off busy Renmin Road: though easy to find, it does require a trip through heavy traffic and a little patience.

Ask the taxi or bus driver to stop on Renmin Road at cāng làng tíng, and follow the signs to the garden. Not all visitors are enthralled by this eerie site; some find it uninspiring and fail to spot its appeal. It is however the oldest garden in Suzhou, with a history of a thousand years. Built by Song Dynasty (960-1279) poet Su Shunqin, the garden draws its name from an even older poem of the pre-imperial period.

Canglang Pavilion has always been a retreat, from the days of its conception. Past the entrance, one is easily flustered by the absence of a centerpiece to this large area, and lush parterres. Let yourself wander through its alleys and contemplate the ponds, past the bamboo grove and up the tiny central hill.

This pavilion is a place to muse in, to sit and

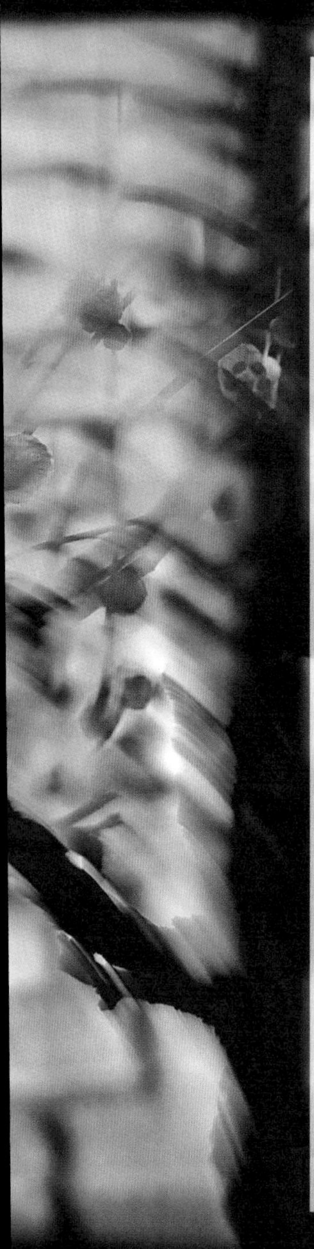

spend the afternoon reading or observing. Music often floats in from a neighboring traditional Chinese arts school, as time stands still and poets whisper through the rustling bamboos at every gentle gust of the moist wind.

Canglang Pavilion has remained an anti tourist trap: a place of genuine depth where photos matter less than impressions, where guidebooks become redundant and millennia of literary melancholy spring to life. You might not have, while in China, the time to learn the country's language and explore its poetic twists. Nor will you probably read the many authors and thinkers who have made the Middle Kingdom a place of such refinement. But if you spend a little time heeding their voices, you might meet them in the wild beauty of Canglang Pavilion.

(Alexis Lefranc)

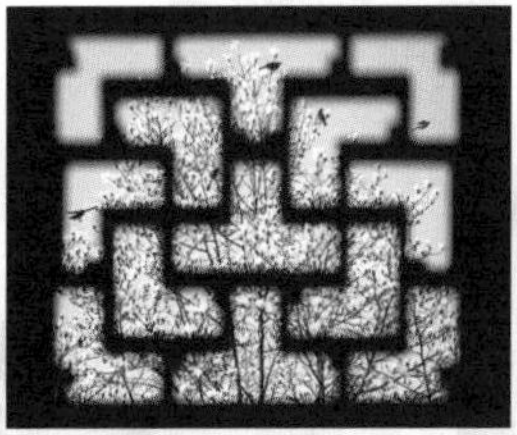

TIPS

Canglang Pavilion:

Tickets: 20 yuan from April 16 to October 30,
15 yuan from October 31 to April 15.

Add: 3 Canglangting Street

Opening hours: 9am-5pm

Linger longer as the feeling grows stronger

ONE winter my friend took me to the Lingering Garden (留园). This was my first visit there. None of us had ever thought there was any place in the world like this garden in Suzhou. It was a kind of beauty that seemed to calm our restlessness and soothe our souls.

The Lingering Garden features imposing scenery and soul-stirring tranquility. It is the beauty in the desolation that may lead people to believe that they are experiencing a prehistoric place. In winter, the cotton-like snow lies upon the windowsills; the broad windows and the frosted door admits a dim light, to enhance the snug cheer within.

Take a stroll along side the winding stream. Browse around the attractive limestone peak, woody hills, and fancy buildings. Peek through exquisite stone gates at the well-kept huts. Observe closely the details that have made the garden synonymous with delicateness and depth. I saw it in the design of a doorway or arch and in the little bridges and quaint balconies. No matter where you look, you would find everyday objects transformed into works of art.

The wind gently murmured through the blinds, or puffed with feathery softness against the windows, and occasionally sighed like a zephyr lifting the leaves. The leaves dropped, and lay heaped up over the roadside, in masses of gorgeous harmonies of green, brown and yellow.

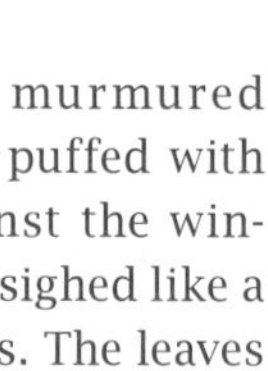

Here, beauty is an all-pervading presence. It waves in the branches of trees and the green blades of grass. It gleams from the hues of the peaks and the precious stones. Go into the pavilion or the tower; spend a winter day by the small fairy isle or the woody hills, and all your little perplexities and anxieties will vanish. There will be jolliness, peace and tranquility with you forever.

(Lin Wenyun)

TIPS

Possessing the typical Qing Dynasty (1636-1912) style, Lingering Garden is renowned for the exquisite beauty of its magnificent halls, and the various shapes and colors of the buildings. It is celebrated for its artistic way of dealing with the spaces between various kinds of architectural forms and garden courts, which has successfully created the feeling of depth.

Special points of interest: Guanyun Peak, Nanmu Palace, Fish Fossil

Tickets: 40 yuan (March 1 to May 31 and September 1 to November 30); 30 yuan (June 1 to August 31 and December 1 to April 30)

Opening hours: 7:30am to 5pm

Add: 338 Liuyuan Road

Public transport: Bus No. 6, 7, 22, 33, 44, 70, 85, 88, 91, 317; Tour Bus No. 1, 3, 5

Find your Aphrodite in Hanshan Temple

IN Greek Mythology, Aphrodite is the Goddess of Love. In China, specifically in Suzhou, the God of Love is a pair of smiling twins named He-He. The first time I saw them was in the form of a portrait found on the bottom of my granny's suitcase.

My grandmother told me the story of the twins, who lived in Hanshan Temple (寒山寺) just outside Suzhou City. A long time ago, two young men named Han Shan and Shi De fell in love with a girl named Xiao Fang at the same time. Out of respect for the girl, and to avoid conflict among themselves, the two lads left home to practice Buddhism. In memory of their decency, Suzhou people named them He-He, meaning Gods of Love and Harmony and worship them so as to bring happiness to marriages.

In Suzhou, a bride will experience the entire premarital routines with excitement and anxiousness. A portrait of He-He that is displayed at the wedding ceremony will assure her that she will be able to build a family with mutual respect and

healthy descendants. The gold statues of He-He are sitting on a lotus plate in front of the Treasure Pavilion of Hanshan Temple, brining love to all those who believe in them.

I decided one day to go to the Hanshan Temple and ask He-He to help me find my Mr. Right. Grandmother told me to look out for any potential candidates while I was in the temple, but I had no luck.

I still believe in the legend of He-He and hope my wishes will be heard. Maybe one day, in the Hanshan Temple, my Mr. Right will be there waiting to offer me his heart.

(Xie Xiongfei)

TIPS

Tickets: 20 yuan
Opening hours:
7am-5:30pm
(from March 20 to October 20)
7:30am-5pm
(from October 21 to March 19)

West Garden（西园）:

Located just outside the western gate of the old city, West Garden has a history of over 700 years. The layout of each pavilion or hall is neatly arranged. The most unique hall is called the Arhat Hall west to the main hall. It has 48 compartments and in total holds five hundred Arhat statues. All of the statues are similar in size but have different facial expressions. This Arhat hall is the only one of its kind in the southeastern part of China.

In Buddhism, Arhat is someone who has gained insight into the true nature of existence and will not be reborn.

Where lovers fall into eternal embrace

THIS is one of Suzhou's lesser-known sights. The Couple's Garden Retreat（耦园）is not that easy to find, and a reward for the adventurous few who dare venture beyond the traditional tourist trail of Pingjiang Road and Tiger Hill.

The Couple's Garden Retreat is one of the spots in Suzhou listed as a World Heritage Site, and rightly so. The garden is in fact a huge town house with several living quarters and halls, accommodating two gardens within its walls.

Tucked away in a fold of Pingjiang Road's northern side, the garden is easily reached on foot. Coming from Pingjiang Road, you enter from the western side and straight into the West Garden. The garden was built and owned by a high-ranking official in the 19th century. More recent than some of the oldest gardens in Suzhou, it encompasses two entwined garden designs, hence the name Couple's Garden Retreat.

Imagine if you will, the lavish receptions and busy house staff, the ladies in silk robes oozing dear perfumes and the blooming rose trees. Imagine poetry readings and songs late into the night, accompanied by local wine and tales of times past. Halls

open through back doors into dining rooms and reception areas. Tiny vestibules with laced windows let you peer into its lush mounds and glittering lakes. Pictures hang on walls and scant displays of calligraphy remind the visitor of the stately nature of this home: proverbs, adages and quotes from classical Chinese authors.

Long, bare corridors form a small maze of ways to the other side of the house, characterized by the large East Garden surrounded by reception halls. Overlooking the central pond, these allow for social gatherings from where much can be seen without revealing oneself. By the pond a platform takes center stage, as if to announce an imminent display of music, grandeur, or untimely embrace.

The Couple's Garden Retreat is one of Suzhou's most powerfully suggestive sights, and an excellent choice for those visitors seeking to escape the crowds and steep themselves in a genuine garden experience.

(Alexis Lefranc)

TIPS

The Couple's Garden Retreat looks like a rectangle, 108 meters long and 78 meters wide. It covers an area of 7,917 square meters and a construction area of 4,496 square meters.

Add: 7 Xiaoxinqiao Lane

Tickets: 15 yuan in slow season (October 31 to April 15)
20 yuan in busy season (April 16 to October 30)

Opening hours: 7:30am-5:00pm

There is no direct bus, but you can walk there from Pingjiang Road. It's really hard to explain how to get there, and the best way is to ask for directions.

Mountain villa and the art of gardening

WHILE studying abroad, lots of my foreign friends have asked me, "What is the Earthly Paradise like?" I always told them, "People there live in beauty; they find and create beauty in their everyday life."

While sitting on the flight back home, I could hardly contain my excitement. This time I planned to visit the Mountain Villa with Embracing Beauty (环秀山庄) again.

Literally a mountain villa embraced in picturesque beauty, the Mountain Villa with Embracing Beauty epitomizes Suzhou's art of garden design. The 7-meter-tall rock mountain is my personal favorite. Gazing at it from where I stand in one of the main parlors of the villa makes me feel as if I were looking into a picture of vast mountains with steep cliffs, deep valleys, intricate caves, and twisted ravines.

The same garden is home to one of the city's oldest embroidery art centers. As you walk through a labyrinth of vase-shaped arch doors and corridors, you arrive at the spectacular

site where dozens of artists sit along windows bent over their work. Needles fly up and down, stitch in and out: turning mere thread into vivid portraits of animals, landscapes and people.

Two artists are working on a two-meter picture of a dragon and phoenix on a yet-to-be-finished yellow background. They have more than 30 types of golden threads dangling before them. I nudge closer. "How long have you been doing this?" I ask one of them. She replies in the typically gentle Suzhou dialect, "Embroidery? 19 years. And this piece I'm working on, about one year and a half, by both of us." When I marvel at the length of time, she explains: "Oh yes, it is, but beautiful things take time to form."

If you are coming to Suzhou for a visit, don't forget this World Heritage Site. Here, the art of garden design will tell you the city and the lifestyle my home folks adore. The art of embroidery will tell you the exquisite work that people of Suzhou have been creating for some 2,000 years.

(Wang Yifan)

TIPS

The Mountain Villa with Embracing Beauty

Covering a floor area of 2,179 square meters, the man-made mountain is the most beautiful among all the man-made mountains in Chinese gardens.

Add: 262 Jingde Road

Public transport: Bus No. 3, 46 and 701; Tour Bus No. 1

Tickets: 15 yuan

Opening hours: 8am-5pm

There are four top embroidery schools in China, namely Suzhou Embroidery, Guangdong Embroidery, Sichuang Embroidery and Hunan Embroidery. It's universally acknowledged that the Suzhou Embroidery tops the four.

Suzhou embroidery is known for its color and needle methods. The embroidery artists have created the skill and technique of "splitting silks and piecing the colors together" from the long-term practice, not only are there abundant colors, but also the feelings, expressions and inherent structures of different images are demonstrated.

Now the double-sided embroidery has already developed into a more skillful stage of three-difference with different colors, different contents and different needle methods on both sides. Besides general requests for the double-sided embroidery, the stitches and silk threads should be taken into consideration to make sure that the colors on two sides do not affect each other, the stitches do not reveal, and to perfect the effect.

Where to find quality embroidery art pieces:

Master Gu Wen Xia's Studio: 334, Yangyu Lane

Master Ren Hui Xian's Studio: 3F and 4F, 641, Shiquan Street

Rock turned into enchantment

CAI Tinghui's Zui Shi Ju, or Drunk Rock Residence, is the smallest of the three private gardens he designed. This one is a maze, like many of the famous classical gardens in Suzhou. It can be a different experience with every trip there.

We were led by an acquaintance of Cai's on a tour of the garden. Entering from the left door, we travelled through a grotto built of yellowstone granite and then along a winding path that twists through a few small caves to a rock stair leading up to the second level.

Suddenly we found ourselves inside a study resembling the rooms of ancient scholars described in old Chinese tales. It featured white walls, black doors and traditional thread binding on the books lining crimson shelves. There were all manner of rocks carved with texts or paintings on boxwood desks.

We walked through a series of small pagodas with dozens more shelves, rocks, books, sculptures and carvings. And then we came upon Cai himself, a sanguine man in his late 50s, with a mischievous hint of the naughtiness, innocence and passion of an eight-year-old boy.

Like so many a successful artist and celebrity, Cai's name card boasts a host of honorifics, telling us he is a famous Chinese epigrapher, vice president of the Suzhou Traditional Chinese Painting Institute and a consultant of the Suzhou Garden Management Office, among other distinctions.

Cai is more humble than all the accolades suggest.

"I'm just a craftsman, with my own idea of aesthetics," he said with pride. "I'm not rich. I just love classical gardens, which allow me to combine my skills with aesthetics."

When Cai was eight years old, he spent most of his time in a classical Chinese garden in Suzhou, home to a friend of his father. He found adventure in the countless caves. He climbed the rocks and ate the fruit of trees in the garden. He was enchanted with his garden world and vowed, "One day, I want to have my own private garden."

Over the years, Cai acquired the skills he needed to do that, from carpentry and sculpture to botany and traditional Chinese painting. He was largely self-taught, with help from elder relatives and friends.

Even today, Cai lights up with excitement when he accompanies us around his 600-square-meter Drunk Rock Garden.

Here, small is beautiful. The garden is tiny compared with many Chinese gardens, but it has encapsulated all the essential elements - pagodas, water, bridges, rocks, caves, trees, flowers and the idea of a distinct view at each step.

"I never designed it all beforehand," he said. "Much of the design comes after the big rocks are in place and I let my imagination fill in the spaces in between."

Cai's largest garden, Zui Shi Shan Zhuang, or Drunk Rock Mountain Villa, on Suzhou's East Mountain Island in the Taihu Lake, was his first and is still a work in progress.

The gardens are open to the public.

(Yao Minji)

A city called the "Oriental Venice"

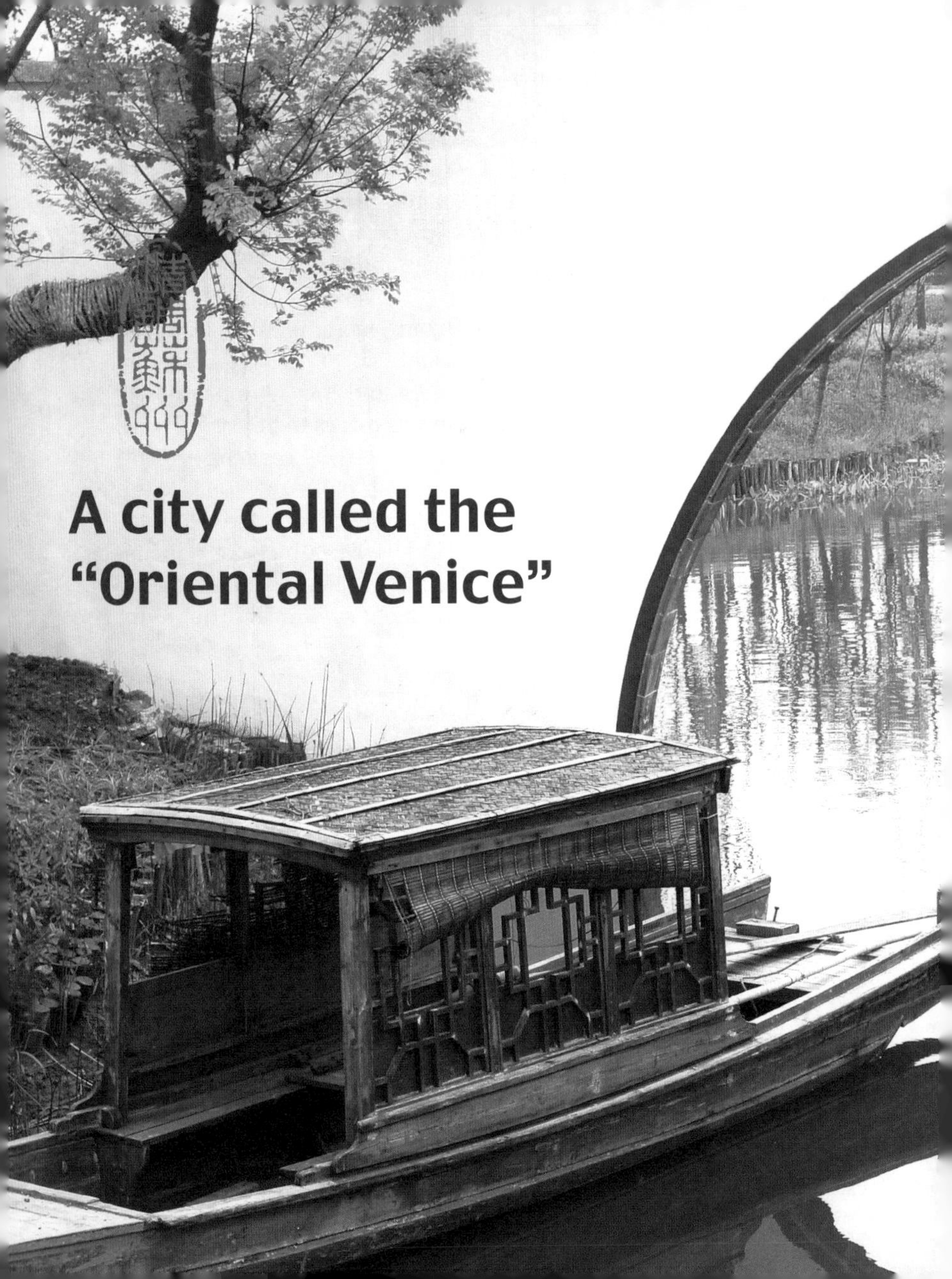

Marco Polo once described Suzhou as "noble, large, and handsome". He marveled at the city's bridgework and architecture. Crisscrossed by many canals, the city came to be known as the "Oriental Venice". Despite modern development, this unique canal network has been preserved and still functions. It carries not only boats, but also the city's history and culture.

It would not be same without water

TWO-FIFTHS of Suzhou's municipal boundaries are in water, including Taihu Lake and the Grand Canal. The city has been called the "Venice of the East." In China, it's more simply referred to as a traditional "water town."

A winding river meanders through the city, and boats can still be seen plying its waters. Suzhou sits on the famed Beijing-Hangzhou Grand Canal.

Suzhou natives love to sleep to the lullaby sounds of rippling waterways.

The city is full of bridges, many old and beautiful. History is written across the spans. Many visitors enjoy taking a day out to visit all the bridges and sense centuries past under their

feet. At minimum, the tour should take in Baodai Bridge, Wu Gate Bridge, Hushan Bridge and Wulong Bridge. Each has a story to tell.

There is something about the combination of bridges and water that is especially evocative on a misty day, when magic seems to hang in the air and a deep sense of being in another world pervades the soul.

Then, too, it's also fun to take a river or canal cruise to see the bridges from an entirely new perspective.

The popular Grand Canal cruise affords not only gorgeous night-time views but also a traditional tea service and a bit of live Pingtan opera performed by a beautiful lute player.

Love of water in Suzhou also extends to several famous ancient wells that are open to visitors at temple sites.

(Chen Ye)

The wall that still stands

THE walls of a city are the first and strongest defense barriers against its enemies. Troy's legendary walls are still standing today and remind people of the tragedy as frequently told in Greek Mythology.

In Suzhou there was also a war, and the walls of Panmen Gate (盘门) were truly unbreakable.

It happened about 700 years ago. The Yuan Dynasty (1280-1367) emperor had his eyes on one of the richest cities in China – Suzhou, and to conquer the city, he needed to break through the newly rebuilt wall.

The walls around the Panmen Gate were unique. They were fortified by a deep moat, with small water gates that allowed boats to come into the city. With all the water gates shut, there was no way that the emperor's army could enter by boat. They were left with only one option – break down Panmen Gate.

Many soldiers had died trying to break it down, but the gate was unmovable. To the emperor's surprise, just when the army was about to give up, the main gate slowly opened. Thinking the city had

surrendered, soldiers poured into through the gate, only to discover that it was a trap. There was an enclosed space between the front gate and the real one leading to the city. With the front gate slowly shutting behind them, the soldiers found themselves trapped between two walls, facing certain death.

The emperor eventually conquered the city, not with his army but through his statesmanship. A few hundred years on, other wars have left their marks, but The Panmen Gate and its surrounding walls still stands. Nowadays, it is the only remaining water-land gate structure in China. It is renowned for its unique structure and rich history. Together with the Wumen Bridge and the Ruiguang Temple Tower, they have become the famous "Trio," one of the most popular tourist attractions in Suzhou.

(Xinlu Cindy Huang)

TIPS

The Trio of Panmen Gate: Panmen Gate, Wumen Bridge and Ruiguang Temple Tower are all connected by the Grand Canal. There were eight main gates in the old city according to history, but some have perished in previous wars. Panmen Gate is the only gate that has been carefully preserved.

Tickets: 40 yuan, with complimentary Suzhou Pingtan shows

Opening hours: 8am-4:45pm

Public transport: Tour Bus No. 2 and 5, or bus No. 7, 30 and 701

盘门
Panmen Gate

To cross the Wumen Bridge, is like to cross the sea of time. Every remaining brick recalls what the fortified gate has seen in the past 700 years. They are standing today as silent witnesses to how the gate has combined water and land to guard the city.

走过吴门桥，就像跨过时间海。每块墙砖回忆着水陆城门在过去七百年中的所见所闻。他们如今守在那里如同无声的见证者，见证城门如何将水陆结合保护着这座城。

Gateway of yesteryear

XUMEN Gate (胥门) is one of the ancient land and water gates that once provided security to Suzhou's walled city.

There is a famous saying in China that includes a reference to the "silver" Xumen Gate.

It is 7.2 meters high and formed by three stone archways. The gate was built in 514 B.C. A few hundred years later, it was closed to provide relief from a serious flood threatening the city. The gate has been restored to become a major tourist attraction in the city.

Nowadays, Xumen Gate is popular as a place to visit during the annual Lantern Festival, when colorful lanterns festoon the area.

Naturally, folklore and history surround the gate's past.

The gate is named after Wu Zixu, a famous general of the Spring and Autumn Period (770-476 B.C.), who is credited with designing the first urban layout of Suzhou as the capital city of the Wu Kingdom. His urban planning survived the test of time and remains basically unchanged today.

Legend has it that Wu lived near the gate and when he killed himself on the king's orders, his head was hung on the gate. There is an imposing stone statue of Wu in the plaza near the gate, a lasting tribute to a man famous in Chinese history.

Like Panmen Gate, Xumen Gate is one of the two surviving old city gates in Suzhou.

Located on the south side of Wannian Bridge, it was officially recognized as cultural heritage in 1982.

Wannian Bridge is only a 30-minute walk from the gate. It dates back to 1740, when the need arose to link two busy commercial parts of the city. In English, the name means "Everlasting Bridge."

It was constructed of purple stone during the Tang Dynasty (618-907) and is a well-preserved edifice with a smooth surface. There are more than 100 stone lion images chiseled on the stone fences on either side of the bridge.

There's plenty of beautiful scenery along the bridge, especially when the dragon boats are out.

(Chen Ye)

TIPS

Xumen Gate is a popular site during the annual Lantern Festival and dragon boat races. The local snack is *zongzi*, or glutinous rice dumpling wrapped in reed leaves.

A grand site to visit

THE Beijing-Hangzhou Grand Canal (京杭大运河) is the longest man-made waterway in the world. Crossing 1,747 kilometers, it is 16 times the length of the Suez Canal and 33 times the Panama Canal.

From Beijing in the north to Hangzhou in the south, the canal passes through a number of provinces and major cities, connecting five major river systems. On one of its southern shores sits Suzhou.

In fact, the city in ancient times figured the canal's inception. In the Spring and Autumn Period (722-481 B.C.), Fuchai, ruler of the Wu state that eventually became present-day Suzhou, was off to the north trying to conquer a neighboring state. He ordered a canal be constructed to facilitate the deployment of troops and munitions.

Work began in 486 B.C., and the various stretches of the canal were finally completed and linked together during the Sui Dynasty (581–618). The canal underwent almost total reconstruction between 1411 and 1415.

Its importance in trade and flood control etched the canal into the heritage of Chinese history. Today it's an attraction for visitors to Suzhou.

The Suzhou branch of the canal originally ran from Wuxi, through Hushu Gate to Feng Bridge, then east to Changmen Gate. Later modifications changed the course a bit. Suzhou's nickname as a "water town" comes from its long association with the canal and its offshoots.

(Chen Ye)

TIPS

Here are some major attractions along the canal:

Hengtang Post House, situated at the intersection of the Xu River and the Grand Canal, served officials in ancient times. Today, all that remains is a pavilion from the Qing Dynasty (1636-1912).

Xushuguan Town, located at the northwest side of Suzhou city and just along the canal, used to be the most flourishing commercial area in China. It served as a tax collection site during the Ming Dynasty (1368-1644). Plans are underway to do restoration work in the styles of the Ming and Qing dynasties to increase its tourism potential.

Tieling Gate, close to Hanshan Temple, was built during the Ming Dynasty as security against invading forces. The three-tier building is the only remaining part of the original fortification structure.

City moat cruise, a moonlight odyssey

IT is impossible to appreciate Suzhou to its fullest without an evening cruise down the ancient moat of the city.

It is one of the top highlights for visitors, an experience not to be missed.

When the streetlights come on and the moon comes out, Suzhou is transformed into a magical place of great enchantment.

I was lucky enough to take a cruise with a beautiful Suzhou girl as my companion.

After boarding, we entered a spacious cabin that is air-controlled so passengers feel cool in the summer and warm in the winter. There was a large LCD TV screen showing music videos and news, and each passenger was served tea.

"Good evening, everyone," said a middle-aged hostess, who was obviously our guide for the evening. "I would like to show you an attractive night vision of this ancient city."

A tingle of excitement was palpable among those in the cabin.

The one-hour cruise started from Xinshi Bridge, passing through Panmen Gate and then under the Panlong, Renmin, Nanyuan and Midu bridges. The return trip passed under the Wannian, Guxu, Ganjiang, Jingde and Nanxing bridges, and the Changmen Gate Drawbridge, before depositing passengers back at Xinshi Bridge.

The scenery along the route was mesmerizing. The whitewashed houses with gray tiled roofs and the greenery along the shores took on a special glow under night lights. From all sides of the cruise ship are sights to delight eyes: Panmen Gate, the statue of Wu Zixu and the dancing night lights of the city.

The cruise guide pointed out some of the history that followed us along the waterway. "It is said Midu Bridge was known as Miedu Bridge in ancient times," she said.

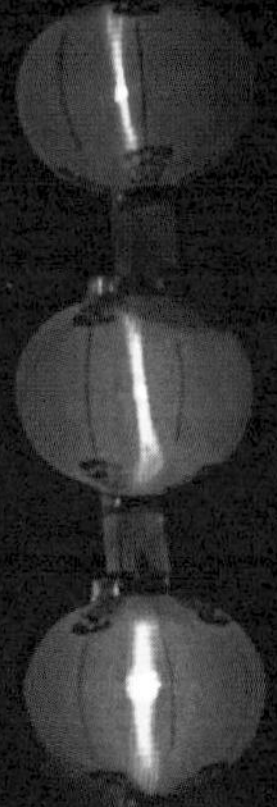

"Mie means 'stop' in Chinese and du means 'cross'. And that's just about the situation that confronted the people who lived here in yesteryear. They had only a ferry boat available to get them across the canal, and the boat was monopolized by greedy businessmen, leaving no transport for common folk."

The story goes that a gentle monk then raised money to build a bridge, hence Midu Bridge.

Adding to the fun, passengers were entertained with a bit of Chinese opera, provided by a lovely woman wearing the traditional cheongsam and playing a lute. She sang Pingtan, the city's famous local opera, in Suzhou dialect.

The music lingered in our minds as we disembarked from a thoroughly pleasurable experience.

(Fei Lai)

TIPS

Opening hours: Daily, at 7:30pm

Tickets: 80 yuan, which includes the tour guide for 30 minutes and live Pingtan show for 15 minutes.

A 'precious belt' for festivals

BRIDGES are part of Suzhou's charm. They crisscross the waterways that give the city a reputation as the "Oriental Venice."

Any stroll through the city will reveal bridges of all shapes and sizes, built from a variety of materials.

Of special interest is Baodai Bridge (宝带桥), one of China's 10 most famous spans.

Where does the name come from? Well, the answer comes when standing on the bridge.

It looks remarkable like a belt across the river. In Chinese, *bao* means "precious" and *dai* means "belt." Legend has it that a local governor named Wang Zhongshu sold his precious belt in order to finance construction of the bridge in the ninth century.

The bridge has undergone several reconstructions. Its current form dates back to 1872. The architectural style of the entire bridge is both complex and attractive, leaving no one to wonder why it was designated a national cultural site and put under heritage protection in 2001.

I was told the bridge is the oldest arch stone bridge among all existing ancient bridges in China.

The residents of Suzhou hold deep feelings for Baodai Bridge. Some say

the bridge improves traffic flow between the Beijing-Hangzhou Grand Canal and Tantai Lake. Others are more esoteric, believing the bridge holds magical qualities when visited during the annual Mid-Autumn Festival.

It is said that during the full moon on the 15th day of the eighth lunar month, a person standing on the bridge will be able to see the moon's reflections in 53 arches.

Baodai Bridge has 53 arches along its 317-meter stone span. It was built without any cement. Local people say the bridge is very strong because of the support of the arches.

Counting from the north side, the 14th, 15th, and 16th arches are high enough to allow boat traffic to flow underneath.

Two pair of stone lions once stood guard on either end of the bridge, but those on the southern side have sunk into the sand of the river and are no longer visible.

The pair that remains has unfortunately drawn some graffiti – no doubt the work of tourists wanting to leave memento messages of their visit.

At the end of the bridge sits the Tantai Temple, built to honor one of the celebrated followers of Confucius. The temple serves as an ancestral hall for nearby villages.

There is a stone pagoda between the 27th and 28th arches of Baodai Bridge, sculpted with gods. Another stone pagoda sits two meters away from the entrance of Tantai Temple, and near the pagoda is a stele engraved with the legend of Baodai Bridge.

(Chen Ye)

TIPS

Admission: Free

Since there are no handrails on Baodai Bridge, take caution while walking there.

Bridging the present and the past in stone

IT'S hard to escape the beauty and folklore of bridges when thinking about Suzhou.

Although Baodai Bridge is perhaps the most famous, Wumen Bridge (吴门桥) is also a sight worth seeing. Of the two, it's survived in better condition.

Wumen Bridge is the main pathway in and out of Panmen Gate. It is 66 meters long and five meters wide, the biggest antique single arch bridge of stone in Jiangsu Province.

I was told the bridge is one of the renowned "Three Scenes at Panmen Gate." It was built in 1084 and later rebuilt during the Qing Dynasty (1636-1912).

It was originally called the Three Bridge because it comprised two wooden bridges on the north shore and one stone bridge on the south.

In 1872, the bridge was reconstructed as a single arch bridge, mainly made from Jinshan granite mixed with reddish-brown Wukang stone.

It's a bit of a walk. There are 50 stone steps on the north and south bridge slopes. Some visitors may feel a bit of puff after the climb

up to the top of the bridge and back.

Standing on the bridge, visitors can watch boats floating gently by and can also see a high pagoda and excellent scenery in the distance.

The great stone bridge, the nearby Panmen Gate city tower and the Ruiguang Pagoda form the backbone of scenic attractions on the south side of Suzhou.

While there, I encountered an old antique peddler, who has been selling his wares at the foot of the bridge for more than 20 years.

"Some of the best years of my life are wrapped up in the area near Panmen Gate," said the silver-haired man, who was wearing a white silk robe and was too shy to give his name.

I stayed and chatted with him for a bit. He said all his antiques come from the countryside. He was a funny old man, but his presence seemed almost an integral part of the charming environment.

Some say Panmen Gate city tower is the best location for sweeping views of old Suzhou, but I tend to think you can't beat the views from Wumen Bridge, with the tranquility of water passing beneath your feet.

(Chen Ye)

Old wells tell stories from the deep past

YOUNG people today can hardly imagine a world without tap water. But in Suzhou, young and old alike often prefer well water for washing clothes, cooking rice and other daily uses. They think it's cleaner.

They like to soak watermelons in a well in summer, using a string bag, because after several hours, the watermelon tastes especially sweet.

There are an estimated total of 600 wells in the old town of Suzhou. Most wells in the downtown area date back about 100 years.

The well with the longest history in the city is located on the south side of Sanqing Hall at the Xuanmiao Taoist Temple.

The current master of the temple kindly offered us a tour to this oldest well.

It's colorfully called the Five Generations Ancient Well, but its history spans more than five generations. The well is believed to be more than 1,000 years old, but its water level is still high.

It is said the well was once a secret meeting place for Taoist priests who believed it gave them energy

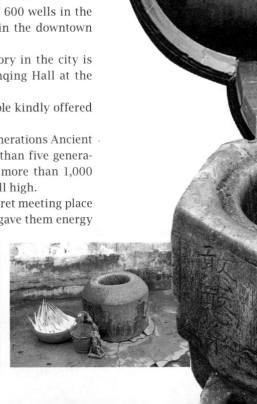

and perhaps immortality.

But that's only hearsay.

Wells, you see, have their own stories to tell.

Liuyun Well, located at the junction of Cang Street and Dingxiang Alley, has a touching tale to it.

According to the story, a banker named Shen Xingshu was rich in material wealth but was unblessed because he had no sons. As he got older, the dream of an heir slipped further away.

Then his luck changed, and a son was born. To commemorate the birth, Shen dug 18 wells in Suzhou.

Liuyun Well is one of those wells. It was dug in 1934. This well has a larger diameter than most, making it easier for residents to draw water.

The old well has been renovated with new granite, though it still retains a traditional look.

(Chen Ye)

History comes alive in relics

ANCIENT towns are part of the celebrated charm of Suzhou and a must-stop on any tour of the city.

Mudu (木渎) is a famous water town located southwest of Suzhou proper, nestled in hills by the Taihu Lake.

Dating back 2,500 years, the township is steeped in history. Legend has it that Xi Shi, one of China's ancient "Four Beauties," lived here as a concubine of Fuchai, king of the Wu Kingdom.

Later, Emperor Qianlong of the Qing Dynasty (1636-1912) is said to have been so enchanted with this place that he visited it six times, listening to opera in the city's famous gardens.

Ten gardens built during the Ming and Qing dynasties have been well preserved and are open to the public. Many a film crew has used the gardens as backdrops for period movies.

Yanjia Garden was originally the residence of the famous scholar Shen Deqian during the reign of Emperor Qianlong. In the garden at Bangyan Mansion, visitors can see rock wall carvings tracing the area's prosperous past. Pavilions, trees and a small lake in the garden give it a poetic, peaceful atmosphere.

On the outskirts of Mudu are mountains with ancient trees, temples and rocks whose distinctive shapes are named after animals they suggest.

The covered wooden bridge in the south of Mudu is a popular attraction. The bridge, which is more than five meters long, features a rare design. The late afternoon rays of the sun cast a serene, timeworn look on the bridge.

The structure has provided shelter from storms for residents and visitors alike over the centuries, and even the legend surrounding it draws on that theme.

It is said the daughter of a wealthy man fell in love with a poor fisherman. Her father, being a magnanimous sort, allowed them to marry. She moved into the rather shabby house of her husband, who soon grieved that he had made her suffer so much for love. He left home, in his small boat, determined to make something of himself and return with riches. She stood every day at the shore, waiting for his return. A carpenter working for her father, moved by her lonely vigil with sadness, finally built the bridge to protect her from the rain.

(Fei Lai)

TIPS

Admission to Mudu Ancient Street is 60 yuan.

Two five-star hotels, four four-star hotels and almost 10 holiday resorts offer accommodation ranging from 100 yuan to 800 yuan a night.

The Zi Lan Xiao Zhu hotel at the entrance of the township is recommended for its decorative Ming and Qing styles. Its luxury rooms feature mahogany furniture.

Tel: 0512-6679 5905

China Garden Hotel (0512-6625 6666) and Tianping Grand Hotel Suzhou (0512-6626 8888) are both four-star hotels.

Shopping in Mudu can be fun. The town is filled with local crafts, including intricate embroidered goods. Food specialties include Qian Sheng Yuan pancakes that are stuffed with black dates, paste and sesame, fresh lake shrimp and fish.

Let our cuisine enchant your palate

Good food leaves a deep, lasting impression. Suzhou's cuisine offers tempting dishes of different ingredients and unique flavor combinations. Whether it is a famous dish from a top restaurant or just a bowl of noodles from a tiny street stall, Suzhou's food will always delight and surprise you. The city is a true master chef.

III

Let's go eating!

NOT all the visitors come to Suzhou purely for its elegant classical Chinese gardens; some others including me are here to investigate the great variety of Suzhou food.

Suzhou cuisine is characterized by exquisite presentation and delicate flavors with subtle sweetness. Taking the famous Song Shu Gui Yu (Sweet and Sour Mandarin Fish) as an example. The chef spends a long time to carve the fish body into a chrysanthemum-like pattern not only for the final presentation but also for the meat to absorb the flavor from the sauce easily and evenly.

Suzhou people are known for their eating specific dishes according to the changing seasons, probably due to their plenty of produce, easy climate and rich gastronomic culture.

"We only eat horse beans during a short time from late spring to early summer when the bean tastes extremely tender, fresh and fragrant," said a friend of mine who was born

and brought up in Suzhou.

Furthermore, Suzhou is one of the few places in China that love using seasonal flower as key ingredients to make dishes and snacks. There is Rose Filling Gao, a cake made from glutinous rice ideally served in summer, and Tang Gui Hua, a sweet paste made of dried osmanthus flower served in autumn and early winter.

In addition, fresh water produce, from fish, shrimp and eel to various water plants such as water chestnut and foxnut are popularly used in Suzhou cuisine.

For those seeking traditional Suzhou flavor, Shiquan Street and Guanqian Street, both located in the center of the old town, are ideal food destinations lined with restaurants featuring traditional Suzhou dishes, small noodle shops boasting Su style soup noodles and snack stores selling Su-style candies that use seasonal fruits, herbs and nuts as ingredients.

The dining environment in Suzhou is quite local characteristic. No matter in small snack shops or classy restaurants, Chinese ink-wash painting or calligraphy is a favored piece of decoration. Pingtan, a vocal art originated in Suzhou, is often used for background music, which may confuse diners into feeling being transported back to old days.

(Gao Ceng)

TIPS

A philosopher once said that when the Chinese had begun pleasing their palates with every imaginable kind of delicious food, French chefs were still eating birds and animals raw in the woods.

Joking apart, there is possibly nothing else that means more to Chinese people than eating.

Each and every Chinese bride would be told time and time again that to catch a man's heart, catch his stomach first. In China, friendship is most often expressed at dinner tables. If you browse through the nation's history, you will find numerous wars fought for food; the most unbelievable one happened several hundred years B.C. when a prince was so angry that he couldn't eat a huge turtle's meat that he destroyed a state.

Suzhou is an indispensable part of China's gastronomic territory. Local meals feature lake-food while snacks boast various flour-made specialties. Suzhou cuisine is known for its fineness, delicateness and sweetness.

Go on a diet? Do it after you leave Suzhou.

The street food of Suzhou

FOOD in Suzhou is as varied and plentiful as it is delicious and bizarre. Street vendor food is cheap and can be found everywhere in the city. It is just unavoidable!

Hot pot is a classic Chinese food and places to eat it are numerous throughout the city. There is a range of different styles of hot pot. Dry hot pot is a dish with meat (chicken, beef, lamb, prawn), chilies, peppers, onions and other spices cooked in a metal pot with a delicious sauce that can be spicy, or not, depending on your preference.

Noodles are of course a very common street food in Suzhou. Here are two of my favorite noodle dishes. Cold glass noodles in a vinegar and sesame oil dressing with cucumber slivers, chili, peanuts and tofu. The flavor of the sesame and chili oil along with cucumber is mouthwatering. Fried noodles are commonplace in Suzhou and are good to have in the colder months. They are mixed with fried eggs, meat, chili and vegetables and cooked in a hot wok while you stand and watch with fascination, anticipating to sample them.

Barbeque vendors appear later in the evening and will cook up sizzling skewered meat or fish and vegetables for you for a very good price. The smells coming from these vendors draw you in from streets away as you follow your nose to the irresistible smell of barbequed food.

(Galvin Yack)

A legendary dish eaten at its legendary source

ASK a foreigner about favorite foods in China, and Song Shu Gui Yu (Squirrel-shaped Sour and Sweet Mandarin Fish) is likely to pop up. Why? The color is attractively bright, the taste is delectable and the shape of the finished dish – with the bushy tail-look of a squirrel – is fascinating when served.

The fish is carefully crosshatched so that when it's fried, it fans out, allowing all the crevices to soak up the sour and sweet sauce.

The dish originated in Suzhou and has a legend to it. Emperor Qianlong of the Qing Dynasty (1636-1912), who was enthusiast about trips south of Beijing, once laid eyes on an altar bearing food for the gods in a Suzhou restaurant and suddenly decided that he wanted to eat the fish placed there. The royal command put the chef in an uncomfortable situation. If he cooked the fish for the emperor, he risked the wrath of the gods. If he didn't cook the fish, he risked the wrath of the emperor.

The chef was nothing if not inventive. He carved the fish in such a way

that it looked like a squirrel after being fried. That way, the gods might not notice that their fish was on the royal plate. The emperor loved the dish, and it entered into culinary folklore.

If you want to try Song Shu Gui Yu in its hometown, visit the Song He Lou restaurant in Suzhou, where legend it the dish was created.

Song He Lou（松鹤楼）is often called "one of the four most famous restaurants in China." It specializes in Suzhou cuisine, with a long menu that also includes Shelled Shrimp in Clear Soup, Deep Fried Eel and Braised Tofu with Crab.

(Zhou Yubin)

TIPS

Song He Lou is located in downtown Suzhou in the middle of Guanqian Street, opposite to Da Cheng Fang. It is a traditional Suzhou-style restaurant, with a reputation known all over China. The average price of a meal per person is at least 100 yuan.

Add: 72 Tai Jian Nong, Guanqian Street

Tel: 0512-6770 0688

Must try dishes: Sour and Sweet Mandarin Fish, Shelled Shrimp in Clear Soup, Whitebait and Water Shield Soup and Braised Tofu with Crab.

You can't beat Old Suzhou

IT'S hard to pick out just one restaurant in Suzhou that exemplifies the best of local cuisine. Some aficionados would nominate Song He Lou or De Yue Lou, two very well-known restaurants.

But many local gastronomes will insist that Old Suzhou (老苏州) is the best of them all, not only for its dishes but also for its reasonable prices.

So we decided to give it a try.

The restaurant, initially opened by celebrated local foodie Lu Wenfu, is located downtown, surrounded by charming residential streets and numerous pubs. It's quite easy to get find. A traditional, cozy interior greets customers with an immediate sense of welcome.

I first asked the waiters about the availability of Shui Ba Xian, the eight seasonal water plants produced locally and commonly featured in true Suzhou-style cuisine.

The eight water plants are: lotus root, wild rice stem, water chestnut, arrowhead, water dropwort, foxnut, water caltrop and brasenia. They become available in the market in different seasons. For example, lotus root is prevalent in August, while water chestnuts predominant in November.

Except for foxnut, which is traditionally

used in dessert soups, the other seven plants are usually stir-fried in main dishes, along with colorful greens and vegetables.

This seasonal dish in Old Suzhou is called He Tang Xiao Chao, or fried water plant. Most of the water plants have a natural sweetness and crispy texture.

Moving on from water plants, there were other tempting courses on its menu. Here are two too good to miss:

Sautéed Shelled Shrimp. To me, a good shrimp sauté requires a clean presentation, with no additional oil and sauce left on the plate and no fishy smell. The shrimp meat should maintain its original tender, bouncy texture. Old Suzhou ticked all the boxes. Its shrimp sauté was clean in presentation, and the pink shrimp meat was served on steamed lotus leaves. The taste was balanced, with a slight herbal fragrance of lotus, and the texture was tender.

Braised Eel with Bamboo Shoots. A classic Suzhou dish. Although many Suzhou housewives make the dish at home, it is often too greasy or fishy. At Old Suzhou, the eel was tender, highlighting its original flavor. Sliced ginger was added to dispel any fishy smell, and the bamboo shoots were soft and rich, absorbing the flavor of the eel and offsetting any fatty taste.

Old Suzhou offers large portions of quality food at prices that won't break

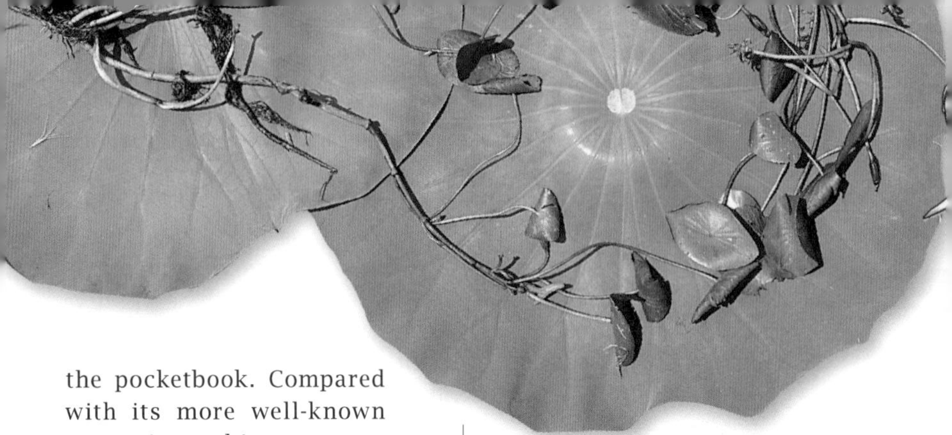

the pocketbook. Compared with its more well-known competitors, this restaurant is delightfully low-key and relaxing. No wonder so many locals choose it for a nice family dinner out.

(Gao Ceng)

TIPS

Old Suzhou restaurant

Add: 658 Shiquan Street (opposite Garden Hotel)

Tel: 0512-6529 1988

Recommendations: Signature dishes of Suzhou cuisine such as Sautéed Shelled Shrimp and Stir-fried Shredded Eel with Hot Oil are truly authentic. Also recommendable is its superb Pork Balls with Crab Meat. A good meal in the restaurant costs only 60 yuan to 70 yuan per person.

TIPS

The eight seasonal water plants (Shui Ba Xian) are available in markets during the following periods:

1. Lotus root, from August to September
2. Wild rice stem, from May to June for spring crop, from September to October for autumn crop
3. Water chestnut, from November to March
4. Arrowhead, from November to March
5. Water dropwort, from November to March
6. Foxnut, from September to October
7. Water caltrop, from September to mid or late October
8. Brasenia, from mid or late April to mid July, from mid-August to early October

Dishes or desserts with Shui Ba Xian as ingredients, such as Sweet and Sour Lotus Roots, Shredded Pork with Wild Rice Stems, Water Dropwort with Dried Tofu Slices, Osmanthus Foxnut, can be found in restaurants at reasonable prices throughout the city.

Hengjie Street outside the Fengmen Gate is a major distribution center. In autumn, you can buy lotus root, foxnut, water caltrop, and wild rice stems and in winter you will find water chestnut, arrowhead and water dropwort.

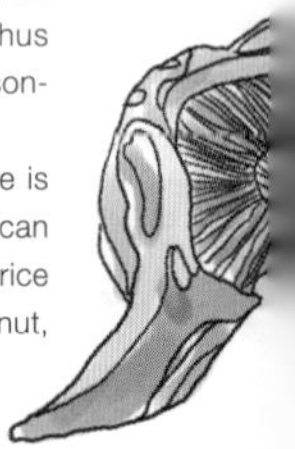

Noodle lovers find a taste heaven

PEOPLE in north China generally prefer wheat-based foods, such as *mantou*, dumpling, and noodles, while their brethren to the south tend to go for rice.

In Suzhou, which sort of straddles the north and south of the country, the locals love noodles.

One local woman recalled noodles as a breakfast staple when she was a young girl.

"But we don't cook them at home," she said. "There are noodle stalls everywhere. You can find one just outside your front door. I still think a bowl of noodles in broth is a good start for the day."

She also confessed that once or twice a week she drives 30 minutes to the Castle Hotel (胥城大厦) just to enjoy the famous ao'zao noodles.

The noodles are a local specialty from the nearby city of Kunshan in Jiangsu Province. The story goes that Suzhou folks were so enamored of the noodles that they brought the recipe from the original ao'zao restaurants in Kunshan and made it their own.

Ao means "magical" and zao means "oven" in Chinese. An odd name given that no oven is involved in the preparation. In Suzhou, is has an even odder connotation because aozao sounds like a word in Suzhou dialect that means "dirty."

Well, "dirty" or not, the noodles are simply delicious. Legend has it that the grandmother in a poor family first concocted the dish because she didn't want to throw any leftovers away. She used fish bones, chicken bones and even fish scales to make a broth in which to boil noodles. Thus was an enduring traditional born.

The Castle Hotel offers two types of ao'zao noodles: one in a red soup of fish, eels and soy sauce; the other

in a white broth made from chicken and duck.

The two soups have distinctive flavors. The red soup is heavier and even a bit sticky. The white has a more crystal clear taste. Which one is better? Well, that's all a matter of taste.

Everyday at lunch and dinner time, the restaurant's dining hall on the second floor is filled with patrons who have come to savor the noodles.

The Castle Hotel also serves other typical Suzhou cuisines, such as shelled shrimp. It is rumored that the restaurant's chef once cooked for China's national leaders in Beijing. No wonder the food is so exquisite.

(Zhou Yubin)

TIPS

Add: 333 Sanxiang Rd

Tel: 0512-6828 6688

Price: noodles 20 yuan; toppings such as fish and duck are 10 yuan; shelled shrimp is 58 yuan.

Tong De Xing's noodle soup

NOODLE soup to Suzhou's people, is like bacon and eggs to Westerners. Breakfast or brunch would not be the same without a hot and tasty bowl of noodle soup with your own choice of topping.

People are very particular about their noodle soups in Suzhou. The temperature of the soup, the type of soup base, the choice of topping, the arrangement of the topping (either on top of the noodle or in a separate bowl) and with or without spring onion, all need to be considered to suit each individual's choice.

It is not hard to find noodle soup restaurants, as they are practically all over Suzhou. Tong De Xing (同得兴), a noodle soup shop that has been around over 20 years, certainly has won a good reputation among all the noodle soup lovers.

Tong De Xing's white soup is made from fresh water ell, pork bones and shrimps, which give the soup a rich yet mild flavor. The best topping that goes with this soup is slow cooked pork belly. The soft, almost melting texture of the pork compliments the chewy noodles. No other noodle soup will ever satisfy you after having this one.

However, the white noodle soup with pork belly is only available from June to September. If you miss the season, don't get upset as there are always other toppings that will surprise you. For example, deep fried fish fillet, grilled fresh water eel, cooked shrimp meat, shredded pork with salted cabbage etc. The list goes on and on.

The owner, Mr. Xiao, is often praised for his devotion to make good noodle soups. He has learned from some of the best masters in this field and managed to develop a recipe that is better than the old ones. His innovation has won him many rewards, but the most important reward for him, is his three noodle soup restaurants which are always packed out.

(Xinlu Cindy Huang)

TIPS

Tong De Xing Shiquan Restaurant:
Add: 624 Shiquan Street

Tong De Xing Gunxiufang Restaurant:
Add: 13 Gunxiufang Alley
(both are more spacious than the original shop, average cost 25 yuan per person)

Tong De Xing (the original shop)
Add: 6 Jiayufang Alley, Renmin Road
(average cost 8 yuan per person)

A dance on your tongue

WU Men Ren Jia (吴门人家) is a fine dining restaurant featuring recipes created during the Qing Dynasty (1636-1912), including the favorite dishes of the Emperor Qianlong.

The old recipes, which fell by the wayside during the "cultural revolution" (1966-1976), have been revived by Sha Peizhi, owner of Wu Men Ren Jia, who served up a signature meal for me to taste.

First was a starter called Huotui Songzi, a crunchy relish of sugar, ground roasted pine nuts and diced cured ham. The blend of nutty and sweet stirred my appetite, and the slight salty flavor of the ham delicately offset the sweetness.

The second dish was Yingtao Rou, a piece of pork - half fat, half meat - that was slowly cooked for about eight hours and

then braised in a secret cherry-red sauce and served with stir-fried seasonal vegetables. The pork had a melt-in-the-mouth texture: fatty but not greasy.

The third dish was the legendary Fish Intestine Sword. A whole fish is grilled and topped with sweet and sour sauce. A short, slender sword is embedded in its intestine. According to Sha, the dish was created by a Suzhou nobleman named Gong Ziguang during the Spring and Autumn period (722-481 B.C.) to be served to a despotic emperor. While serving, our waiter pulled out the sword, just as Gong did when he killed the emperor. Luckily, our lives were spared and our palates rewarded.

For dessert, we had a variety of sweet red bean paste congee, seasoned with sweetened osmanthus. The dish had a silky texture and the taste was delicately flowery.

The dishes danced in my mind for days after leaving Suzhou.

(Gao Ceng)

TIPS

Wu Men Ren Jia

Add: 30 Panru Lane, Yuanlin Road

Tel: 0512-6728 8041

Sugar Congee is 18 yuan a portion, a big bowl quite enough for two to three persons. Snacks such as Pan-Fried Turnip Pancake, Eyebrow Pancake and Ermianhuang Noodlesare popular with patrons. Signature offerings also include local cuisine, including Stir-fried Shredded Eel with Hot Oil, Duck with Eight Delicacies, Pork in Cherry Sauce, Sweet and Sour Mandarin Fish, Wu Men Shelled Shrimp and Sautéed Sliced Fish in Rice Wine Sauce, to name just a few.

Osmanthus gives a flavor

ONE of the joys of Suzhou is Tang Gui Hua, or sugared sweet-scented osmanthus, which originated centuries ago in the small township of Guangfu in Suzhou.

Today it is commonly used across the Yangtze River Delta area as a flavor enhancer, but it is only in Suzhou where every family has a special way of cooking it.

Each time I visit Suzhou, I am always happy to see Tang Gui Hua still popular with daily meals. Its light fragrance evokes childhood memories in me.

Tang Gui Hua is used in traditional Chinese desserts such as muffins, sweet rice cakes and sweet dumplings. Sometimes it is also used in non-dessert dishes. Used sparingly, it imparts a distinct flavor that makes a dish seemed lost without it.

Of all dishes, lotus root with Tang Gui Hua is my favorite. Filled with sticky rice in every hole, the whole lotus root is put in a sweet soup flavored with Tang Gui Hua and sugar, and steamed for one to two hours until it is soft and glutinous. The lotus root is then sliced into thick pieces for serving. It is one of the most popular dishes during the Chinese New Year.

In addition, Tang Gu Hua is used with Ji Tou Mi (foxnut) in sweet soup. It is one of the traditional Suzhou cuisines too good to be missed.

Besides being sweet, the osmanthus, or sweet tea olive plant, can be salty if dried without adding sugar or honey. I rather like the salty version, which strengthens the inborn fragrance of the flower.

(Gao Ceng)

TIPS

The fragrance of osmanthus, the Flower of Suzhou, pervades the city in Autumn. Yaoshang Village in the northwest of Guangfu Town, Wuzhong District is a famous osmanthus attraction.

A seasonal food best served during autumn and winter seasons, Tang Gui Hua is available in large supermarkets as well as Cai Zhi Zhai and Ye Shou He on Guanqian Street.

Come in Autumn and you will see osmanthus; come in Spring, you will see plum blossoms. From mid or late February to early or mid-March, Taihu Lake Linwu Hill and Guangfu Xiangxuehai have the best plum blossoms to offer.

The true taste of Suzhou one pastry at a time

IF you have never tried Macaroons, you cannot confidently say that you've been to France. If you miss Huang Tian Yuan's (黄天源) pastries in Suzhou, you will possibly lose the chance of tasting the most delicious dessert in the world.

In Guanqian Pedestrian Street, you will find many centuries-old shops but only one, Huang Tian Yuan pastry shop, has visitors waiting in line to buy their treats.

Owners of the pastry shops explain that Suzhou is wealthy in glutinous rice, which is made into various pastries after being ground up. Suzhou people are brought up with the sweet, soft, aromatic glutinous pastries and so no wonder they speak so sweetly and gently. Local people value their delicate and exquisite lifestyle, which is also embodied in making pastries, requiring at least 10 procedures.

The varieties of the pastries will dazzle you. Visitors to Suzhou tend to taste all kinds of delicious pastries they can find, but local people seldom do that. They try to follow the Confucius proverb "Eat in moderation."

My favorite, a dual-filled pastry, is a cold snack served only early summer. It's offered only for a short period of time on the market so you may easily miss it. Just as the name implies, it has two fillings. The thin and soft surface of the pastry looks semi-transparent. One bite, and you will first taste the sweet and soft bean paste followed by crisp sesame. The delicious fragrance suddenly activates your sense of smell and invigorates you. It's marvelous how the two fillings blend together so well without any added flavors.

When early summer comes, I

patiently wait in line to buy some dual-filled pastries and take them back home. I love the taste of one flavor after the first bite and then a different flavor after a second bite. Even while writing this article, I can feel the sweet and fragrant tastes in my mouth. My mum often says that children from Suzhou cannot bear to live far away from home, as they will always want to come back for the sweet pastries.

(Yang Jingru)

TIPS

Different types of pastries are available at different times of the year.

Based on the Chinese Lunar Calendar, the following pastries are available at these times.

January - Rice Balls

February 2 - Chengyao Cake

March - Sweet Green Rice Balls

April 24 - Fairy Cake

May - Rice balls filled with minced meat and Dual-filled pastries (sweet)

June 24 – Xie Zhao Rice Balls

July - Cowpea Cake

August – Glutinous Rice Balls

September 9 - Chongyang Cake

October - Radish and Rice Balls

November - Winter Solstice Rice Balls

December – Sweet Rice Cake with Sweet Tea Olive Blossom

Special recommendations:

Sweet Green Rice Ball

Where to buy: when March arrives, almost all the pastry stores and snack stores in Suzhou will sell sweet green rice balls. Besides the most famous Zhengyi brand in Kunshan, there are some stores in the city proper of Suzhou, for instance, Wan Fu Xing and Huang Tian Yuan.

Scones with Sweet Fermented Rice

Where to buy: Cai Zhi Zhai shop, which is famous for its Suzhou-style snacks. The hand-made scones with sweet fermented rice in Cai Zhi Zhai are one of the best. It's available in Guanqian Pedestrian Street. The scone only appears on the market for a short period, usually around Qingming Festival in April every year.

Add: No. 91, Guanqian Pedestrian Street

Tel: 0512-6522 8079

Dual-filled pastry:

Where to buy: Huang Tian Yuan pastry shop. The pastry generally appears on the market in June.

Add: No. 86, Guanqian Pedestrian Street (beside Temple of Mystery)

Tel: 0512-6770 6106

Meat-filled Mooncake:

Where to buy: Castle Hotel (333 Sanxiang Road) and Changfa (65-80 Lindun Road)

These two shops are centuries-old stores selling the best meat-filled mooncakes. When the Mid-autumn Festival approaches, people will be queuing up by the roadside to buy their mooncakes. There are over 50 chain stores of Changfa in Suzhou, selling the traditional meat-filled mooncakes.

Classic bean curd remains true to original recipe

"SPEND 200 yuan (around 30 U.S. dollars) and get two packs of Jinjin (津津) Bean Curd for free." The promotional poster is prominently displaced on a huge board in front of a shopping mall in downtown Suzhou. In Suzhou, using a specialty local bean curd to drum up sales is smart marketing. It's a popular food with many locals.

"While many Western-influenced Chinese children choose McDonald's or KFC for their snacks, some of us still retain our love of traditional bean curd, not only for the taste but also for its health benefits," said Zhang Jie, who was born and grew up in Suzhou.

Jinjin Bean Curd, a kind of dried bean curd, is first deep-fried and then preserved in a sauce derived from various flavorings. Its dark brown wrinkled skin envelopes a yellow honeycomb interior that gives the curd a layer of flavors and textures. The outer skin is comparatively dry and maybe even a little crispy. The taste has a savory richness. The curd is juicy inside, absorbing all the flavors of the sauce. The taste is nutty, almost meat-

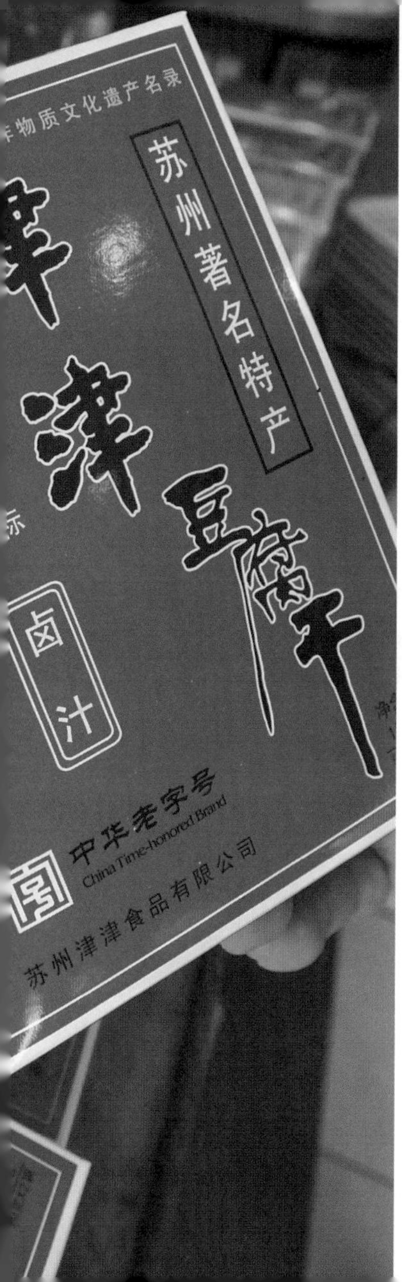

like, and the texture is tender, fluffy and a bit glutinous. The curd is flavored with aniseed, fennel and Chinese cinnamon, which spring forth in an unforgettable aroma when a package is opened. Suzhou locals often accompany this popular snack with warm rice wine. And every serving ends with licking all the sauce up with the fingers.

I had the good fortune to meet Zhang Bomin, a food consultant at the Suzhou Jinjin Food Co. who specializes in preparing bean curd. He explained that sourcing the ingredients and using time-honored recipes are the secret of producing this fine bean curd. In the preparation, precise frying heat is also crucial. Masters of the art with long experience do it to perfection. There is also a strict order in which various fragrances and seasonings should be added, according to the original recipe. What results is a classic flavor from a classic recipe.

The bean curd comes in two kinds of packaging. One is simple plastic for curd that is purchased and eaten the same day as it's made. The other is a vacuum pack that gives the curd a longer shelf life but lessens its juiciness.

(Gao Ceng)

TIPS

You can buy Jinjin Bean Curd at Ye Shou He Food Store, located at 69 Guanqian Street and Changfa Bakery Shop, a bakery chain with more than 50 outlets in Suzhou featuring various local snacks and Western pastries.

Delectable dumplings make restaurant a favorite stop

FROM the very moment I stepped into Ya Ba Sheng Jian (哑巴生煎) (Dumb's Fried Dumplings), I was struck by the clean, home-like environment. It was quite different from other traditional Chinese snack restaurants, exuding a sense of warmth and delicacy. In the restaurant, customers can watch chefs making raw *sheng jian*,

or pan-fried dumplings filled with minced pork, and then frying them to perfection. Before the plump, shining dumplings are completely done, they are sprinkled with sesame seed and chopped green onion, adding both flavor and a tempting appearance.

Sheng jian is a very popular dish in Suzhou. Being somewhat of a glutton for them, I have my own ideas how they should be. A good *sheng jian* must be crisp at the bottom and juicy inside. A tasty meat juice requires very fresh pork mince.

The juice goes spurting out when I bite a little hole on the surface of one of Ya Ba Sheng Jian's dumplings. The hot liquid bursts on the tongue, and it's not so much rich as a little sweet, which is a bit different from other dumplings I have tasted. Sweetness is a common flavor of traditional Suzhou cuisine.

Then I come to meatball inside. It is big, fresh and fragrant. Definitely the best *sheng jian* I have ever tasted.

Ya Ba Sheng Jian does the crisp bottom to perfection. It is neither overdone nor too soft. It has the taste of thin toast with a slight crackle upon biting it. The sound adds to the pleasure of eating the dumpling.

Aside from pan-fried dumplings, this restaurant also serves zongzi, or traditional Chinese rice pudding; Suzhou-flavored noodles with shrimp, sliced eel or vegetables; and toufu jelly. All the dishes are popular with restaurant regular. And no wonder! Despite its fame, Ya Ba Sheng Jian is not content to rest on its laurels. It never lets down its high standards in providing memorable dishes to local residents and tourists alike.

(Gao Ceng)

TIPS

Besides their signature *sheng jian* (8 yuan for eight dumplings), you can also try their wonton, *tangyuan*, a kind of glutinous rice ball with sweet fillings and various Chinese noodles.

Add: 12 Lingdun Road

Tel: 0512-6720 8077

无锡
北桥互通
相城互通
阳澄湖互通
黄埭互通
绕城高速西北段
东桥枢纽
相城区
通安互通
苏嘉杭高速
绕城高速
沪宁高速
天池山互通
苏州市
上海
光福互通
木渎镇
藏书镇
吴中区
西山互通
东山互通
石湖互通
绕城高速
苏沪高速

Mutton - A tasty way to good winter health

WHEN the weather turns cold, it's time to turn your attention to Cangshu mutton (藏书羊肉).

The Chinese believe that mutton, served as soup or in other dishes, has health-giving properties to protect you when icy winds are rattling the windows. The mutton comes from goats.

Cangshu mutton is a local specialty in the Suzhou area. Mutton restaurants normally operate only for about six months every year, but the food is so good that many people don't need a change in climate to enjoy it. Nowadays, you can find the restaurants open as early as the warm days of September.

Cangshu is famous for its unique ways of cooking the meat. Sometimes it is stewed slowly in big barrels. The most popular cooking methods are boiling and stewing.

Served stewed in soup, the mutton is tender and delectable. Its nutrition is often amplified by the addition of aromatic medicinal herbs or other wholesome flavorings.

Cangshu mutton restaurants all use the same logo, so they aren't hard to spot. Many people prefer to drive to the source in Cangshu, though the specialty restaurants proliferate throughout the Suzhou area. It's said the food is best at the source.

(Fei Lai)

TIPS

Restaurants sporting Cangshu Mutton signs are everywhere. A meal usually costs between 100 yuan and 120 yuan per kilogram, but some simple mutton broth can be ordered for only 10 yuan.

Restaurants in Cangshu proper are said to be the best places to enjoy this regional specialty. The town is adjacent to Mudu and has a street dedicated to its favorite meal.

There are also some delicious Shuangfeng mutton noodle shops in Taicang. Take the Sukun Highway and exit at Shuangfeng. Drive toward Shuangfeng and soon you will come across a street of the restaurants.

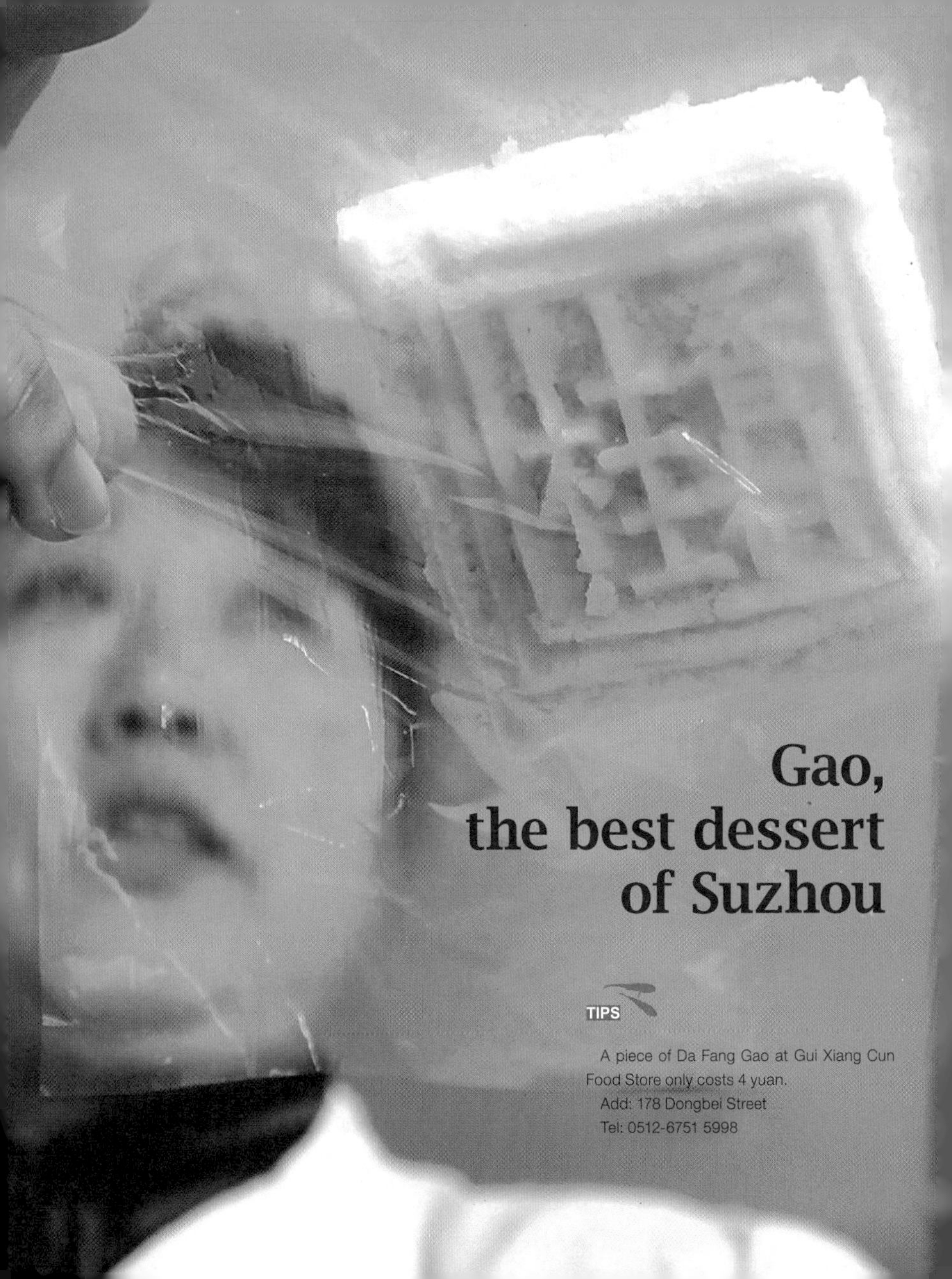

Gao, the best dessert of Suzhou

TIPS

A piece of Da Fang Gao at Gui Xiang Cun Food Store only costs 4 yuan.

Add: 178 Dongbei Street

Tel: 0512-6751 5998

SUZHOU people are said to have a sweet tooth, which is perhaps why the city's desserts are renowned in China. None is more prized than *Gao*, a specialty cake made from glutinous rice, lard and sugar.

When in the city, I met a middle-aged journalist surnamed Yu and his waistline betrayed his particular fondness for the celebrated cake. "I know eating too much of it is not good for my health," Yu confessed. "However, it's hard for me to resist the temptation of the unique texture and flavor." Yu is not alone in his passion for Gao. Walk into any food store and you will see Suzhou locals eagerly buying up large quantities of the cakes.

Suzhou's signature Gao comes in various shapes and colors, often reflecting seasonal ingredients. The cake is moist, tender and rich in sweetness.

Tourists wanting to take Suzhou-style Gao home with them queue up in places like Huang Tian Yuan, a nationally known food store in the city, to buy machine-made, vacuum-packed cakes. But locals prefer to buy gao that is freshly hand made in places like Gui Xiang Cun(桂香村). It's a small shop with a pastry kitchen that turns out various varieties of cakes, especially the traditional Da Fang Gao, which is square, white cake made of rice, with a sweet or savory filling steamed in the early morning during spring and autumn seasons. Its crust is soft and fluffy, while the filling is fresh and silky. Six different kinds of fillings are available: mint, red bean paste, black sesame seed, rose, *baiguo* (a mixture of seasonal fruits and nuts), and meat.

Besides the signature Da Fang Gao, sold seasonally, other varieties of the cakes are available all year around, such as Gui Hua Gao, a glutinous rice cake spread with preserved osmanthus, and Mei Gui Tang Nian Gao, made of glutinous rice, rose and sugar. Both have a moist but fine tenderness, with a bouncy texture, flowery aroma and moderate sweetness.

(Gao Ceng)

Candy is sometimes the best medicine

TIME-HONORED Cai Zhi Zhai(采芝斋) specializes in selling traditional Suzhou-style candies among other popular local food products.

The shop's signature candies include *zong zi tang*, a maltose shaped like a pyramid, and *cui-ong tang*, a rectangular hard candy with pine nut filling.

Quite different from Western sweets, Suzhou-style candy relies on seasonal dried fruits, flower blossoms, herbs and various nuts for the main ingredients, which add layers of flavor and texture.

Four kinds of *zong zi tang* are available, including rose flavored with a bright pink color, strong floral fragrance and smooth sweetness, and mint flavored with a refreshing after-taste. For those who prefer nuttiness, the original flavor comes with an abundance of pine-nut filling.

Cui song tang is popular because of its unique textures, with a crunchy skin outside and a fluffy filling inside. The candy originated in the Qing Dynasty (1636-1912). The crunchy texture reflects an experienced candymaker's precise temperature controls when heating and converting the syrup.

I recommend eating the candy with a cup of Biluochun, a Chinese green tea produced in Suzhou that is noted for its floral fragrance and long, sweet after-taste. That's what the Suzhou

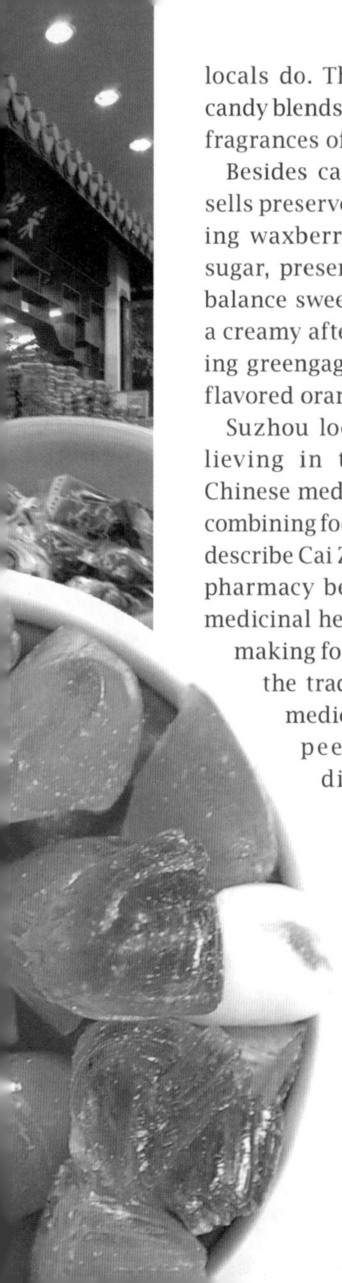

locals do. The sweetness of candy blends with the natural fragrances of the tea.

Besides candies, the shop sells preserved fruits, including waxberries coated with sugar, preserved plums that balance sweet and sour with a creamy after-taste, refreshing greengage and delicately flavored orange peel.

Suzhou locals, firmly believing in the traditional Chinese medicine concept of combining food and medicine, describe Cai Zhi Zhai as a half pharmacy because so many medicinal herbs are used for making food. According to the traditional Chinese medicine, the orange peel stimulates digestion while ginger candy helps warm the stomach and dispel cold.

The store's reputation was no doubt enhanced by Empress Dowager Cixi (1835-1908), who once praised its *bei mu* candy, made from the fritillaria bulb, for helping cure her cough.

The store's stocks follow seasonal patterns. In the heat of summer, *wu mei tang*, a cold drink made from black plums, is sold to quench thirst and relieve heat. In spring and autumn, locals, especially the elderly, queue up in the morning to buy *jiu niang bing*, a steamed cake made from wheat and unfiltered glutinous rice, with either rose or red bean paste filling.

(Gao Ceng)

TIPS

Cai Zhi Zhai
Add: 91 Guanqian Street
Tel: 0512-6522 8079

Cai Zhi Zhai boasts over 300 kinds of food products in such five categories as candies, cakes, roasted seeds and nuts, preserved fruits, salted collections, coming in more than 1,000 different packaging styles. Its *bei mu tang*, *song ren tang*, *zong zi tang*, shrimp roe, ginger candy and soft candy among others, are among the best-known Suzhou specialties.

The retail flagship store is on Guanqian Street while more than 40 franchised outlets can be found throughout the city. Cai Zhi Zhai offers a great variety of food products at reasonable prices, and its gift boxes range from less than 100 yuan to 300 yuan.

Crabs put Yangcheng Lake on the map

WHEN thinking about hairy crabs (大闸蟹), the image of Yangcheng Lake immediately comes to mind.

Every autumn, people from all over China visit the lake to savor what are considered among the best crabs in the country. About three-fourths of the lake administratively belongs to Suzhou.

My mother always tells me that a good hairy crab should look alert and menacing, with large pinchers. The females have juicy roe and extra padding, which is the tasty yellow fat that makes the crab so succulent. To eat a crab, one first pulls off the legs and removes the shell to get to the tasty hot roe. Then the rest of the meat is eaten.

Good crabmeat often tastes sweet. I prefer male crabs because they have *gao*, a special thick, ropy white fat. The meat is traditionally dipped in a sauce of Chinese vinegar and sliced ginger. Crab is considered to be *yin* (cold energy) by the Chinese. The ginger adds *yang* (hot energy) food to balance the meal. In Chinese culture, *yin* and *yang* are two opposing principles in nature, so it might be said a meal of crab carries its own culture code.

The early second half of the year is the best time to enjoy fresh hairy crab at Yangcheng Lake because that is the height of the harvest season. There are numerous restaurants serving farmhouse-style crab feasts near the lake. Although they have a certain sameness in appearance about them, there's no mistaking the distinctive aroma when removing their shells.

Qing Shui An is typical of lakeside restaurants. It boasts a home-like, comfortable environment with

traditional Chinese interior décor. Patrons can order a range of crab sizes, but the general rule is: Bigger is better.

Crab eaten at the lakeside has that unmistakable taste of freshness. It is smooth and tender, with a lovely sweetness. One crab is never enough. The next time you visit Yangcheng Lake, be sure to order a big plateful.

(Gao Ceng)

TIPS

Some small restaurants opened by local fishermen located near Yangcheng Lake are superb places for enjoying fresh hairy crab in season. Every year, from October to November is the best time enjoying the seasonal crab.

Crab banquet accessories

WHEN eating Suzhou's most famous Hairy Crab, you will need to put all your table manners aside. Put on a pair of gloves and make good use of the crab banquet accessories. Alternatively, you can also use your teeth. Before you do that, just make sure you have dental coverage from your insurance.

However, for local people, teeth and fingers are all they use when eating crabs. Some people are so skillful that after taking out the meat, they are able to put all the shells back together, like the crab had not been eaten.

The Dazha Crab has more fat inside the shell compared to sea crabs. This crab fat is considered a delicacy by Chinese people. The meat inside the leg is also very tasty, but requires some work to extract.

To make shell cracking easier, a person during the Ming Dynasty (1368-1644) invented a device renowned through generations, this was a three-piece tool set for opening the shell and cracking open the legs during a crab banquet. This was further developed into the ultimate eight-piece tool set called "Crab Eight" (蟹八件).

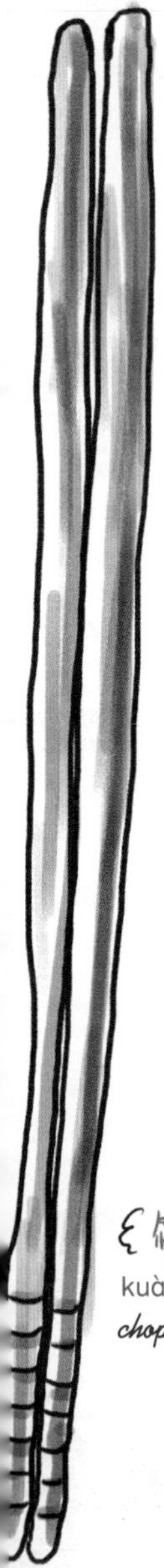

筷子
kuài zi
chopsticks

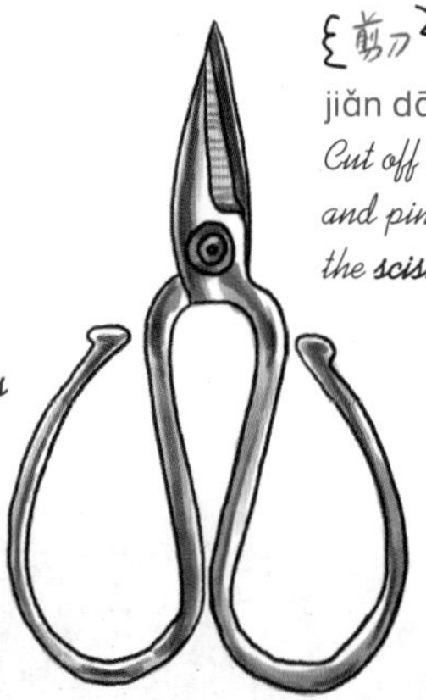

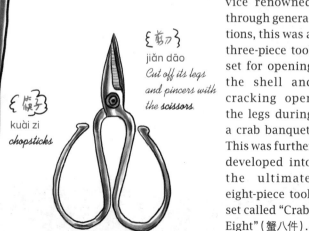

剪刀
jiǎn dāo
Cut off its legs and pincers with the ***scissors****.*

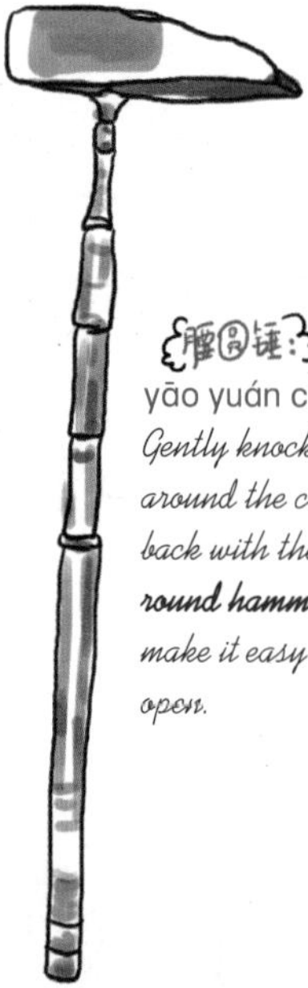

腰圆锤
yāo yuán chuí
Gently knock around the crab's back with the ***round hammer*** *to make it easy to open.*

The set of accessories contains a pair of scissors, a hammer, a spoon, a bowl, a hatchet, a stick, a platform and a pair of chopsticks.

All are boxed as a whole pack.

The "Crab Eight" is now sold more as a souvenir. However, having a set of these accessories may still come in handy, especially after having discovered how tasty the Dazha Crab is.

(Fan Yi)

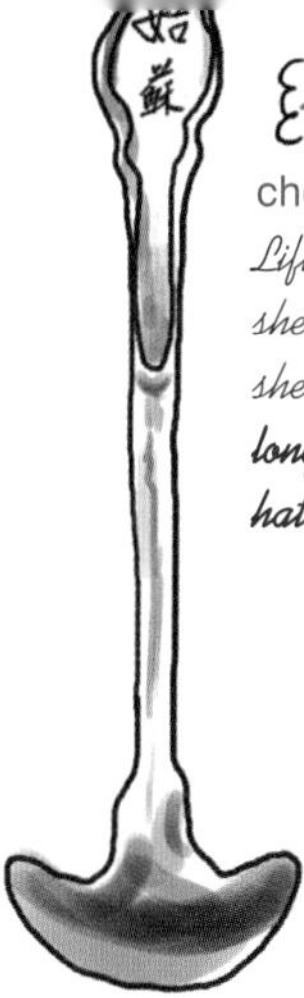

长柄斧

cháng bǐng fǔ

Lift the back shell off its belly shell, with the ***long-handled hatchet****.*

签子

qiān zi

Pick, hook or poke out the meat from its legs with the ***stick****.*

长柄勺

cháng bǐng cháo

Scrape out and eat its roes with the ***long-handled spoon****.*

剔凳

tìdèng

Put its pincers on the ***platform*** *(an iron chopping block) and smash them with the* ***round hammer****.*

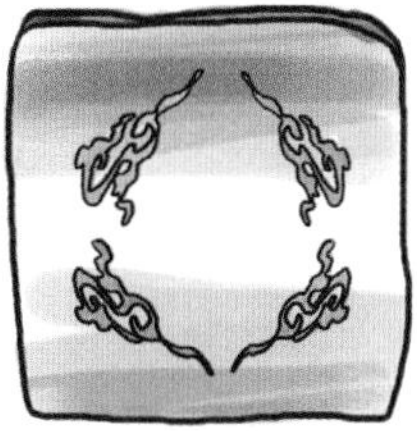

盆

pén

Put its back shell in the ***bowl****.*

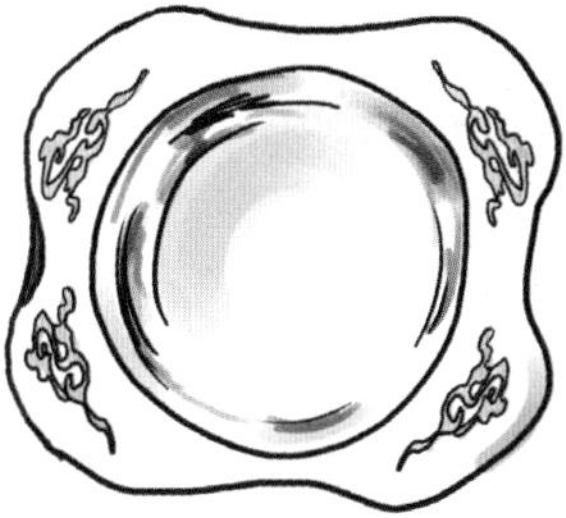

TIPS

Once nearly lost in history, this tool set was reinvented by tradition-cherishing manufacturers in Suzhou. You can buy a set from Gusu Bronze Scissors Ltd at No. 91, Guanqian Road, on the eastern side of Cai Zhi Zhai. They sell a Crab Eight set made of Chinese copper (1,800 yuan per set, in a rosewood case) or stainless steel (400 yuan per set in a paper box, or 600 yuan in a bamboo case).

Sold in the same shop are also brand-made bronze scissors, which is another traditional Suzhou handicraft. Palm-sized with a sharp cutting edge, these special scissors are sold at 60 yuan per pair in paper box.

Tel: 0512-6918 7275

139 6210 5876

A favorite haunt of crabs

"The beauty's leg"

"The beauty's leg" in Yangcheng Lake (阳澄湖) is a scenic spot that provides visitors an ideal vista of the surrounding countryside and an array of farmhouse restaurants with great cuisine. This is a place to throw away the cares of the world and enjoy tranquility and a sense of inner peace. If you visit in autumn, you can treat yourself to the famous local freshwater crabs. There are two recommended places to eat crab: one is the Zha family farmhouse restaurant. Its phone number is 130 5288 1813. The other is the Hu farmhouse restaurant. You can contact them on 139 5240 8185. Both places are located in the center of "the beauty's leg," near the Yangcheng Lake Holiday Resort. The price for two standard-size crabs is 120 yuan, including one male and one female crab. (Yes, there is a taste difference!) You can also buy extra to take home with you.

How to get there: Take the No. 87 bus east from the North Bus Station to the Qingshuicun stop

Lotus Island

Lotus Island is an eco-destination in Yangcheng Lake famous for fresh water crab, yellow rape flowers, sunflowers and Hangzhou chrysanthemums.

The island is another great place to taste lake food. But most of the farmhouse restaurants there don't open until crab season in September.

How to get here: walk north along Xinghu Street and then take a ferry to Lotus Island in the center of "the beauty's leg."

Repulse Bay Street in Weiting Town

Located in the south of the Yangcheng peninsula, Repulse Bay Street is part of the Yangcheng Lake Holiday Resort. There you can find more than 10 restaurants and nearly 70 shops specializing in crab and other lakeside specialties. In addition to the food, tourists will delight in the beautiful lakeside

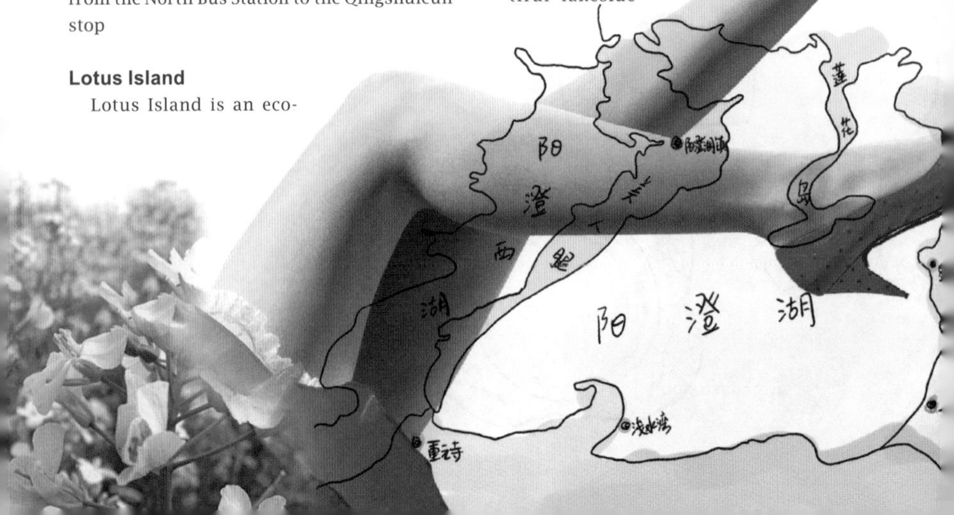

landscape. A quiet stroll is an afternoon's delight. Overnight accommodation also is available.

Tips for visitors: average cost per person for a meal is 30-100 yuan; fresh crabs are available from September to December.

How to get there: Bus No. 109 or 169 to Repulse Bay stop

Yangcheng Farmhouse in Weiting Town

Yangcheng Farmhouse is located on the Yangcheng peninsula next to Yangcheng Lake and the ancient Chongyuan Buddhist Temple. The farmhouse offers accommodation, dining, entertainment and meeting rooms. The farm spans 99 acres, some of it in orchards. The farmhouse dining rooms can accommodate 600 people. The cuisine draws heavily on lake products and on vegetables and animals raised on the farm, including chickens and ducks. The farm also provides areas for fishing, barbecues and fruit-picking.

Lotus House, another restaurant on the little island to the south of the farm, is decorated in rustic simplicity and can serve 150 diners. It's an ideal spot to enjoy views of the Chongyuan Temple and listen to its bell chimes.

The phone number is 0512-6542 7535.

Tips for visitors: average cost of a meal per person is 60-80 yuan. Local fresh crab is available from September to December.

Tel: 0512-6507 7666

How to get there: Bus No. 109 or 169 to the Yangcheng Farmhouse stop

Yangcheng Farm Houses

Yangcheng Farm Houses, located in the Yangcheng Lake town, operate about 50 shops specializing in fresh crab. Most are open from September through December, and many are run out of farmers' own homes. It's a treat to taste the fresh food in a rustic, home-style setting. The farmhouses are managed by the Yangcheng Farm House Management Co.

Tips to visitors: average cost of a meal per person is 50-60 yuan (including crab).

Specialty: fresh crab from Yangcheng Lake and fresh local farm produce

Tel: 0512-6917 3952

How to get there: Bus No. 109 or 169 to the Yangcheng Farmhouse stop

Seven signature dishes

IF you are a gourmet interested in local specialty cuisine, then Suzhou is a must stop on your destination list. I have chosen seven Suzhou delicacies that will provide an adventure in eating not to be forgotten.

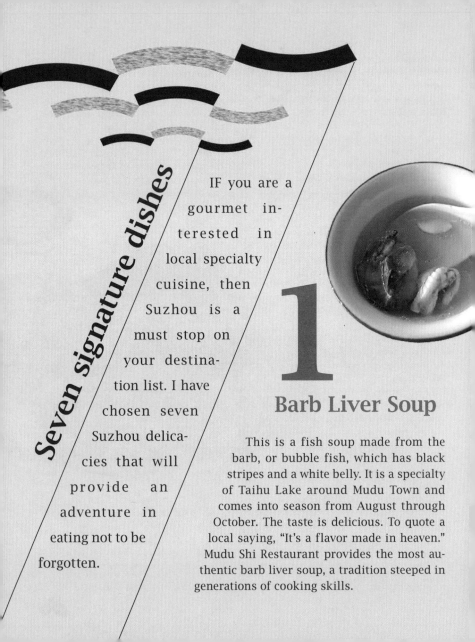

1 Barb Liver Soup

This is a fish soup made from the barb, or bubble fish, which has black stripes and a white belly. It is a specialty of Taihu Lake around Mudu Town and comes into season from August through October. The taste is delicious. To quote a local saying, "It's a flavor made in heaven." Mudu Shi Restaurant provides the most authentic barb liver soup, a tradition steeped in generations of cooking skills.

2

Squirrel-shaped Mandarin Fish

This would rank near the top of famous traditional Suzhou dishes. The fish is prepared to resemble a squirrel. The mandarin fish is noted for its delicate flavor. It is prepared by deboning the fish and then frying it in hot oil before bathing it in a sweet and sour sauce. The end result is fish crisp on the outside, and tender and delectable inside. The dish is perfect in color, aroma, taste and appearance.

The braised mandarin fish served by Song He Lou Restaurant on Guanqian Street is said to be the most renowned. The restaurant has a history dating back over 200 years.

3

Cangshu Mutton

Cangshu locals cook mutton in a special way. It is prepared in a large wooden barrel. The dish is traditionally eaten in autumn and winter and is said to have originated in the Ming Dynasty (1368-1644). Every autumn signboards advertising Cangshu mutton are seen on almost in every corner in Suzhou.

Cangshu mutton uses goat meat as its base. Cooked by locals, it may appear in several dishes, including boiled mutton, mutton soup and stewed mutton with brown sauce. The unique cooking method gives the meat a special taste that removes the normal mutton odor. When local cooks are asked how they remove that aroma, they always shrug their shoulders, uncover the pot and let people have a look. The white soup inside always comes as a taste surprise.

Kunshan Ao'zao Noodles

4

Kunshan Ao'zao noodles are often served with stir-fried fish in red oil, and the most famous of the noodles are spiced with duck and white soup broth.

The broth is prepared with the scales, gills and meat of black carp. Toppings include fried carp or spiced duck made from Kunshan Dama duck stew. All the ingredients are authentic and locally sourced.

You don't have to travel to the city of Kunshan to enjoy this delicacy. The Xucheng Restaurant in Suzhou bought the secret recipe from the Kunshan Ao'zao Restaurant long time ago.

Taihu Lake White Shrimp

5

White shrimp is a local delicacy in Taihu Lake. They are often called crystal shrimp because of their small bodies and extremely thin shells. The shrimp are really delicious when boiled, without special seasonings. If you are not skillful in peeling off the skins of the shrimp, just simply use your hands.

6 Huang Tian Yuan Cake

Huang Tian Yuan is the premier cake maker in Suzhou. The people of Suzhou are famous for their sweet tooth. Huang Tian Yuan provides distinctive cake products in different seasons, including sweet rice cakes, rice cake with lard, rice dumplings with rice cake soup in the lunar January, Qing dumplings for the Qingming Festival, fairy cake for the fourth day of the lunar April and double ninth cake for the Double Ninth Festival.

7 Yangcheng Lake Hairy Crabs

There are crabs almost everywhere on dining tables of China, but the famed Yangcheng Lake hairy crab comes only from Yangcheng Lake in Suzhou. Generally speaking, the crabs have black backs, white bellies, yellow fur and golden claws.

The claws of the crabs are so strong that it's said the creature can crawl on glass. Apart from the delicious flavor, authentic Yangcheng Lake hairy crabs have an unmistakable sweetness that means you can forego the vinegar-ginger sauces that typically accompany the eating of other crabs.

Not all the crabs fished up from the lake or sold in shops as Yangcheng Lake hairy crabs are authentic. To make sure you get the real thing, it's best to visit Yangcheng Lake yourself and sample this delicacy in a local restaurant. The long and narrow island, shaped like Italy, in the middle of Yangcheng Lake is called Lotus Island. It is a delightful place accessible by boat. Crabs there are considered the best you can get.

Little left to be desired

IN Suzhou, we take pride in our local history and culture, but that does not mean we don't also appreciate foreign imports, especially of the epicurean variety. At Ah Mi Xiang (阿咪香), a modest Korean restaurant on Shiquan Street, locals and visitors alike can enjoy an array of flavorful and reasonably priced Korean and pan-Asian dishes.

The restaurant itself is moderately sized, with two to four person booths spaced in close but comfortable proximity on the first floor, while the second floor accommodates larger parties.

An interesting feature of this place food-wise is the variety of their banchan, or appetizer dishes. Recent offerings have included savory pieces of Japanese pancake, sweet potato fries, and pickled bean sprouts. One of my favorite dishes here is the spicy rice cakes, or glutinous bite-sized pieces of dough slathered in a tangy sauce. According to some Korean exchange students, it's sweeter than the spicy rice cake in Korea, but they assured me that it's equally tasty.

Discovering Ah Mi Xiang's chicken and shiitake mushroom soup was a fortuitous accident, but it has since become another oft-craved favorite. The tenderness of the chicken, the chewy freshness of the mushrooms, and the savoriness of the light, golden broth blend perfectly into a charming bowl of comfort food goodness. This dish can be paired with their stir-fried vegetable udon (thick noodles), or with their kimchi pancakes. The portions are pretty generous as well, so you don't have to spend a lot to fill your stomach.

(Duola Gong)

TIPS

Ah Mi Xiang Korean Barbecue restaurant

Add: 403 Shiquan Street, Canglang District, Suzhou

Tel: 0512-6518 9277

Public transport: Bus No. 47, 204, 501, 511

Sweet Secrets

THE English translation of this restaurant's name, "Sweet Secrets," may sound rather cavity-inducing, but do not be misled by this cutely deceptive moniker. Tian Mi Mi (甜蜜蜜) is actually a small Hong Kong-style eatery that offers full meals as well as specialty beverages and desserts.

Situated on a smaller road running parallel to Guanqian Street, the restaurant has retained a pleasantly low-key atmosphere during my visits. They seem to maintain a favorable balance of just enough diners to create a warm, jovial buzz of conversation but not so many as to create a ruckus or overwhelm the wait staff.

What I love most about Tian Mi Mi is the variety of styles represented in their menu. Their full meals and sweets consist of juicy plates of roast duck or *chashao* (sweet marinated barbecued pork); steaming bowls of noodle soup with greens and wontons; pan-fried noodles with beef and string beans; or generous servings of fried rice with eggs and shrimp, etc.

A personal favorite is the Singapore-style glass noodles, which are tossed in turmeric (giving it that characteristic yellow coloring often mistakenly dubbed "curry") and mixed with strips of pork, assorted vegetables, and shrimp.

I've also found Tian Mi Mi an ideal place to sit and chat with a friend over bowls of sweet goodies or glasses of refreshing drinks. Their dessert menu boasts pages of sweet fixes ranging from fruit salads doused in sago nectar to mango pudding to glutinous rice balls in warm, thick red bean soup. Drinks range from Hong Kong milk tea and coffee to assorted teas, fruit smoothies, and shakes.

(Duola Gong)

TIPS

Tian Mi Mi Hong Kong-style tea restaurant

Add: No. 41, Bi Feng Fang, Pingjiang District (close to Lindun Road)

Tel: 0512-6581 1837

Average cost: 80 yuan per person

Recommendations: Double-layer steamed milk, Chashao Hot Pot Rice, Signature Sago Cream, Signature Almond Tofu Spaghetti, Honey Peach Baked Rice

A curious encounter with Pingjiang Road

Strolling along Pingjiang Road is like walking in a dream.
The street could be empty, with only the occasional sound of footsteps.
Or it could be full of beautiful blossoms dancing in a cool breeze.
Its shops and cafes beckon the browser and entice the curious.

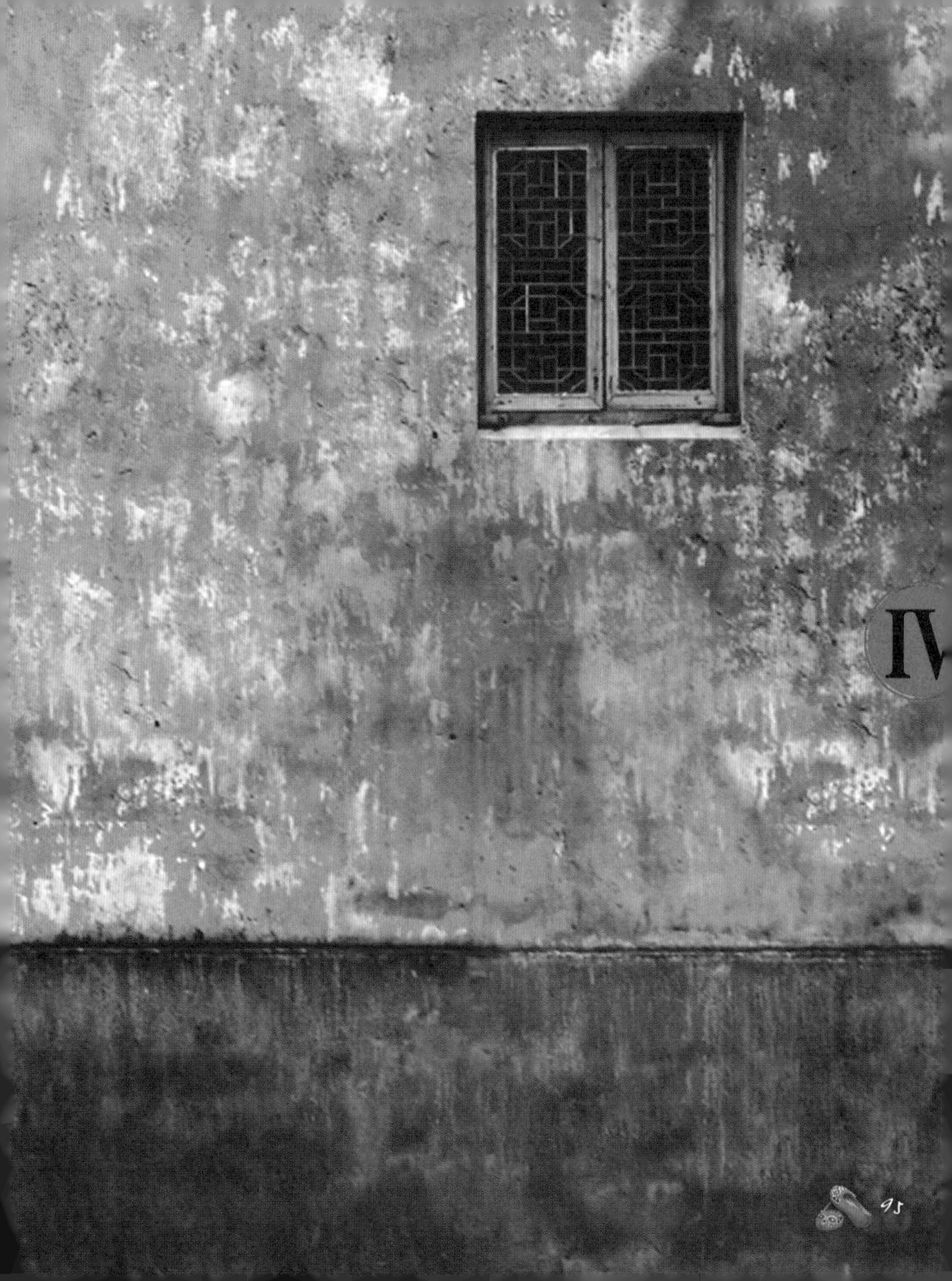
IV

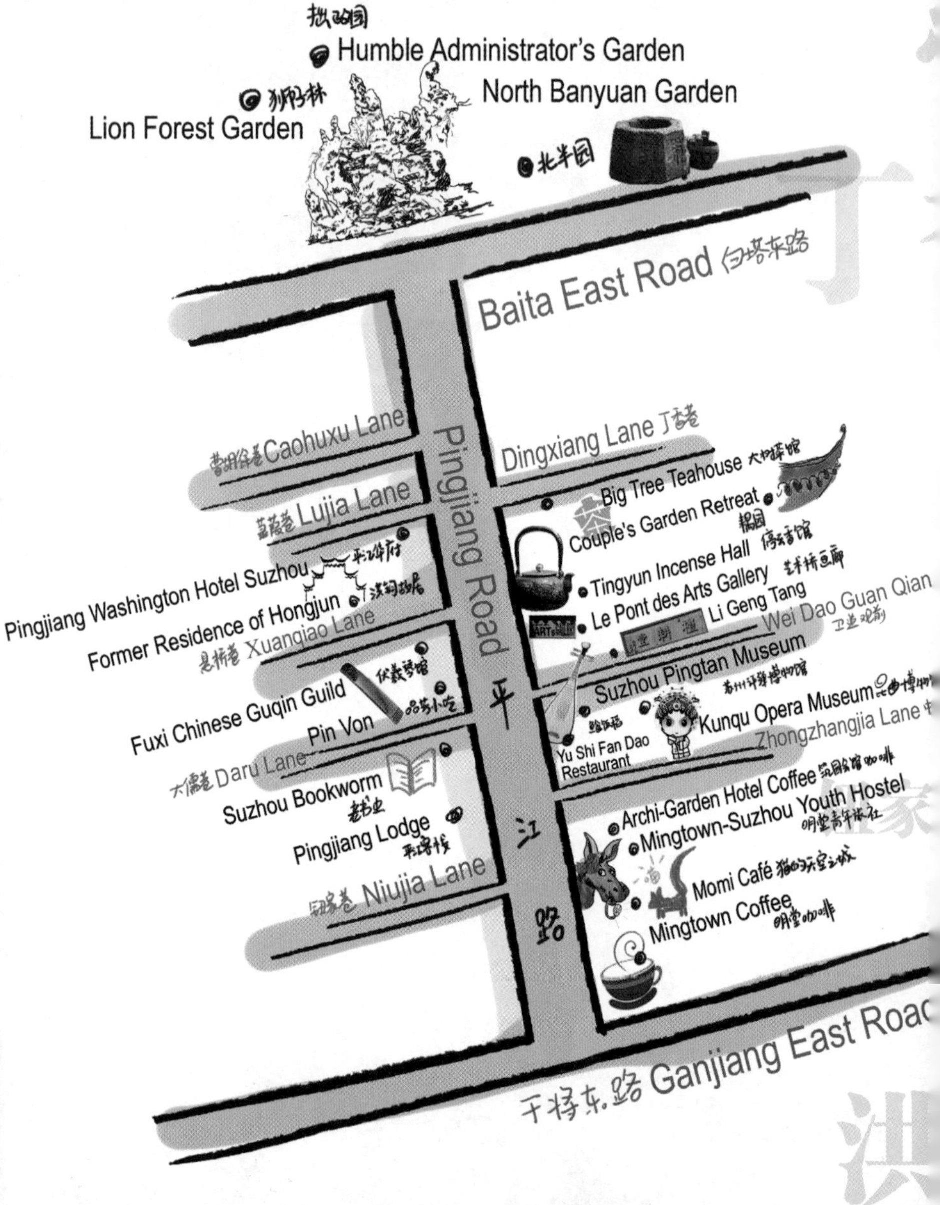
拙政园
Humble Administrator's Garden
狮子林
Lion Forest Garden
North Banyuan Garden
北半园
Baita East Road 白塔东路
Caohuxu Lane
Lujia Lane
Pingjiang Road
Dingxiang Lane 丁香巷
Big Tree Teahouse 大树茶馆
Couple's Garden Retreat
耦园
Tingyun Incense Hall 停云香馆
Le Pont des Arts Gallery 艺术桥画廊
Li Geng Tang
Wei Dao Guan Qian
卫道观前
Pingjiang Washington Hotel Suzhou
Former Residence of Hongjun
Xuanqiao Lane
Fuxi Chinese Guqin Guild
Pin Von
Suzhou Pingtan Museum
苏州评弹博物馆
Kunqu Opera Museum
Yu Shi Fan Dao Restaurant
Zhongzhangjia Lane
大儒巷 Daru Lane
Suzhou Bookworm
老书虫
Archi-Garden Hotel Coffee
Mingtown-Suzhou Youth Hostel
明堂青年旅社
Pingjiang Lodge
Momi Café
Niujia Lane
Mingtown Coffee
明堂咖啡
平
江
路
干将东路 Ganjiang East Road

Pingjiang Road

Each step on the stone road has an echo, that of this ancient city and with a slight hint of coffee espresso. All the houses along the road are antique-like, yet you can still find bars and Cafés inside, and that is the uniqueness of this road — a mixture of modern and classic.

踏在石板路上的每一步都有着回响，或如此城市一般古老，或带着些许浓缩咖啡的香气。所有路边的房子都感觉古老，但是你还是在其中找到酒吧或者咖啡馆。这就是这条路的与众不同之处——现代和古典的融合。

A lady of renewable charms

HAVE you been to Pingjiang Road?

That's the first question friends asked me when I returned from a trip to Suzhou. The popularity of this street is not hard to understand.

Often compared with the famous Guanqian Street in Suzhou, Pingjiang Road boasts a creative, laid-back environment without pretensions.

It takes less than 20 minutes to walk from one end of the road to the other, but in between are an array of twisting narrow alleyways, small, stylish shops and eateries that can keep a visitor for hours.

Unlike most reconstructed cultural or historical streets in tourist areas, Pingjiang Road blends old and new in a unique coupling of ancient-style buildings, contemporary shops and ordinary residences.

The foundation stones of older buildings date back to the Song Dynasty (960-1279), and the buildings underwent renovation during the Ming Dynasty (1368-1644).

The name Pingjiang comes from the earliest known map of the ancient city, drawn in 1229. It is clear from historical comparisons that the layout of Suzhou hasn't changed much from the city's earliest days.

Pingjiang Road, which runs parallel to the Pingjiiang River, is criss-crossed by countless small lanes. On one side of the river, are hostels, postcard shops, incense stores, yogurt vendors and other commercial facilities. On the other, old residences still stand along small lanes and are inhabited by local people.

Many of these old houses once belonged to influential intellectuals of their times. Suzhou was famous for her scholars. The local government has refrained from turning all these old houses into museums or tourist spots. Rather, people in the area just live ordinary lives in a continuum with the past.

One might describe Pingjiang Road as an ageless lady of renewable charms. As night falls, the old lady dons her best evening gown. The quiet stone walls suddenly come to life with reflections from the street lamps and the Pingjiang River. It is a sight of pure beauty.

(Yao Minji)

TIPS

The street is especially beautiful at night, when street lamps light up the Pingjiang River.

Gang Gang, the celebrity dog

PINGJIANG Road is a place famous for its cafes, shops and old buildings. However, there is one thing from Pingjiang Road that has left quite an impression on me: people with their dogs and especially one celebrity dog called Gang Gang.

The name Gang Gang comes from Suzhou's own dialect and describes his chubby body and his "thick head".

Gang Gang's owner lives not far from Pingjiang Road. It all started as a routine to walk Gang Gang along this street, but soon the owner discovered that Gang Gang would "play dead" if he was too tired to walk. Well, hats off to Gang Gang as he really plays "dead" well. No matter how hard the owner tries to move him, his exceptional weight and blank look become his best leverage. However, if the owner yells out "Let's go home"! He immediately stands up and waves his non-existing tail, and quite happy to run along.

His presence is one of Pingjiang Road's biggest attractions. Tourists will often laugh themselves to death when they witness Gang Gang's performance. The locals, who have seen it before, will give the owner a sympathetic

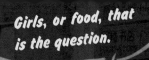

Girls, or food, that is the question.

look and shake their heads. Videos of Gang Gang's performance have received massive hits on the Internet. He was even interviewed by several foreign TV channels due to his surge in popularity.

Just like many popular male celebrities, Gang Gang is also a "lady's man". He will not hesitate to work his charm whenever he sees a pretty woman. With his innocent yet "handsome" face, women will often give him a gentle pat, or even a cuddle. Yet Gang Gang does not chase all the girls, only those who fit his criteria of "pretty." Women who have failed to get Gang Gang's attention would try to prove their prettiness by bribing him with food. The result? Well, we have to say food is more important to Gang Gang than a few girls.

The people, the street, and most of all, Gang Gang, have made Pingjiang Road an unforgettable place for me.

(Xinlu Cindy Huang)

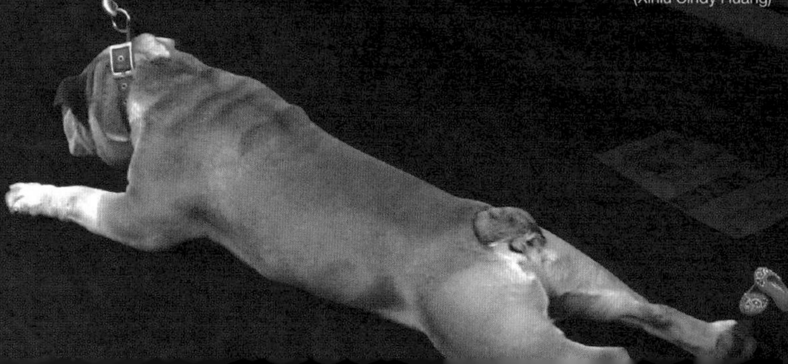

If you are a cat  person

FIRST I have to say, I am a true cat person. My cat's name is Mishka and he has been living like a king since I adopted him from an animal shelter.

The first time that I went to Pingjiang Road, I was amazed to see the number of cats along this narrow street. Almost every five steps I would run into a cat that was sleeping in the sun or in front of a shop. There was one sitting in front of an art gallery that even had some star quality. Every time someone wanted to take a photo of him, he would look at the camera and throw a pose, with a few purrs if he was in the mood.

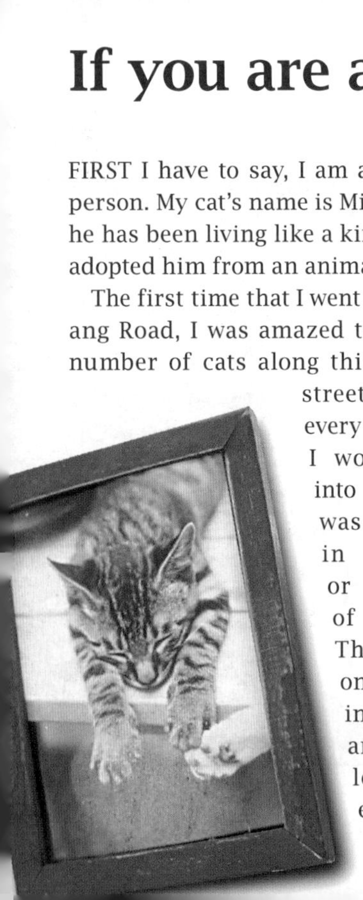

One shop called "Momi Café" attracted my attention. Its Chinese name means "City in the Cat's Sky" (猫的天空之城). I first thought it was just a cafe, but it is actually also a shop that sells postcards, books and gifts. What impressed me the most was that the cat theme was everywhere in this cafe. There were images of cats on cups, postcards and also on the wall. When I was talking to the owner of the cafe, she even pointed to her cat, which was sleeping in its bed in the middle of the cafe and said to me: "Over there, that's the real boss."

My encounter with Pingjiang Road's

cats had a happy ending. On my way back, I was followed by this small kitten. Judging by her look, she was most likely a street cat but was well fed, maybe by the shop owners or just strangers. I could not help but take her home with me. She was eventually adopted by my aunt, who is also a true cat person. She was given the name "Chou Niu", which means ugly doll but in a nice way and has lived like a queen ever since.

(Xinlu Cindy Huang)

TIPS

Momi Café

Pingjiang Shop add: 25 Pingjiang Road

Tel: 0512-6755 7912

Business hours: 10am-11pm

Shantang Shop add: 49 Xiatang, Tonggui Bridge, Shangtang Street

Tel: 0512-655 65211

Tongli Shop add: 22 Fuguang Street, San Bride, Tongli

Tel: 189 1355 2810

Who we are: We are a café, a bookshop, a post office, and also a place to escape.

What we recommend: Hand-drawn map of Suzhou, our special selection of books, postcards (over 300 different types to choose from). Last but not least, our homemade white tea. All ingredients are naturally grown or imported with careful selection.

Romantic lanes

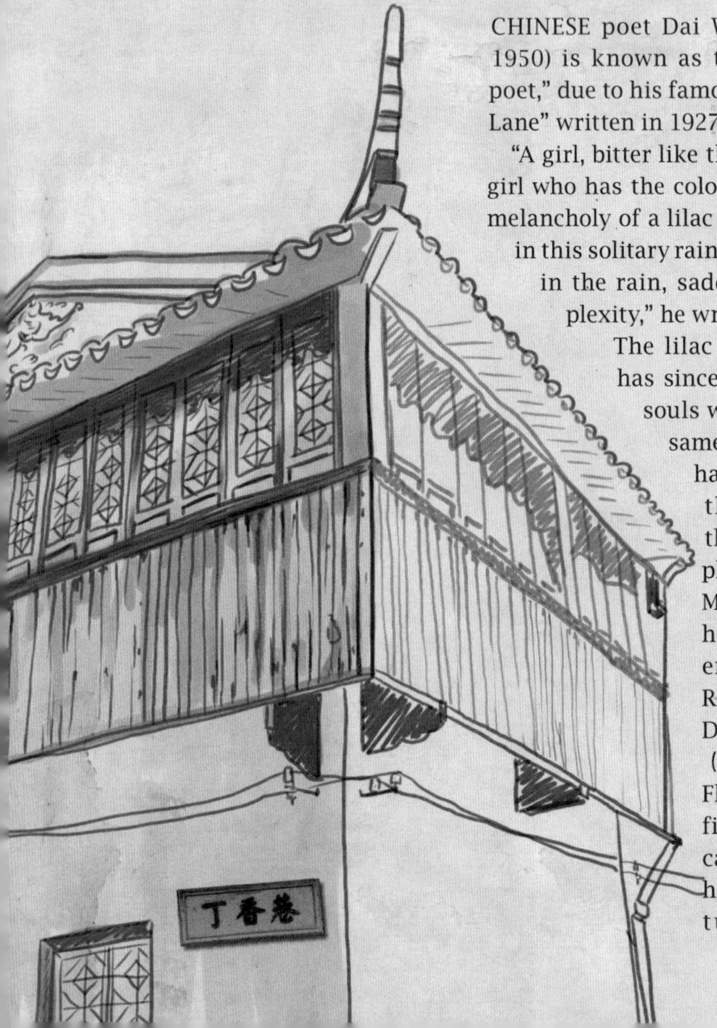

CHINESE poet Dai Wangshu (1905-1950) is known as the "rainy Lane poet," due to his famous poem "Rainy Lane" written in 1927.

"A girl, bitter like the lilac flower, a girl who has the color, fragrance and melancholy of a lilac flower, wanders in this solitary rainy lane, saddened in the rain, saddened with perplexity," he wrote.

The lilac flower-like girl has since captured many souls who have felt the same solitude, or who have wondered for the location of the poem's metaphoric rainy lane. Many say it is right here at the east end of Pingjiang Road. It is called Dingxiang Lane (丁香巷), or Lilac Flower Lane. It is filled with classical style Chinese houses and cultural history.

Since the release of the poem, it is considered particularly romantic to walk on this lane in the rain.

There are many similar lanes in the city. They are famous for their former residents, most of whom are scholars or beautiful women.

Among them, Xuanqiao Lane (悬桥巷), or Hanging Bridge Lane, is perhaps one of the most well known, for it once housed the legendary courtesan Sai Jinhua and her husband, scholar-official and diplomat Hong Jun.

Sai Jinhua, whose name means "prettier than golden flowers," was a legendary courtesan of the late 19th and early 20th centuries.

Today it is difficult to determine exactly which suite in the residence in Xuanqiao Lane housed the legendary courtesan, but that doesn't stop visitors intrigued by the tales of this beautiful woman.

In addition to Hong Jun, famous men like historian Gu Jiegang (1893-1980) and writer Ye Shengtao (1894-1988) all had their roots in Xuanqiao Lane.

The narrow and twisting lanes, scattered all around, are a highlight of the city, encapsulating its rich history and culture with beautiful delicacy, elegance and style.

(Yao Minji)

TIPS

Dingxiang Lane is a small lane at the east of Pingjiang Road. What writer Dai Wangshu wrote beautifully in "The Rainy Lane" might well be here, it depends on how you feel.

No ticket is required for Dingxiang Lane, which means you can wander around freely.

Half a garden?

THROUGH a circular door, a delicate garden provides an instant feeling of refreshment. Banyuan Garden（半园）, or "Half Garden," is only about 1,000 square meters. Its design, which plays on its name, proves that doing things by half can sometimes be distinctive.

A small stone bridge, with a handrail on one side, crosses a pond in the center of the garden. To its left, a small hillock supports half a summerhouse. The structure sits against a wall, giving the impression that the other half is on the other side.

A pathway under a typical Chinese roof goes halfway around the garden, looking out on a half stage that extends to the round door. Again there is the illusion that the other half is outside the door.

The garden was first built by a retired Suzhou official and scholar. He called it Zhi Yuan, or "Stop Garden," to express his desire to retire from his government career and retreat back to mountains and waters.

The garden was later sold to a local governor, who changed the name to Pu Yuan, or "Garden of Simplicity," keeping the theme of the original plan.

The garden's last known owner was another local official, who changed its name to its present form.

Three owners gave it different names, but they all expressed the same concept held by many Chinese scholars: It is better to enjoy the beauty of simplicity by half than overdoing things.

(Yao Minji)

TIPS

The Scholars Hotel Pingjiang Fu

"Pingjiang" is the old name for Suzhou, and Fu means more than just "home." It means "home for a scholar or government official." This establishment is a Suzhou-style guesthouse built on the basis of the Banyuan Garden. Give them a call if you want to stay at the hotel or visit the garden. A bit pricey, though.

Add: 60 Baita East Road

Tel: 0512-6770 6688

The following list includes other hotels renovated from old houses:

Pingjiang Lodge

Built on the site of the old residence of two rich families – the Fangs and the Dongs – from the Ming Dynasty (1368-1644), this hotel is located in the vicinity of other old homes of famous scholars.Pingjiang Lodge has 42 courtyard-front rooms, with the rates ranging from 580 yuan to 1,688 yuan.

Add: 33 Niujia Lane, Pingjiang District

Tel: 400 710 1818

Archi-Garden Hotel

The Archi-Garden Hotel is the former residence of the wealthy Zhang family during the Qing Dynasty (1636-1912). It combines modern facilities with old-style architecture. Only four guestrooms are available.

Add: 31 Pingjiang Road

Tel: 0512-6581 0618

Suzhou Higher Hotel, Pingjiang Road Branch

This venue fuses the concept of a traditional Suzhou garden with contemporary design and comfortable, tranquil accommodation.

Add: 62-67 Pingjiang Road

Tel: 0512-6777 7189

400 886 6868

Youth hostel offers adventure at a budget price

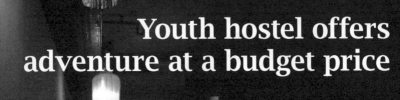

AT the first glance, the popular Mingtown Youth Hostel (明堂青年旅舍) looks a bit like a university dormitory.

The reception desk has posted a list of answers to the most frequently asked questions from visitors. Just opposite is a notice board with information on room prices, floor layouts and Internet connection, and an array of notes posted by hostel guests.

The lobby also has computers for public use, which appear to be popular with young guests. The bicycles parked just inside the door give the area a student atmosphere, as do the long corridors and dim lighting, with young people scurrying about holding beer cans, books, cameras and snacks.

Like many other venues on the historic Pingjiang Road, Mingtown has been rebuilt from an old-style house with a wood-structured roof.

Modern laser lighting pours down from the roof through wooden slats. Old pictures of the area on the wall, lit by lantern-shaped lamps, add a sense of nostalgia, reminding guests that this place has been here for hundreds of years.

To say the least, Mingtown is popular among backpackers, Chinese and foreign. It's close to the city's most famous tourist attractions but offers accommodation at a reasonable price.

In 10 minutes, you can walk from Mingtown to the famous Guanqian Street, the Suzhou Museum and the Humble Administrator's Garden, Couple's Garden Retreat, among other tourist hot spots.

Service is geared to backpackers and includes free wireless, a DVD library, bicycle rentals and local guides.

While a hostel might not appeal to older, more well-heeled travelers, it does provide a cheap, laid-back place to stay and meet new friends.

(Yao Minji)

TIPS

They offer "multi-person" rooms other than the standard single and double bedrooms. How do they do that? Bunk beds! You will love it!

Add: 28 Pingjiang Road

Tel: 0512-6581 6869

Food to mend the body and warm the soul

IN Suzhou, people equate eating with good health. That probably explains why dishes drawing on seasonal herbs are so popular. And if you think that "herbal cuisine" doesn't sound very tasty, you have a great surprise in store when stepping off the rich food circuit.

San Wei ("three flavors") restaurant (三味养生馆) is located on Pingjiang Road. The restaurant is probably the only riverside eatery serving herbal cuisine. It's not a big place, but it makes up in atmosphere what it lacks in size. A great sense of tranquility washes over people who sit beside its windows, watching the world go by.

Each dish on the menu is accompanied by an explanation of its nutritional value and the body functions it addresses. Patrons can pick dishes that they think might particularly help their own health conditions.

Hawthorn tea, for example, is said to be a good appetite stimulant. I chose it as a great way to start a meal. Red date tea is touted as particularly good for women - helping both their outward appearance and their inward well-being.

For hot dishes, I chose Jiu Niang Yu (fish steamed with fermented glutinous rice), Mei Gui Fu Ru Kou Rou (meat with rose and fermented bean curd) and Pork Rib Soup. All the dishes were highly recommended by locals.

Fermented glutinous rice, called *jiuniang* in Chinese, is a traditional favorite sweet of Suzhou locals. It can be either added to sweet desserts like dumplings and pastries or used in conventional dishes like fish braised in soy source or dry-fried prawns. I tried it with the fish for the first time. Delicious! The sweetness of jiuniang delicately balances the flavor of the fish.

Rose oil is frequently used in dishes in Suzhou. It is added to rice cakes and pastries, and also as a flavor enhancer for meats. Meat with rose and fermented bean curd is a dish unique to the San Wei Restaurant. Dipping soft chunks of meat in soy sauce flavored with rose is an exquisite taste experience hard to describe.

Most dishes served at San Wei are steamed, which is considered the lightest and healthiest way to cook food in China. People looking to shed a few kilograms will find a friend in San Wei. Even beyond all the health claims, the cuisine and atmosphere at San Wei are so relaxing that one has the sensation of experiencing the soul of Suzhou at its best.

(Gao Ceng)

TIPS

San Wei Restaurant

Signature dishes include Jiu Niang Yu and Mei Gui Fu Ru Kou Rou. Average price for a meal per person is around 60 yuan.

Add: 163 Pingjiang Road

Tel: 0512-6755 3033

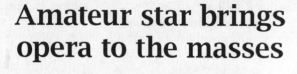

Amateur star brings opera to the masses

LV Chengfang was putting the finishing touches on her performance face as we entered the Fuxi Chinese Guqin Guild (伏羲琴馆) in the middle of Pingjiang Road alongside the Pingjiang River. She was carefully drawing eyeliner up and out beyond the ends of her eyes to form the "phoenix eyes" typical of a traditional Chinese beauty.

Lv was preparing for her daily Kunqu Opera performance, which starts at 7:30pm every evening in the teahouse. On weekends, there is an additional matinee.

In the past year, Lv has performed more than 400 times, a track record impressive even for a professional Kunqu Opera performer. And Lv is not even a professional. She is one of the most well-known amateur Kunqu Opera performers in the Suzhou area.

Kunqu is one of China's oldest operatic forms, with a history dating back more than 600 years. It originated in Suzhou and has influenced the style of many Chinese operatic forms, including Peking Opera.

Kunqu was designated one of the "Masterpieces of the Oral and Intangible Heritage of Humanity" by UNESCO in 2001.

Known as "mother" of many Chinese operas, Kunqu is marked by its delicacy and elegance, created not only by its music and vocals, but also by the graceful and symbolic gestures, refined costumes and distinctive make-up of its performers.

Some diehard enthusiasts believe that every step,

every rhythm, every gesture of Kunqu Opera must strictly adhere to the original style of the genre. Sometimes, one word or one posture can endure for several minutes, making it very laborious for modern, younger audiences to appreciate.

Even in its birthplace Suzhou, Kunqu Opera usually remains out of reach for ordinary citizens. Its long reputation as an art form for the upper classes has confined most performances to theaters, museum or upmarket restaurants.

Lv said she prefered to popularize Kunqu. And although she would not rank among the best Kunqu performers in Suzhou, her talent and devotion did attract audiences. Her interpretation is designed to make the opera more accessible.

"I only hope that there will be more amateur performers like me who want to popularize this beautiful ancient art," she said.

(Yao Minji)

TIPS

It is a teahouse with Kunqu Opera and Chinese Guqin performances.

Add: 97 Pingjiang Road

Tel: 0512-6581 2905

Average price per person: 80 yuan

Performing time: 8pm to 10:30pm (an additional show is available on weekends and holidays at 2:30pm to 5pm)

No extra charges for performances

Sculptor finds himself in his artwork

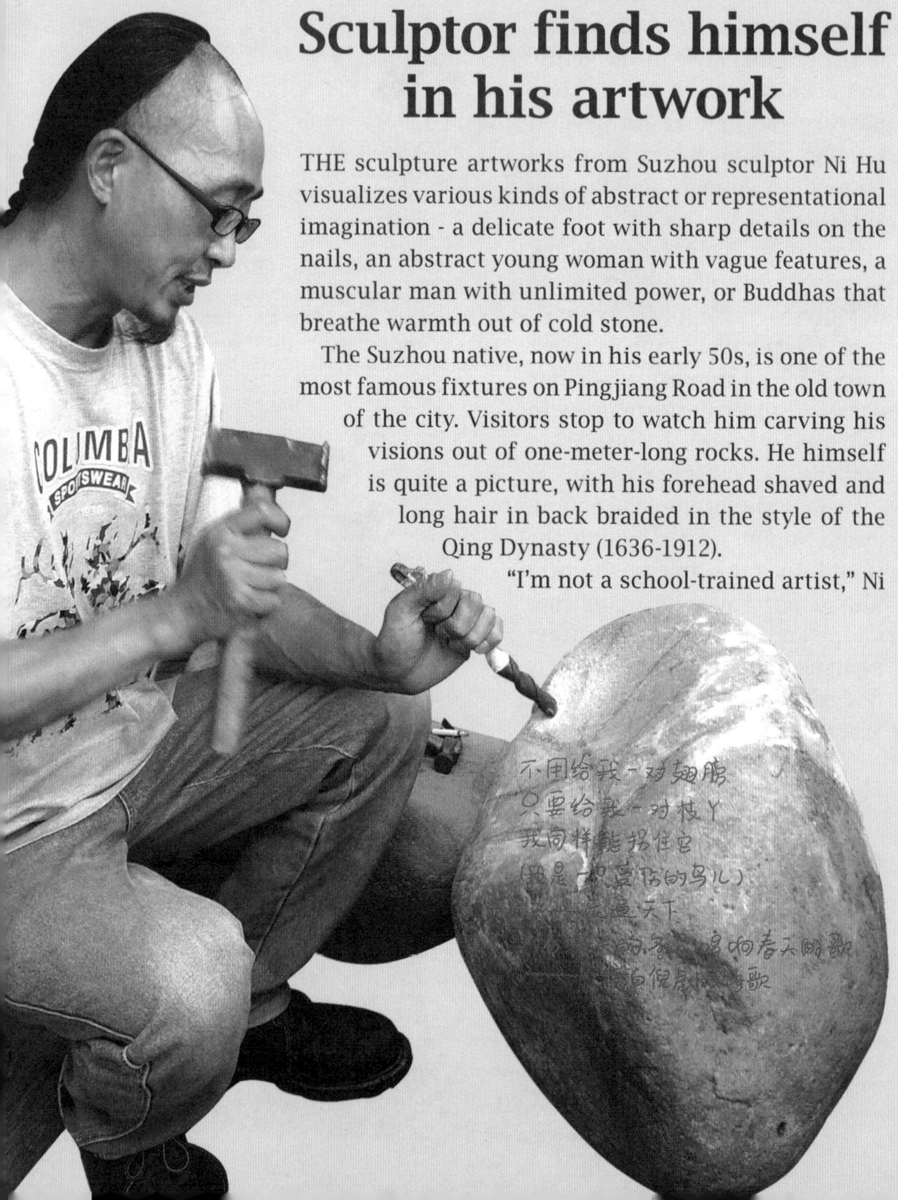

THE sculpture artworks from Suzhou sculptor Ni Hu visualizes various kinds of abstract or representational imagination - a delicate foot with sharp details on the nails, an abstract young woman with vague features, a muscular man with unlimited power, or Buddhas that breathe warmth out of cold stone.

The Suzhou native, now in his early 50s, is one of the most famous fixtures on Pingjiang Road in the old town of the city. Visitors stop to watch him carving his visions out of one-meter-long rocks. He himself is quite a picture, with his forehead shaved and long hair in back braided in the style of the Qing Dynasty (1636-1912).

"I'm not a school-trained artist," Ni

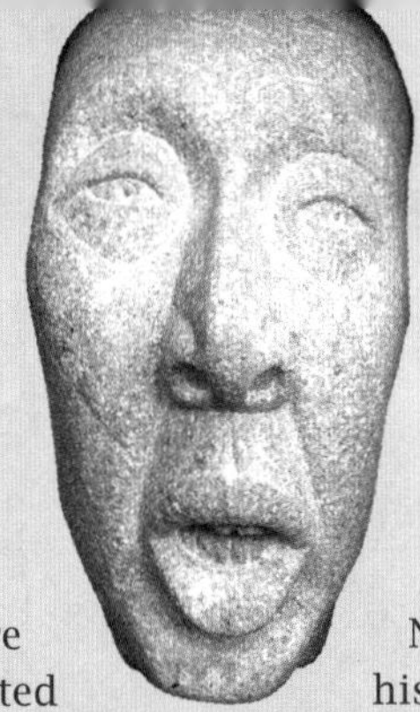

said. "I've known many hard times in my life. "

He added, "Art is not the exclusive domain of well-trained artists. It is just a matter of expressing yourself through all kinds of media."

Ni's self-portrait sculpture has a face with exaggerated features. The eyes are crafted much smaller than his, sitting under swollen eyelids. Under the eyes is a big nose with large nostrils, perched just above an open mouth with thick lips.

It is not the prettiest of faces, and etched in rock, it looks even more cold and coarse.

Some would say it doesn't look like Ni much at all. But the sculpture conveys a unique strength of character, and, like his other works, there is a power and originality that cuts to the soul.

The artist quit his job in a state-owned factory in the early 1990s and tried his hand at a succession of jobs - taxi driver, shop assistant, craftsman and others. He was lost.

"It was a very painful period," he said. "As a married man, I couldn't support myself, not to mention fulfilling my responsibilities toward my family. Neighbors and relatives all thought I was useless."

One evening when he was out walking with his wife, a truck packed with trash passed by and a large stone dropped from the back of it. The stone rolled onto the street, and Ni immediately likened it to his own feckless existence. He took the rock home and decided to find some meaning in it and, by extension, in himself.

With rudimentary tools he had on hand, Ni carved a sleeping Buddha out of the rock. It was the dawn of a new life.

Sculpture is not his only medium. Ni has also organized a street performance troupe to express his feelings in another mode. The troupe members dress themselves up as sculptures and give performances, sometimes for money.

"It's always difficult to balance art and commerce, but my goal is simple – to feed myself and my family," Ni said.

(Yao Minji)

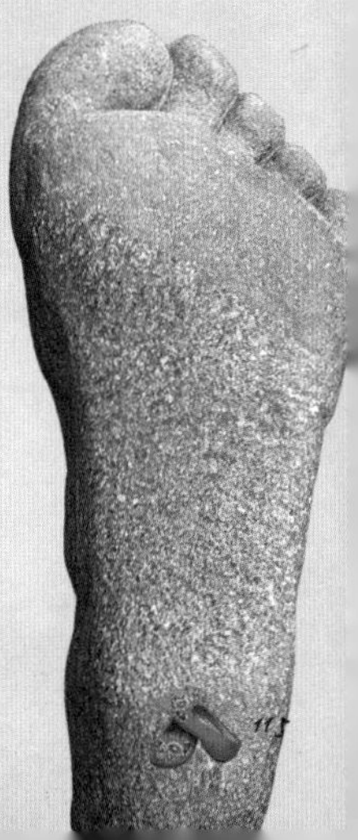

Taste fresh flavors on Pingjiang Road

Shang Xia Ruo

The Chinese-style courtyard is penetrated with the passion of western food, and all the elements are expressed in the traditional Chinese courtyard, table wares, tables, and chairs. The official cap chair, painted in white and matched with visually striking seat cushions, add an artistic touch. Sitting in the double cane chair at the entrance hall, you will be directly attracted by the black tiles and white walls of the hall.

Nargile is strongly recommended, as you can feel the fantastic alien cultural shock by tasting it.

Add: 255-257 Pingjiang Road, Pingjiang District

Tel: 0512-6581 5779

Business hours: 11am-11pm

Tao Ye Pu Dessert Shop

Hidden in the streets, with ink-and-wash lanterns illuminating its signboard. The walls there are red.

It's not very big, with three small tables, and five to six stools. Outside the window, flows the tranquil Pingjiang River.

Specialties: Double-layer Milk with Red Bean, Chilled Mango Sago Cream with Pomelo

Add: 46 Pingjiang Road

Tel: 0512-6215 7565

Tingyun Incense Hall

It sells various incenses (eaglewood, sandalwood, natural incense products and incense wares), tea (Japanese antique tea sets), flower (various ikebana wares) and paintings (literati and zen paintings).

Add: 125 Pingjiang Road (entrance to Xuanqiao Lane)

Tel: 0512-6581 5845

138 1526 6078

Higher Garden

This garden is situated on the other side of the river where Higher Hotel stands. It has a peculiar old-style yard. Looking through the arched door, you are greeted by a tiny courtyard and several delicate tearooms perfect for drinking tea and enjoying Pingtan.

Time to appreciate Pingtan: Monday to Friday, 7:30pm-10pm; Saturday and Sunday, 2pm-5pm. Minimum consumption: 78 yuan per person.

Add: 64 Pingjiang Road (Higher Hotel)

Tel: 0512-6581 0618

La Rive Gauche in the old city

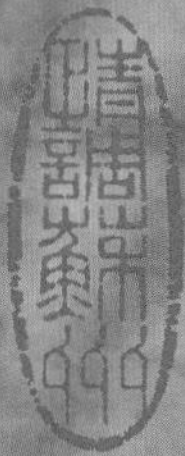

La Rive Gauche, or Left Bank, is an enchanting part of Suzhou.
Here, history dating back some 2,500 years echoes across lanes and through ancient stone buildings.
A bell in an old tower chimes.
Nostalgia swells.
Be prepared to park your soul here, mon ami.

V

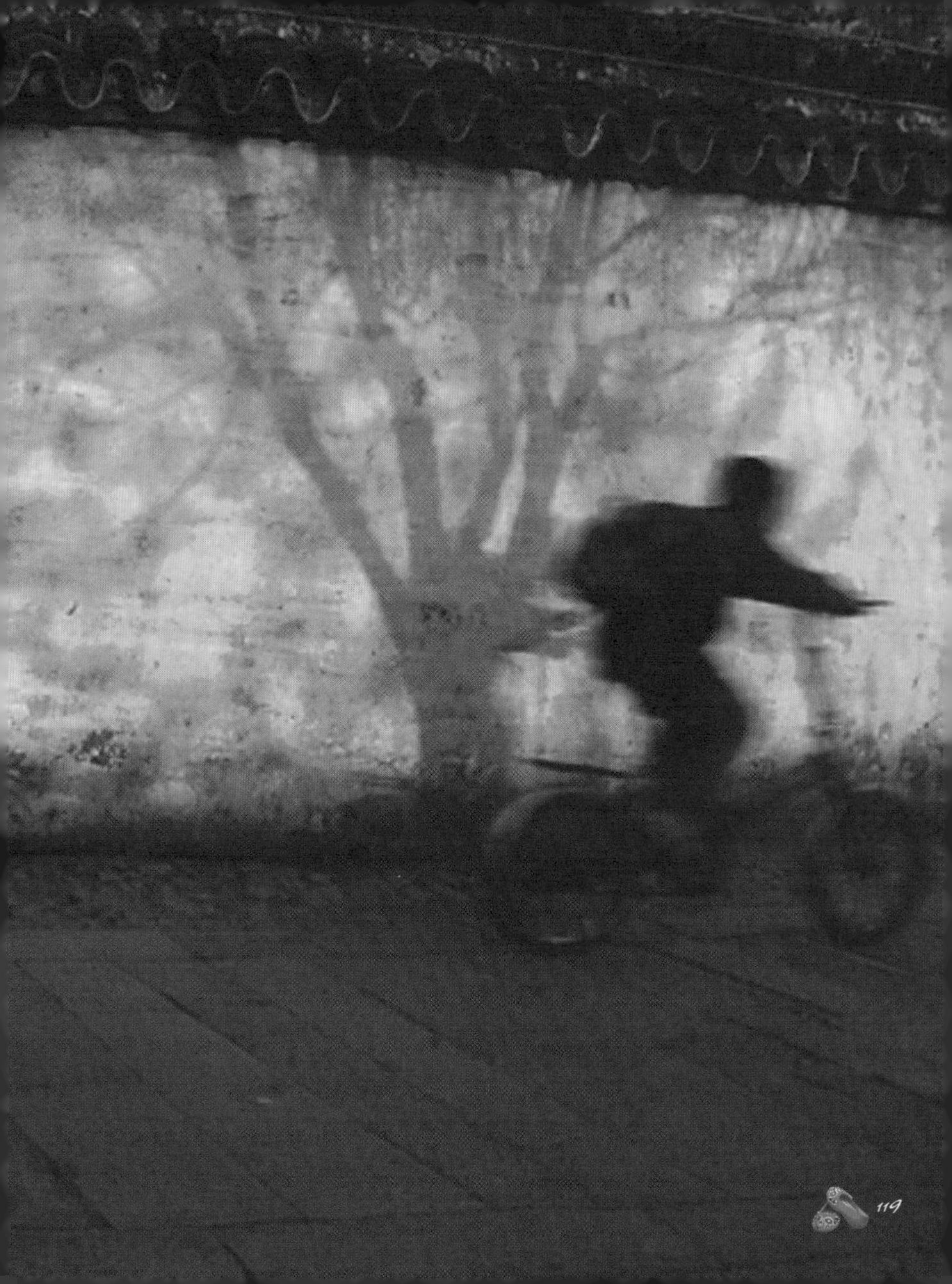

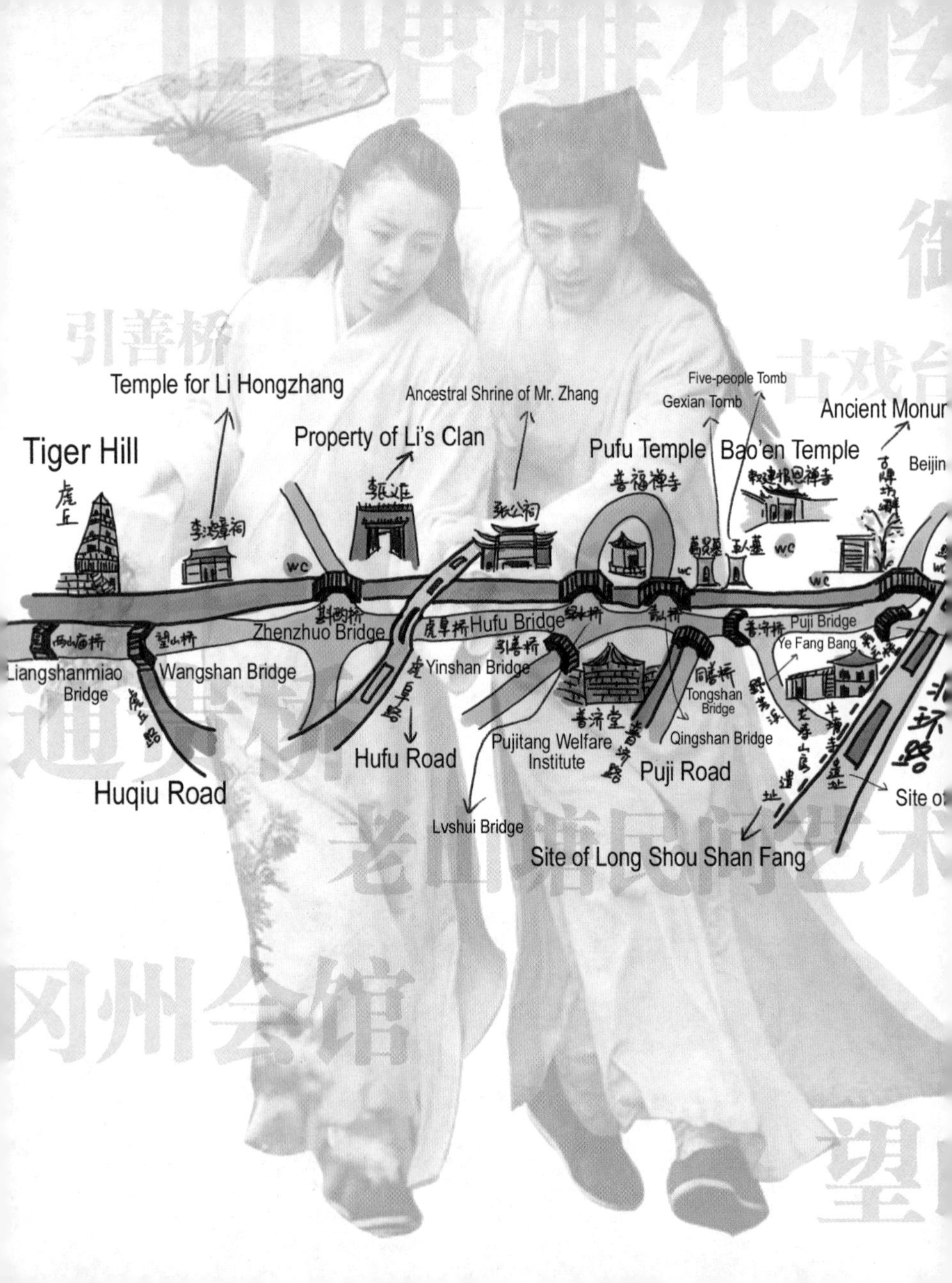
Temple for Li Hongzhang
Ancestral Shrine of Mr. Zhang
Five-people Tomb
Gexian Tomb
Ancient Monur
Tiger Hill
Property of Li's Clan
Pufu Temple
Bao'en Temple
Beijin
Zhenzhuo Bridge
Hufu Bridge
Puji Bridge
Ye Fang Bang
Liangshanmiao Bridge
Wangshan Bridge
Yinshan Bridge
Tongshan Bridge
Qingshan Bridge
Pujitang Welfare Institute
Hufu Road
Puji Road
Huqiu Road
Site o
Lvshui Bridge
Site of Long Shou Shan Fang

观音阁

山塘桥

张公祠

五人墓

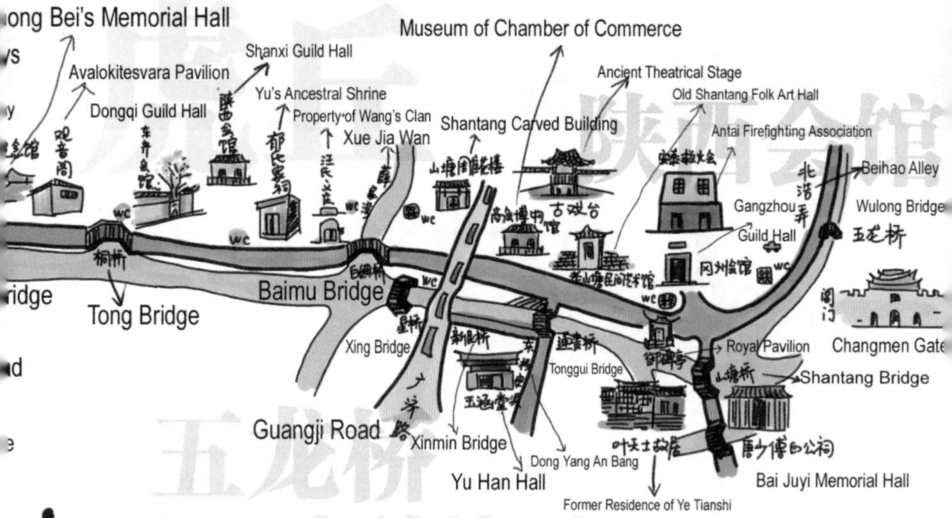

五龙桥

唐伯虎从山塘出发，追秋香去了

阊门

普济堂

Grandma's old street

SHANTANG Street（山塘街） is over 1,100 years old. It is a 3.5 kilometers long street that connects the modern shopping district of Suzhou to historic scenery - Tiger Hill, It is like a ribbon that ties Suzhou's present to its remote past.

The street combines almost all of ancient Suzhou's features. The stone and brick alleys run parallel to the water canal, with ancient local-style houses along the canal bank. Local people had been living in these houses up until about 10 years ago. The street was then refurbished and preserved as a historical site of Suzhou.

My cousin's family and my grandparents were living in one of those old houses along Shantang Street when I was little. I remember spending my childhood wandering around the alley, watching boats carrying local goods to different shops along the canal bank. My grandfather would often spoil me, with some cakes from the local shops, when we went to the morning market. I still consider myself very lucky to be able to hold such fond memories of this street.

As a tourist, you can choose to walk all the way from one end of the street to the other. There are plenty of local craft shops and lots of food stores

to satisfy your stomach. I definitely recommend the Plum Blossom Cake and the Flowering Apple Cake if you have a sweet tooth. They are both my childhood favorite and unique to Suzhou.

If you have some spare time, stop by the teahouse and enjoy a cup of tea while enjoying a Suzhou Opera performance. If you are in hurry, a boat tour is great option. The tour will take about an hour and you can simply sit back and absorb the scenery along the canal.

It doesn't matter which way you choose, I am sure that Shantang Street will not fail to impress you.

(Xinlu Cindy Huang)

TIPS

Apart from the street itself, Shantang Street has other attractions that will interest tourists. They are: Yu Han Hall, Suzhou Business Association Museum, Southeast China Boat Culture Museum, Ancient Theater Stage, Tonggui Bridge, An Tai Fire-fighting Association. Group tickets cost 45 yuan per person, including entry to Yu Han Hall, Suzhou Business Association Museum, Southeast Boat Culture Museum, An Tai Fire-fighting Association and a 40-minute boat tour.

There are also some new tourist spots including Chinese Southern Community Memorial, I.M Pei Family's Ancestral Hall, Pufu Temple, Yifeng Garden, etc; all of which offer free entry to the public.

What we recommend: The perfect schedule to enjoy Shantang Street will be walking along the street during the daytime and taking the boat tour during the night. Pick a restaurant in the street to have dinner and then go to the teahouse for a Suzhou Opera (Pingtan) performance.

Before you go, we also would like to remind you that there are people riding bikes in the street so you need to watch out for the traffic. The stone streets are not suitable for high heels. Make sure you wear a pair of comfortable shoes.

History, culture entwined along old street

TRADITION, culture and history. These three themes intermingle with great charm on Suzhou's Shantang Street.

This roadway has a history dating back about 1,200 years. It still retains the characteristics of the old lanes that once dominated the city, interconnecting communities of houses and shops.

Shantang Street is 3.5 kilometers long, stretching from Tiger Hill to Changmen Gate. It was once a lively commercial center, drawing people from across the region to trade. In 2002, the old street underwent renovation and was reopened to the public two years later.

A casual stroll is the best way to visit this street. View the museum that housed the chamber of commerce in ancient times.

The people sights are perhaps the most interesting. Here you can glimpse life as it has churned on through generations amid architecture of a traditional style. You can still see old women washing laundry in the canal alongside the street. Some very old, beautiful houses are tucked along the way.

The eastern section of Shantang Street is a residential and business area; the western part has a more countryside atmosphere, with less bustle.

There's an ancient theater along the street that used to stage Chinese operas. The wealthy residents of the city enjoyed the performances from high box seats, while the hoi polloi were relegated to standing and watching down below. Of course, common people could enjoy the performances without paying.

The theatre is still operating, keeping up the opera tradition. But it's all amateur performances nowadays, staged by opera buffs who don't charge anything and don't earn anything. This is art for pleasure's sake.

(Caterina Bernardini)

Afternoon tea, China-style, with retro ambience

PEOPLE normally associate "afternoon tea" with the British, but China has its own version of the popular tradition of taking a break between lunch and dinner.

In Suzhou, Rong Yang Lou (荣阳楼) is the best place for "afternoon tea," China-style. Here traditional Chinese tea is served with wonton and *sheng jian* (fried buns) instead of cakes and scones.

Hidden in the residential section of the famous Shantang Street, Rong Yang Lou can be a bit of a challenge to fine. There are a multitude of fruit stalls and small grocery shops surrounding it. Look for a large oven with boiling oil on top of it. That is where the restaurant's famous You Jian Tuan Zi (fried dumpling) is made.

You'll know you are in the right place if you see students eating with their grandparents after school,

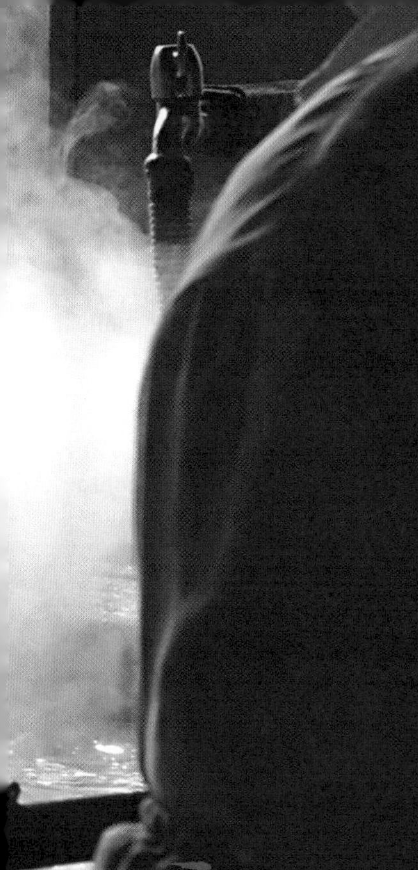

middle-aged women having a short break before they start dinner, and most importantly, the *ayi* who make *sheng jian* right opposite to the counter with skillful, fast movements.

Don't worry that a quick camera snap will disturb them. They are used to it.

What Rong Yang Lou lacks in décor and service, it makes up for with tasty snacks cooked the way they have been for generations. It's the retro charm of the place that is beguiling. You sit at plastic tables and wait for *ayi* in the kitchen to shout out your order number. Then you fetch the food yourself. This is a place with a definite 1980s feel to it.

The menu hasn't changed over the decades. The wonton is still served in a broth that uses lard. No cholesterol correctness here. The *sheng jian* is filled with sweet meat, evoking memories of the past. No wonder this place is so popular with locals!

Rong Yang Lou is also famous for its seasonal offerings of Gao. There many varieties of Gao, and the list changes according to festivals and season. For example, Qing Tuan is popular in spring, especially around the Qingming Festival. You will see long queues of local people waiting to buy gao in front of Rong Yang Lou.

"The food here follows original recipes and never changes," one local said. "And there's another advantage. The price hardly changes either."

(Zhou Yubin)

TIPS

Add: 329 Shantang Street. (Go west from Xinmin Bridge and keep your eye to the left. It's about a five-minute walk.)

Opening hours: 6am-4pm

Must try: *sheng jian* (fried buns), wonton (try their spicy sauce, too)

Average price per person: 10 yuan is definitely enough.

Barrelled bliss for newlyweds

A WEDDING is an auspicious event for the Chinese, steeped in traditions the bride and groom and their families must follow.

To ensure a happy life together and the arrival of a baby, certain foods are a must, including peanuts, lotus seeds and jujubes because their Chinese names all carrying meanings related to fertility.

In Suzhou and points south in China, the wedding food comes in a small wooden barrel called Zi Sun Tong (子孙桶), or "descendants' barrel." Some say the shape of the barrel reminds them of a mini-version of a wooden toilet.

Why put food in a toilet? Why would a toilet be part of a wedding gift in the first place?

The answer lies in the ancient traditional furniture style of Suzhou. In olden times, for example the Qing Dynasty (1636-1912), the bed was the most important piece of furniture in the house. The richer the family, the bigger and fancier the bed.

Unlike modern beds, the ancient version usually had pillars at each corner and was encased by curtains, creating an isolated space akin to a small room. A wooden toilet sat alongside.

As the furniture closest to the newly wedded couple, the wedding toilet – a gift from the bride's parents – would be crafted of top-quality wood and artful designs.

No one would use a wooden toilet nowadays, but it has become a symbol of fertility at weddings. Artisans today make these ceremonial pieces smaller and in exquisite designs. But the number of craftsmen who retain a skill passed down through generation is declining.

Looking for Zi Sun Tong and other traditional wedding gifts, people head for Kuai

Yuan, which sells a range of nuptial presents. Kuai means "chopsticks," which, of course, always come in pairs and carry a nice wedding connotation.

(Zhou Yubin)

TIPS

Kuai Yuan is at 137 Shantang Street. Each set of Zi Sun Tong is 180-360 yuan. Tel: 189 1543 3202

Enjoy the quietness

IN the last few years two streets famed for their water features have taken precedence with travelers in Suzhou. They are Shantang Street and its major rival Pingjiang Road.

However, if a complaint is to be leveled at both locations it is that they are highly commercialized and often crowded. One place where time has however not quite caught up yet is Sheng Jia Dai（盛家带）.

This street is located between Shiquan Street and Soochow University's main campus, and is most easily accessed by leaving the former location and turning towards the campus' south gate after passing the 1937 Nanjing Memorial Statue.

The first indication one has of arriving is being met by a small coffee shop that faces onto a wooden overhang shading the road. This hangs with grapes in the summer. But a few steps further and you find yourself standing on a bridge looking down the canal. Trees overhang into it, and their reflections, caught and captured shimmer out of it.

At this juncture one has the choice of walking on either bank. Personal preference would lead to the northern one that runs beside Soochow University.

The reason being twofold: Firstly, as the path is slightly narrower the only traffic likely to be encountered is bikes. Secondly, more traditional residences are found on this side, with many of the doors welcomingly open.

With residents tending to be older, one can therefore still find riverside washing taking place, witness meals being eaten within a traditional setting, or experience Chinese chess being played. More generally the opportunity to be transported back to a previous era still exists, but this is fading fast.

In short, Sheng Jia Dai is a relaxing escape and a welcome break from the busier streets adjoining it, albeit assuming one avoids rush hour.

(Gareth Morris)

TIPS

Sheng Jia Dai is a south-to-north riverfront lane between Shizi Street and Shiquan Street, right across the river from Soochow University.

The following are also recommendations if you want to experience everyday life in Suzhou:

Huxiangshi Lane, to the east of the middle section of Pingjiang Road

Gaoshi Lane, north section of Zhongjie Road, to the north of Madalu Lane

Wuzixu Alley, to the east of the north end of Jiqing Street

Fan Zhuang Qian Lane, to the west of the middle section of Renmin Road

Gu's Garden Lane, to the west of Pingjiang Road, to the north of Nanshizi Street

Zhu's Garden Lane, to the east of the middle section of Jiqing Street

Huang Fu Ji Lane, to the east of the middle section of Jinfan Road

Huajie Lane, to the east of the southern section of Yangyu Lane

Liji Lane, the middle section of Cangjie Street

China's Picasso and his Peachblossom Hut

MAYBE you haven't heard about it, but Peachblossom Hut is definitely a special sight to see in Suzhou.

Its fame originates from Tang Bohu (Tang Yin), a great Chinese artist who can be considered a counterpart of Picasso – or even more versatile than Picasso. And Peachblossom Hut（桃花坞）is the place where our Chinese Picasso lived, of which Tang wrote a poem Chinese people know well.

Tang lived in the mid-Ming Dynasty. In his early years, he followed the national educational programme and applied himself to customary examinations, and once even achieved first place in the provincial exams, and was hence known as *jie yuan.*

However, he was destined to be a rule-breaker. He repeatedly failed later school exams and then dropped out of school and became a painter and poet. In later years he received the title of Literary Master of the Wuzhong district of Suzhou.

Failure in exams also amplified Tang's wilderness and eroticism. He frequently portrayed feminine beauty, and sometimes even pornographic figures in his paintings, many of which are nowadays more popular among collectors than his paintings of other themes.

Furthermore, according to a folk tale, Tang once had a crush on a maid serving a retired official. He then followed her and served in the palace for three years, until he finally won the maid's heart. All

唐伯虎

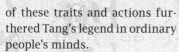

of these traits and actions furthered Tang's legend in ordinary people's minds.

Peachblossom Hut has been known through the years for its artistic air. Today, various ancient buildings and art museums are still located nearby. You can also see Peachblossom woodcarvings and paintings here. Such colorful and delicate paintings are regarded most suitable for traditional festivals.

(Fan Yi)

TIPS

Tang Yin, known as "Tang Bohu" (1470-1523) is a renowned Chinese artist and writer from the Ming Dynasty (1368-1644). A great figure in the history of Chinese Brush Painting, Tang is known best for works depicting natural scenery and people, and most of his works are nowadays collected in the National Palace Museum in Taiwan. In November 1991, one of Tang's works was auctioned by Christie's New York for 720,000 U.S. dollars.

Historical sights near Peachblossom Hut:

1.Five-Peak Garden at 47 Changmen West Street

Tickets: 2 yuan

Opening hours:

April 16 to October 30, 7:30am–5pm (when ticket service stops);

October 31 to April 15, 7:30am–4:30pm (when ticket service stops).

Tel: 0512-6727 5866

Public transport: Bus No. 54, 501, 31.

2.Taibo Temple at Xiatang Street, Changmen Gate. Built in memory of Tai, founder of the Wu Kingdom. The temple is currently closed to the public for renovation. Outdoor archways and its exterior decoration are still open to tourists.

Public transport: Bus No. 54, 501, 31.

3.Memorial Temple of Tang Yin at 10 Qianxin Street, Liao Alley, and the nearby Former Residence of Tang Yin at No. 13 West Xi Da Ying Men

Public transport: Bus No. 146, 32, 88.

4.Pu Garden at 8 Jiaochangqiao Road, currently the Peachblossom Wood-Carving Painting Museum. Visit by appointment only.

Tel: 0512-6751 4356

Public transport: Bus No. 1, 101.

5.The former Suzhou Kunqu Opera School at No. 53 West Xi Da Ying Men, currently the Suzhou Kunqu Opera Club.

Visit by appointment only.

Tel: 0512-6752 0097

Pei's masterpiece houses ancient secrets of Suzhou

SUZHOU is a city steeped in history and culture, with ancient houses, classic gardens and museums everywhere you look.

It is easy to pass by an old building without even noticing the small sign on its gate indicating that it once housed a famous scholar. These old houses have intriguing stories to tell to those who stop and listen to.

Suzhou Museum(苏州博物馆) is not an ancient building, but inside its contemporary façade one can marvel at the march of history that how the city's culture evolved over centuries.

The museum is surrounded by three most famous Suzhou gardens - the Humble Administrator's Garden, Residence of Loyal King (忠王府) and the Lion Forest Garden.

It was designed by one of Suzhou's famous native sons, I.M. Pei. As one of the world's greatest contemporary architects, Pei spent part of his childhood in the Lion Forest Garden.

The garden, dating back more than 600 years, is most famous for its sophisticated arrangement of giant rocks. Pei blended his childhood memories of Suzhou gardens into the design of the museum.

Passing through the entrance court and then stepping into the great hall, guests are always amazed at the stunning garden-like settings.

The eye-catching water pond and a bridge connect two sides of the venue in natural lines. The modern glass and metal structure blends in traditional wood and stone elements.

The main exhibition area is divided into four parts: the Lotus Treasure from the Wu Kingdom, the National Treasures Retrieved from the Ruiguang Pagoda, Legacies from the Region of Middle Wu, and Paintings and Calligraphy from the Renowned Wu School.

This is an ideal place to get acquainted with the sweeping panorama of the Wu culture that built Suzhou.

The Celadon Lotus-Flower-Shaped Bowl with Saucer is just one example of the city's precious ancient relics. It represents a special porcelain craft of the local area, and few examples have survived.

The jade burial ornament piece in an adjacent exhibition room is also an astonishing item to view. Visitors invariably marvel that the shining jade pieces actually date back thousands of years.

In addition to antiques, there is replication of a scholar's studio from the Ming Dynasty (1368-1644) that is also worth seeing. It shows the simple comfort that wise men chose to surround themselves as they mused on philosophy, art and other classic disciplines.

(Yao Minji)

TIPS

Add: 204 Dongbei Street

Tel: 0512-6757 5666

Opening hours:

9am to 5pm (admission is not allowed after 4pm); usually it takes one to two hours to look around the museum.

Admission: Free (closed on Mondays, except on national holidays)

Traffic: Tour Bus No. 1, 2, 5; Bus No. 202, 313, 923, 529, 40, 78 at Suzhou Museum Stop (also Humble Administrator's Garden or Lion Forest Garden Stop)

Special notes:

1) A free ticket is needed for entry, security check is required and no drinks are allowed.

2) Volunteer tour guides may be available depending on chance.

Caught in time

SOOCHOW University (苏州大学) is a multi-campus institution. It has vast new grounds over in Dushu Lake Higher Education Town, and boasts amongst other things one of the largest and most distinctive regional libraries. The university itself also houses students in several other locations, most of which are found in close proximity to the city center.

With this in mind, it is fortunate for any would-be visitor that the heart of this educational knowledge base lies within the original campus, which was established by Methodist missionaries over 100 years ago, and is accessible from multiple subway stations after a short walk.

Entering from the West Gate one could be excused for feeling that he or she had been transported back in time to a bygone era. The buildings somehow seem to have captured the essence of yesteryear and transported it into the here and now. This is accentuated by the fact that most of the buildings in one's immediate eye view consist of the distinctive red and grey brick facade that so often typifies the Victorian period.

With the old Dongwu University Gate but a stone's throw away from the entrance, a collection of pagodas and miniature gardens skillfully woven into what is a canopy of green and scattered throughout the

grounds, and the old Bell Tower with its hard wood interior overlooking an impressive grass square, it is unsurprising that this location appeals to educators, students, tourists and film producers alike for its undoubted natural beauty.

What stands out most for me about this campus is how this environment has a very different face for each and every season. In spring the campus is awash with buds as a fresh green color encapsulates and adorns the world around. By summer a thick multilayered canopy of trees provide the backdrop to a setting of peace and tranquility.

Autumn by contrast bears witness to a kaleidoscope of color as red, brown and golden leaves not only constitute the floor covering, but also act as a light filter from the sky above. Winter though is probably the most magical season. When the snows fall, the university is blanketed in white and, with the campus nearly deserted, this world within a world seems to be caught in time: clocks ticking slower that one would imagine.

Walking through the university one is removed from the ever-quickening pace of life in modern day Suzhou. During the day a visitor can behold the beauty of man and nature, new and old. By night, with the stars and moon overhead, one is transported to a purer time, where moral integrity was a sought-after norm, and innocence a virtue.

(Gareth Morris)

TIPS

With its main campus located along the city moat of Suzhou, Soochow University has experienced the vicissitudes of life in its 110-year evolution.

Passing through the original school gate of Dongwu University, the special sign symbolizing the century-old history of the university, you will be greeted by its famous Square Pagoda, Bell Tower, ancient verdant trees along the river, Keyuan Garden with clear water and rustling trees, mysterious Suntang Hall and elegant Lintang Hall. Every building in the university has its own story.

If you are interested in strolling in Soochow University, we suggest you enter from the gate on Shizi Street, where you can find the most unspoiled scenes, no matter when it's rainy or shiny.

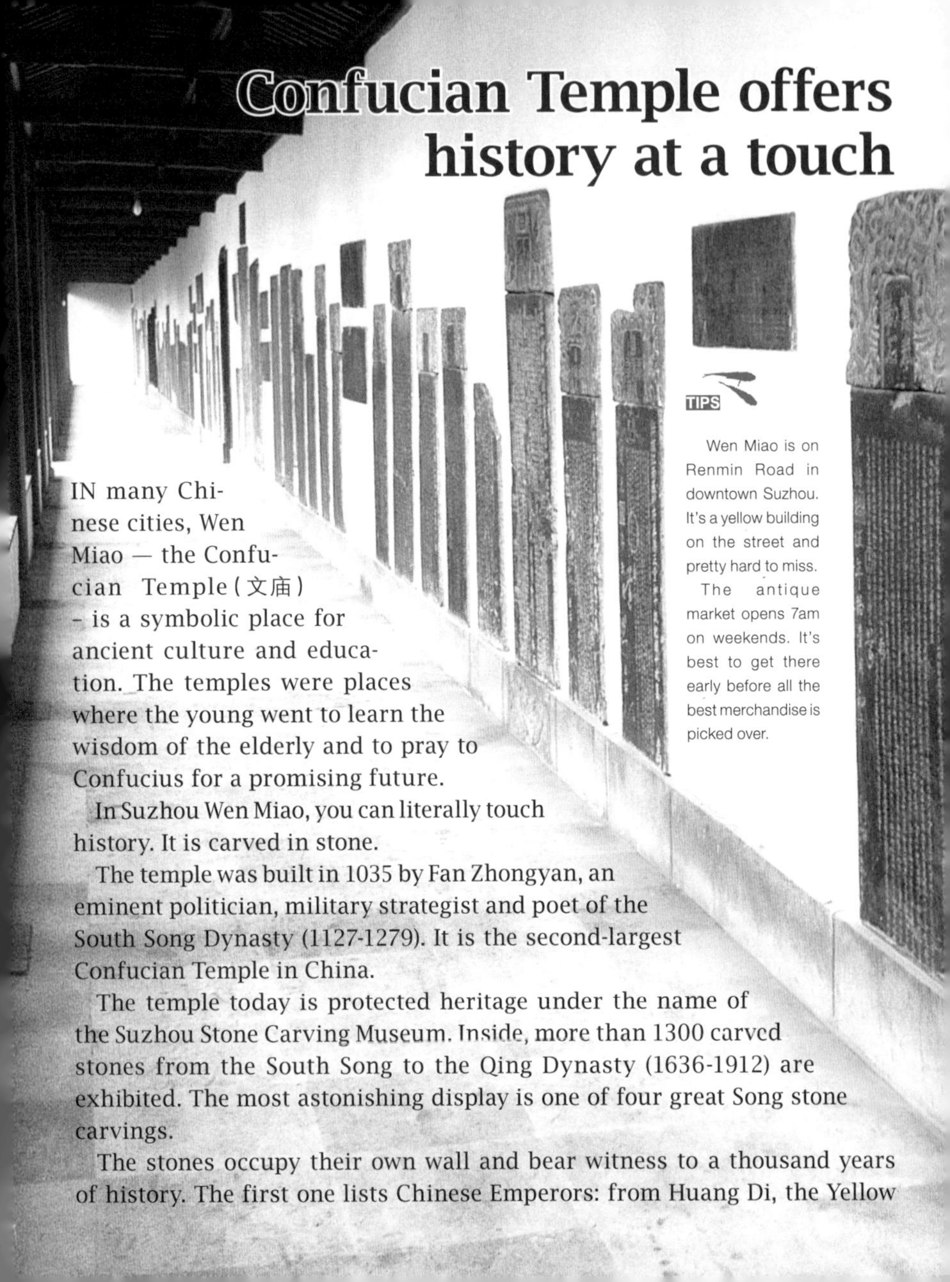

Confucian Temple offers history at a touch

TIPS

Wen Miao is on Renmin Road in downtown Suzhou. It's a yellow building on the street and pretty hard to miss.

The antique market opens 7am on weekends. It's best to get there early before all the best merchandise is picked over.

IN many Chinese cities, Wen Miao — the Confucian Temple (文庙) - is a symbolic place for ancient culture and education. The temples were places where the young went to learn the wisdom of the elderly and to pray to Confucius for a promising future.

In Suzhou Wen Miao, you can literally touch history. It is carved in stone.

The temple was built in 1035 by Fan Zhongyan, an eminent politician, military strategist and poet of the South Song Dynasty (1127-1279). It is the second-largest Confucian Temple in China.

The temple today is protected heritage under the name of the Suzhou Stone Carving Museum. Inside, more than 1300 carved stones from the South Song to the Qing Dynasty (1636-1912) are exhibited. The most astonishing display is one of four great Song stone carvings.

The stones occupy their own wall and bear witness to a thousand years of history. The first one lists Chinese Emperors: from Huang Di, the Yellow

Emperor, who lived somewhere between 2696–2598 B.C., to Emperor Li Zong of South Song Dynasty (1127-1279).

The other three carving stones depict a national map of the North Song Dynasty, a map of Suzhou City from 1229 and one of the oldest astronomy map in the world, which is considered even today remarkably accurate.

There are also more than 200 smaller stone carvings, many of them bearing government edicts of the time. Other stones relate commercial transactions of the times and show a highly developed economy in Suzhou in the late Ming and Qing dynasties.

Museum notwithstanding, Suzhou Wen Miao itself is worth a visit. The Dacheng Hall occupies the temple's main building. Dacheng means "great and final achievements" in Chinese, which was probably especially true for the students who applied themselves diligently.

The hall is constructed of machilusnanmu, one of the most valuable woods in China. Ancient instruments such as Zhong and Qin are displayed in the hall, in honor of the prominence music and art held in ancient scholastic culture.

The temple, it seems, has modern day uses, too. Weekend mornings, it is turned into an antiques bazaar and draws big crowds. Treasure-hunters would enjoy a prowl there as long as they are careful to distinguish between authenticity and fakes.

(Zhou Yubin)

Uncovering hidden gems

SUZHOU has many little treasures tucked into out-of-the-way corners, and one of the sweetest by far is a small museum that is dedicated to holidays and festivals, and the rituals of life in Suzhou as it used to be.

Entrance to the Folk Custom Museum (民俗博物馆) is free, and it is a family-friendly museum that will have the kids begging to go back a second time. Housed in an old mansion with a courtyard, the museum is loaded with displays kids love to see: doll-house rooms with families of little clay people carrying out their special traditions.

In one display you can see everyone cleaning the house from top to bottom in preparation for the New Year holiday. Everything must be mended, polished, and fixed, with no "old business" carried over into the New Year.

Then look at the replica of a Qing-era kitchen with the unique kind of wood burning stoves they used to have. There is a little cleaver and other tools. Every Suzhou kitchen had a Kitchen God back then and there is a little altar to him. The superstition was that he would make a report to the Emperor on the status of the household – sort of like Santa's list of who's been naughty or nice – and therefore he has a special day for required tokens of respect!

In one beautiful home, the one-year-old child has been placed on a big table, surrounded by objects such as an abacus, a book, some money, a piece of jewelry, and more. Many in the family are gathered around the table to see which object will take the child's interest first. If he reaches for the abacus we predict he'll be very good at numbers. If he

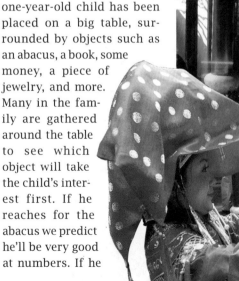

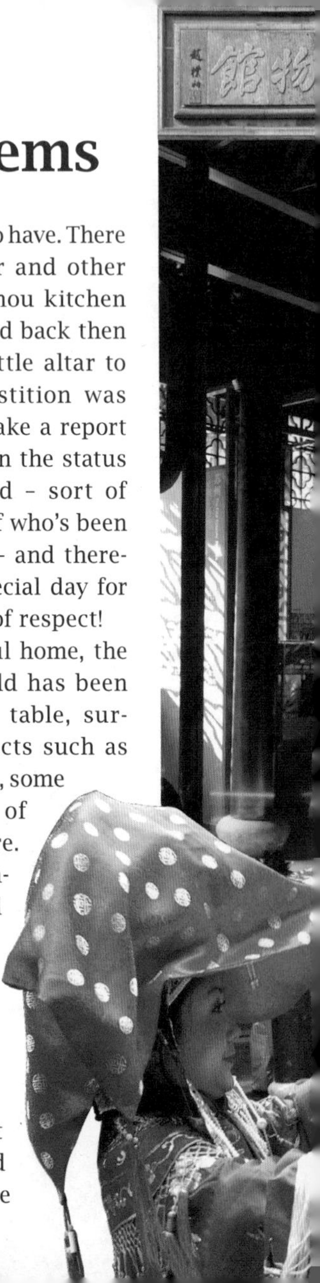

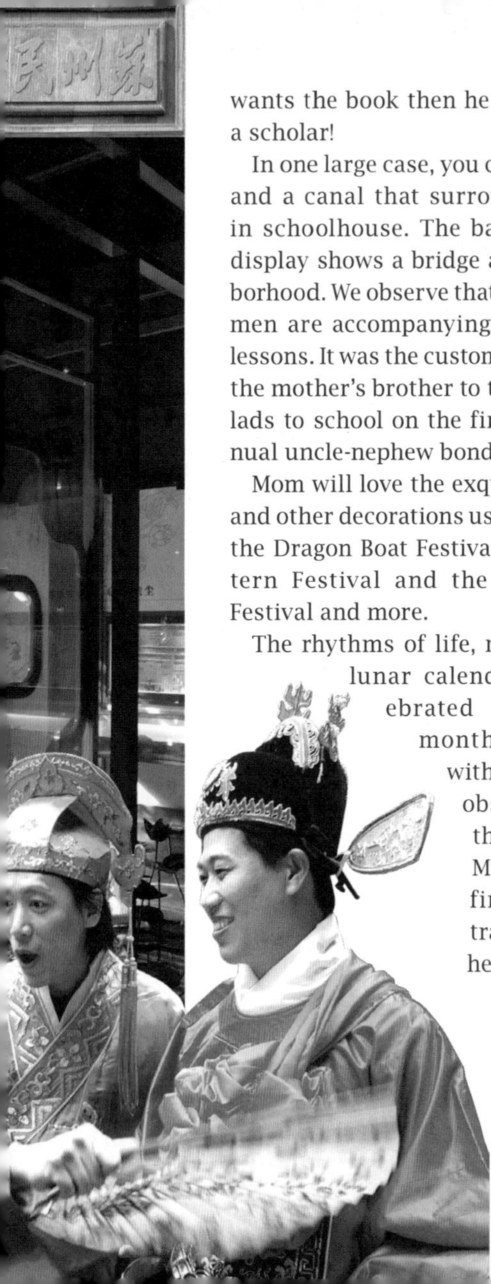

wants the book then he will surely be a scholar!

In one large case, you can see a street and a canal that surround a walled-in schoolhouse. The backside of the display shows a bridge and the neighborhood. We observe that several young men are accompanying boys to their lessons. It was the custom in Suzhou for the mother's brother to take the young lads to school on the first day: an annual uncle-nephew bonding tradition!

Mom will love the exquisite lanterns and other decorations used to celebrate the Dragon Boat Festival and the Lantern Festival and the Mid-Autumn Festival and more.

The rhythms of life, marked by the lunar calendar, were celebrated every single month in Suzhou with some special observance, and the Folk Custom Museum does a fine job at portraying this rich heritage.

(Susan Blauvelt)

TIPS

Find it! Get to the Suzhou Museum, walk along the pedestrian street as far as Humble Administrator's Garden.

Take a right turn to Yuanlin, 200 meters. Tall door in a big wall, on the right. Tiny sign: "Museum Hours." That's it!

The museum is the boyhood home of I.M. Pei, world-famous architect, and designer of new buildings for the Suzhou Museum.

On the roof of the first hall, see a sculptural group of portraits depicting the Eight Immortals, the original "superheros" - each with their own ordinary-looking object that can be turned into a weapon at will!

Don't miss the murals of Old Suzhou, teeming with little stories.

A luxury place to stay

FOR five-star luxury amid the exquisite classical architecture of Old Suzhou, it's hard to beat the Pan Pacific hotel in the downtown of the city.

Its classical gardens and ancient style of architecture blend seamlessly with the modern conveniences of luxury rooms and fine dining.

The hotel itself has become something of a tourist attraction in the city.

It's located with easy access to a wide range of attractions, including Taihu Lake, Hanshan Temple, West Garden Temple, etc.

The hotel is magnificent just to stroll through. Its abbeys and corridors, elaborate wooden pillars and carved windows hark pleasantly back to glorious eras of yesteryear.

Outdoors, the hotel has scenic gardens and sculpted bridges that evoke a feeling of tranquility.

It is near the famous Panmen Gate

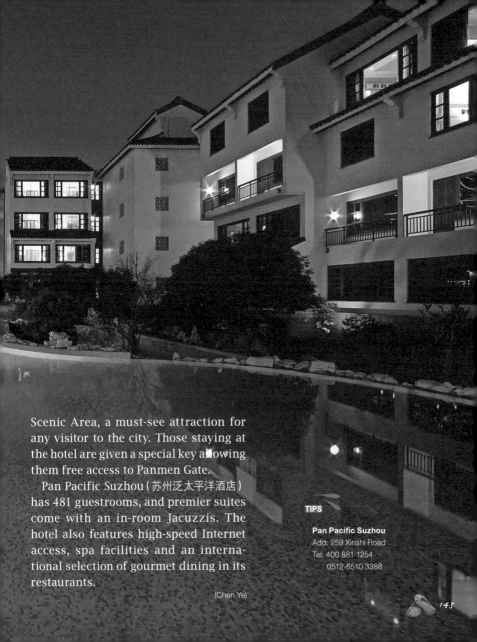

Scenic Area, a must-see attraction for any visitor to the city. Those staying at the hotel are given a special key allowing them free access to Panmen Gate.

Pan Pacific Suzhou (苏州泛太平洋酒店) has 481 guestrooms, and premier suites come with an in-room Jacuzzis. The hotel also features high-speed Internet access, spa facilities and an international selection of gourmet dining in its restaurants.

(Chen Ye)

TIPS

Pan Pacific Suzhou
Add: 259 Xinshi Road
Tel: 400 881 1254
0512-6510 3388

Paradise is not lost in modern Suzhou

THE name Shangri-la is always guaranteed to conjure up visions of mystical harmony in a hidden paradise, though the term wasn't coined until the 1933 novel "Lost Horizon" by British author James Hilton.

If it's a modern-day paradise you are seeking, you can't beat the Shangri-la Hotel (香格里拉大酒店) in Suzhou.

It was the first international hotel built in Suzhou New District.

Like all hotels in this five-star international chain, the Suzhou Shangri-la places guests in the lap of luxury. You sense it the minute you walk through the door and inhale the beautiful light fragrance dispersed by the hotel's air-conditioning system.

This is a place to be pampered and spoiled, whether you are taking one of the daily tours organized for guests to see the city or just luxuriating in the pool or spa bath.

From gentle massages to a refreshing work-out in the gym, guests are invited to relax and throw off the cares of the world.

The hotel has 300 elegantly

appointed rooms and suites catering to international comforts with a Chinese touch.

When it comes to fine dining, the Shang Palace is the premier Chinese restaurant of the hotel, famous throughout the city for its cuisine. It features one large dining hall and six private dining areas. The team of Chinese chefs specializes in Huaiyang and Cantonese cuisines.

The accent here is on fresh, regional ingredients, such as shrimp from nearby Taihu Lake. Steamed and accompanied by Suzhou's popular sweet Ji Tou Mi balls, the shrimp dish is a sensation you won't soon forget.

Noodles here are also excellent. So, too, is the Song Shu Gui Yu, or Squirrel-shaped Mandarin Fish in Sweet and Sour Sauce, which originated in Suzhou.

(Caterina Bernardini)

TIPS

The hotel has a grand view of the city's SND, lit up at night. The hotel is not far from the Shanghai-Nanjing Expressway and only eight minutes from the Suzhou Railway Station. If you want to go shopping, a two-minute walk will take you into the commercial district.

Add: 168 Tayuan Road, Suzhou New District

Tel: 0512-6808 0168

Stylish Suzhou

No matter you believe it or not,
Suzhou is a stylish city.
Take noodles everyday as breakfast,
Stroll in the flower market in the whole morning,
Find the fun in selecting the antiques,
And enjoy shaping when darkness approaches,
I am leisurely and energetic,
I am unique and irreplaceable.

VI

A good time together with books

IN Suzhou, it is very rare to find a place that both foreigners and Chinese go to and integrate. Foreigners usually go to places that cater for a Westernized palate while the majority of the Chinese go to places that serve traditional and local food.

So, when I was introduced to the Bookworm (老书虫), I was quite blown away. As soon as you walk through the door, you see a mix of Chinese and Westerners. For this alone, the Bookworm is an unusual place in Suzhou.

The Bookworm is found near the end of Shiquan Street (known to many simply as Bar Street) in a building that is traditionally Chinese. Living up to its name, it's like a library – all available wall space is lined with books of every type and genre in many of languages.

During the day, The Bookworm has a unique feel to it. It's somewhat between a pub and a coffee shop where you can't help but feel relaxed. Even in the evening, when the people drinking tea have been exchanged for people drinking beer, the feeling is still very relaxed and calm.

Throughout the year, monthly and even weekly, there are always different events that can be found there. Around Christmas, the bar opened up to a French Market selling handmade Christmas items and different types of French food. On occasion, it showcases local talent and local bands come and show off their musical ability.

Similar to this is the "open mike night" that occurs weekly where budding musicians step into the spotlight. There is a mix of music that ranges from country to pop and indie. This night alone is one of my favorite things about China. Each time it's different and everyone who takes part is received well and given genuine applause regardless of their ability.

The Bookworm is a friendly place where the Chinese and foreigners can go, mingle and have a good time together. It is a place to drink tea, meet friends for a good meal or just a night out. It's a place that is well worth a visit.

(Adamo Faccenda)

TIPS

Bookworm

Add: No. 77, Gun Xiu Fang, Shiquan Sreet

Average cost: 20-30 yuan per person for tea or coffee, 50 yuan per person for meals.

It boasts a large number of original editions and shows by expat performers.

Starbucks

Jinji Lake Store: Room 103-1 Rainbow Walk, 158 Xinggang Street, SIP

Tel: 0512-6767 1396

Times Square Store: Room 104, Building D, N6, Suzhou Times Square, 74042 South Cuiyuan Road, SIP (close to the Landscape Bridge of Huachi Street).

Tel: 0512-6696 6255

Tower Store: Room 103, 1st Floor, Suzhou Tower Mall Store, 38 Renmin Road, Canglang District.

Tel: 0512-6518 8623

Noah International Hotel Store: 1-2 Floor, Noah International, 58 Shishan Road, SND.

Tel: 0512-6805 0858

Dio Coffee

SIP Store: 78 Suhui Road, Suzhou Industrial Park

Tel: 0512-6761 7006

SND Binhe Road Store: 1701 Binhe Road, Suzhou New District

Tel: 0512-6831 0030

Xueshi Store: No. 1-13, Xueshi Street, Canglang District

Tel: 0512-6510 8809

Mingtien Coffee

Sports Center Store: 1st, Stadium of Sports Center, 1151 Sanxiang Road

Tel: 0512-6828 8716

SND Tayuan Store: Room 101, Building B, No, 136 Taiyuan Road

Tel: 0512-8918 8988

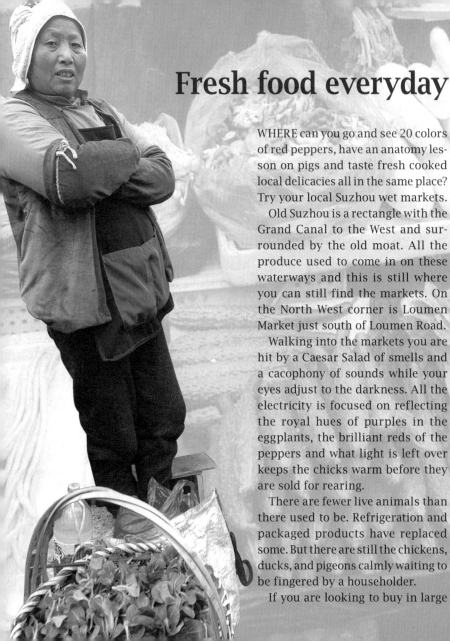

Fresh food everyday

WHERE can you go and see 20 colors of red peppers, have an anatomy lesson on pigs and taste fresh cooked local delicacies all in the same place? Try your local Suzhou wet markets.

Old Suzhou is a rectangle with the Grand Canal to the West and surrounded by the old moat. All the produce used to come in on these waterways and this is still where you can still find the markets. On the North West corner is Loumen Market just south of Loumen Road.

Walking into the markets you are hit by a Caesar Salad of smells and a cacophony of sounds while your eyes adjust to the darkness. All the electricity is focused on reflecting the royal hues of purples in the eggplants, the brilliant reds of the peppers and what light is left over keeps the chicks warm before they are sold for rearing.

There are fewer live animals than there used to be. Refrigeration and packaged products have replaced some. But there are still the chickens, ducks, and pigeons calmly waiting to be fingered by a householder.

If you are looking to buy in large

quantities, head to the Xi'er Road Market at the corner of Dongda Street across from Panmen Gate. This quarter is the domain of the restaurant supply traders.

My favorite market is on the south east corner of Suzhou just outside the moat on Hengjie Street and Moye Road. There is the large covered market but the action outside on Hengjie Street is the most interesting. You can find winter quilts, the old fashioned thermos jugs with the red peony, a hundred types of pickled vegetables, dripping golden brown duck hanging by their necks freshly extracted from the cookers, hand-knitted gloves for 15 yuan and beautifully dressed sales girls flogging sheep inners.

Although stainless steel bun steamers are quickly replacing bamboo, Suzhou market scene is all still very much old China and very much alive. Get out there and eat it up while it lasts!

(Patrick Donahue)

TIPS

Suzhou's best wet markets:

Loumen Market just south of Loumen Road

Xi'er Road Market at the corner of Dongda Street across from Panmen Gate

Hengjie Street Market at Hengjie Street and Moye Road

Feathers, fins and miniature mountains

TUCKED away in a small area at the center of Suzhou is the Pet Market – a small labyrinth of tiny alleyways filled with an array of colorful, exotic sights to amaze and delight you.

As the name implies, the Pet Market sells animals of all shapes and sizes for you to view, wonder at and buy.

Goldfish are sold in their thousands along with other more tropical species that are both freshwater and marine. Large marine and freshwater tanks are on display, showing their colorful occupants. Other types of marine animals on offer are several different types of terrapin species in varying degrees of size, shape and color. You can also find newts at the market that will delight and astound you with their strange shapes and translucent bodies.

If you prefer your pets to have feathers and beaks you will be overjoyed with the amount of different bird species. Big or small, quiet or loud; you will find them all here. Spend some time teaching minor birds to say "hello" or fall in love with the lovebirds in their rainbow feather coats. There are also cockatoos, parakeets, budgies and many different species of finches chirping, squawking and hopping around.

For the more exotic discerner of animals there are lizards and snakes. Chameleons have been known to be seen here, although you do have to keep a close eye out for them, as they don't want you to see them!

More traditionally you can find a good selection of wide-eyed little puppies. Poodles, German shepherds, Bassets and even bulldogs add their bit to the noisy little streets. Feline lovers won't have to do without their beloved pets, with kittens of all

types to "oooh and aaah" at.

Adjacent to the animals are several little alleyways that sell plants and garden or house ornaments. The plants can be bought as seeds or fully grown in beautifully crafted ceramic and clay pots. There is a great selection of Bonsai trees that have been lovingly grown with every twist and notch of every branch, trunk and leaf in perfect miniature. Bonsai's varieties of Oak, Elm, Ash, Cypress and almost any tree species you can think of including evergreen and Chinese species.

Bamboo plants grown with twisting and elaborate stems, Orchids of all descriptions and colors and many other plants are interlaced with traditional limestone rock statues.

The Chinese love for mountains is depicted in these limestone statues that are both wondrous and beautiful to look upon, with twisting rocks that have been weathered and eroded away throughout the eons. These depictions of "Huangshan," or Yellow Mountain, and the Limestone towers and conical hills Southeast of Guilin, China, can keep you mesmerized for hours. They come in all sizes and degrees of color and are inset on exquisite red wood plaques. Truly magnificent!

(Galvin Yack)

TIPS

To catch the real fantasy of Suzhou, the pet and plant market is a must-go for travelers, after a cruise along the Guanqian Street adjacent to it.

You need to be well trained to bargain and enjoy all the fun here. Meanwhile, vendor food is something that easily catches your eyes over the venture of pets and plants. Try the sweet porridge, if you are lucky enough to meet the old vendor who has been the porridge king of the area for a decade.

As an open-air market, shops usually won't be closed until 5pm. The chaos even extends to 8pm in summer time.

Add: 172 Pishi Street, Pingjiang District (north to Guanqian Street, the famous commercial pedestrian area)

Arts live well in Suzhou

SUZHOU has a long history of refinement. It has been a center for visual and performing arts for centuries while Shanghai and Singapore were still muddy backwaters and mangrove swamps. The city's is renowned for its paintings, sculptures, ceramics, and crafts such as silk embroidery, carpentry and jade carving. There has been a renaissance over the last five years supported by the demand for well-appointed offices, sophisticated restaurants and decorations for the homes of arriving expat families and a rising middle class who have walls to decorate and floor space to cover.

The greatest concentration of galleries and shops with high-quality artistic wares is on renovated Pingjiang Road. In the center of the five block street is Le Pont des Arts Gallery located at number 112-115. Here they have contemporary work of local and foreign artists. A wander up this lovely street will take you past beautiful textiles, delicate ceramics, wood and woven crafts and fine art displays.

There is even a grouping of handicapped artists' small studios showing traditional calligraphy, paintings or get your own face sculpted in a miniature clay bust.

Shiquan Street between Moye Road and Renmin Road has half a dozen art galleries. Many of these combine traditional Chinese paintings with antiques and decorative stone pieces. The Pureland is located at 659 Shiquan Street.

If it is jade that catches your fancy, just behind the Suzhou Hotel on Shiquan Street there are perhaps 100 skilled carvers working away in their shops in the winding back streets.

The most impressive boost to the contemporary art scene in Suzhou is the True Color Museum, 219 Tongda Road. It is privately owned and open free of charge from 10am to 5pm. There are cutting-edge conceptual displays and multi-media works.

So the Arts are alive and well in Suzhou and they are not all confined in museums. Although there are still lots of room for the development of an appreciation for the arts in Suzhou, the city is off to an excellent start with a wide palette of choices.

(Patrick Donahue)

TIPS

Galleries and Sources of Fine Arts in Suzhou:

Le Pont des Arts Gallery, 112-115 Pingjiang Road

Pureland Gallery, 659-3 Shiquan Street

True Color Museum, 219 Tongda Road in SIP , 0512-6596 8890

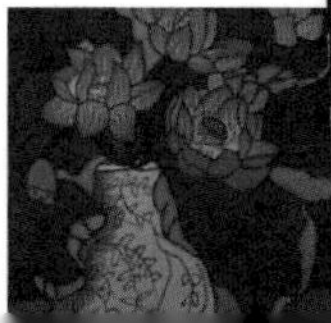

Shoppers' paradise

SUZHOU is a great place to find bargains but you've got to know where to go. Start at the Pearl Market (Zhen Zhu Cheng) 45 minutes north of the city in Weitang of the Xiangcheng District. Here you can pick up a necklace with real pearls for as little as 10 yuan.

There is also the jade market. Tucked just south of Shiquan Street, next to the Master-of-Nets Garden, the market is a labyrinth of small jade carving shops. These people are more artists than merchants and don't seem in a hurry to close a deal.

For clothing, head to Metro Shopping Center (Mei Luo Shang Cheng) at the corner of Guanqian Street and Renmin Road. Or, check the Jiu Guang Department Store on the east bank of the Jinji Lake if you are quite tolerant of price. They have lots of name brand lines and lots of sales.

For children's clothing, go to Gong Yuan Road. Things are cheap but you need to check everything closely. For children aged three to 10 try Baby Bear in Singa Plaza (Xin Du Guan Chang). Here you find good-quality, branded goods at very reasonable prices.

If you are looking for famous Suzhou silks you can try the No. 1 Silk Factory on Panmen Road where there's a great selection of bed comforters. Or try the Silk Museum at 66 Renmin Road.

One thing to remember when dealing with the Suzhou natives, they are not really into bargaining. So if you want something, you might ask for a little "discount" but don't push it or you and the seller will both lose face, be unhappy and you will almost always walk away empty handed. So, unless it is clearly a tourist trap, ask for a 10% discount and be satisfied if the seller accepts.

Happy shopping!

(Patrick Donahue)

TIPS

Great bargain shopping in Suzhou:

Pearl Market (Zhen Zhu Cheng) in Wei Tang

The Jade Market south of Shiquan Street, next to the Master's of the Nets Garden

Children's clothing on Gongyuan Road

Baby Bear for children's clothing in Singa Plaza, SIP. (Xin Du Guan Chang)

No. 1 Silk Factory on Panmen Road

Silk Museum at 66 Renmin Road

Giant, Silverstorm, Trek and Decathelon for bicycles

Restaurant 101

YOU will find every province of China represented in Suzhou's vast array of restaurants, and the different cuisines of these regions will never fail to amaze and delight you. The signs of each restaurant indicate which kind of provincial food they specialize in, so ask a native if you want to eat Hunan tonight, or Harbin-style.

In the spirit of "Viva le diversity" we offer the following list of tips for your maximum enjoyment:

In Suzhou, everyone at the table shares their food. Ordering dinner means deciding what everybody wants to eat, so to facilitate the discussion, the waiter will hand you one menu.

The waiter will often as not bring everybody hot water to drink, or some weak hot tea.

Food choices are often made on the basis of what is "good for your health." Some of the things Suzhou people eat that seem strange to a Westerner, will be immediately justified if you inquire. Sheep's blood soup? Why, it's good for detoxing your lungs! Eat the hide of a pig? Of course! It's good for a woman's skin and the health of her ovaries! This kind of "folk wisdom" is quite common, and as you observe the strength and agility and overall wellbeing of the older generation in Suzhou, you must concede that they seem to know quite a bit about staying healthy.

Forget rich desserts. Restaurants will offer watermelon and other fresh fruit, as a general rule. Maybe ice cream.

In the noodle shops you see on every street, which are very delicious and inexpensive, chopsticks might be in a big jar on the table for you to help yourself. However, many restaurants, to prove sterile conditions of plates, glass, and cup, will give you a shrink-wrapped set upon your sitting down.

Napkins? No. There might be a package of tissues on the table. Sometimes if you ask for paper, they will bring you a little package of tissues, and add a few yuan to your bill.

Conversely, toothpicks are frequently offered on the table. Don't be surprised to see someone cover the front her mouth with one hand while she picks her teeth.

Suzhou people are not very comfortable with "splitting the bill" or doing what Americans call "Dutch Treat." They will fight to pay the check every

time. You'd better be quick if you want to reciprocate ...

Tipping? The good news is that in all but the most high-end restaurants, tipping is not expected and not generally practiced either. Before I got wise, I even had a server chase me down the street shouting, "You left your money on the table!" The bad news is that your server will not check in frequently to see if you want anything else. Need more tea? Signal, or call out "Fu wu yuan er!" and your server will come right over.

(Susan Blauvelt)

TIPS

Using chopsticks is easy, once you know the technique:

Wedge one chopstick between the web of your thumb and index finger, and the fourth finger. The thumb exerts a little pressure so that this chopstick stays in place.

The chopstick on top is grasped with the end of the thumb and the index finger. Those two hold it, and move it against the stationary stick to pick up the food.

Beginners can fold a wad of tissue between the sticks, held together with a rubber band, and then use the above method. Children can learn this way, too!

Chopsticks are the norm, but you can ask for a spoon, if you like. Some places even have forks.

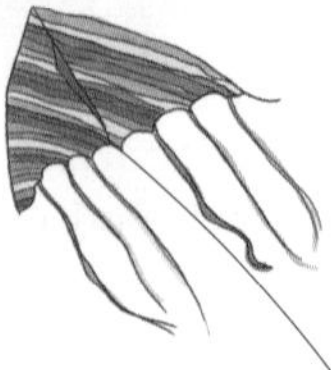

Off the beaten track

LIKE many cities in China, Suzhou is not known for its parks; however, in Guihua Park（桂花公园）, it does have one of some acclaim. It is the perfect place to spend a morning or afternoon safe in the knowledge that almost all of the family will be adequately catered for.

This hidden gem lies a 15-minute walk south of Shiquan Street and despite being more rudimentary in places than the aforementioned site, is larger, less crowded and subsequently more peaceful. The only downside is the potential effort involved in getting there, although onsite parking and numerous buses remove a significant amount of this the so-said difficulty.

When arriving at the central gate one is able to access the park from one of two entrances. Go straight ahead and just beyond the exercise area, after crossing a wooden bridge spanning a small waterway, lies one of the city's larger canals. In contrast, by turning left one is first met by a managed pigeon coop and feeding area. This is followed a little further on by a decent-sized children's play area.

However, irrespective of which route one initially opts for, the secret is to navigate towards the center of the park. This is because with the exception of the entrance, Guihua is in effect a self-contained site, with water lying to the east and south, and residential buildings walled off to the west. Also, at the far southeast corner of the park a real treasure is to be found. A replica old-fashioned wall, beautifully lit at night, with a mock, but full size, guard

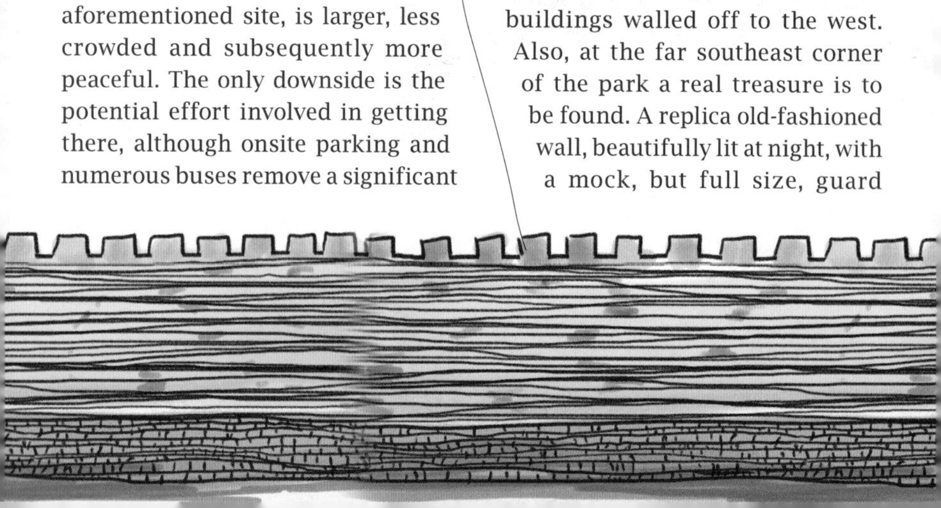

tower stands tall. These offer great partial views of the city's skyline.

As if this were not enough, with fewer visitor numbers, it is not uncommon to find large swathes of the park deserted, and with a wooded path leading away from Gui Hua at its rear, one also has the additional benefit of leaving from an alternative exit. In fact, this route that meanders westward has paths running on the north and south perimeters of an earthen, tree-covered ridge. With beautiful flowers adorning the pathways in the summer and numerous rest spots tastefully provided, a tranquil stroll is in the offering.

(Gareth Morris)

TIPS

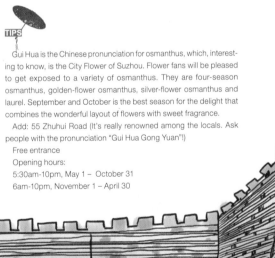

Gui Hua is the Chinese pronunciation for osmanthus, which, interesting to know, is the City Flower of Suzhou. Flower fans will be pleased to get exposed to a variety of osmanthus. They are four-season osmanthus, golden-flower osmanthus, silver-flower osmanthus and laurel. September and October is the best season for the delight that combines the wonderful layout of flowers with sweet fragrance.

Add: 55 Zhuhui Road (It's really renowned among the locals. Ask people with the pronunciation "Gui Hua Gong Yuan"!)

Free entrance

Opening hours:

5:30am-10pm, May 1 – October 31

6am-10pm, November 1 – April 30

A sweet place for cycling

ON my third day in Suzhou I went out and bought a bike. It wasn't a fancy bicycle with gears either, despite the fact that it plainly said "Fashion" right there on the frame ...

I recommend getting basic transportation like this if you are going to be spending much time in Suzhou. You can also borrow the "free bicycles" that the city provides, which are available at many places. (See "TIPS" on Page 340). It's fun!

You don't need to exert yourself too much when riding around this town. Suzhou is a luxuriously level city, which you might not guess since it is surrounded by many lovely hills. But the city itself, which is really like three small cities side-by-side, is very flat, and therefore it is a paradise for part-time pedallers.

Then add the joy of discovery, and Suzhou gives you that in spades. Around every corner of the old town, Suzhou City, there is evidence of her long history in the buildings that really do look like the ink wash paintings they sell. Whoever said "God is in the details" must have ridden around Suzhou, noticing all the arched bridges, with the different kinds of lion and dragon finials, crossing the hundreds of canals, and the small parks everywhere with little pavilions and statues of beloved ancient poets. Getting "up-close and personal" with the Suzhou street scene can be pretty rewarding.

Let's talk safety. Suzhou streets are designed for cyclists and have dedicated bike lanes on both sides of

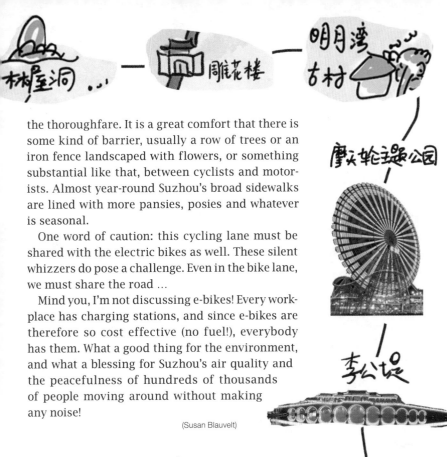

the thoroughfare. It is a great comfort that there is some kind of barrier, usually a row of trees or an iron fence landscaped with flowers, or something substantial like that, between cyclists and motorists. Almost year-round Suzhou's broad sidewalks are lined with more pansies, posies and whatever is seasonal.

One word of caution: this cycling lane must be shared with the electric bikes as well. These silent whizzers do pose a challenge. Even in the bike lane, we must share the road …

Mind you, I'm not discussing e-bikes! Every workplace has charging stations, and since e-bikes are therefore so cost effective (no fuel!), everybody has them. What a good thing for the environment, and what a blessing for Suzhou's air quality and the peacefulness of hundreds of thousands of people moving around without making any noise!

(Susan Blauvelt)

摩天轮主题公园

李公堤

狮子林

昆曲博物馆

科技文化中心

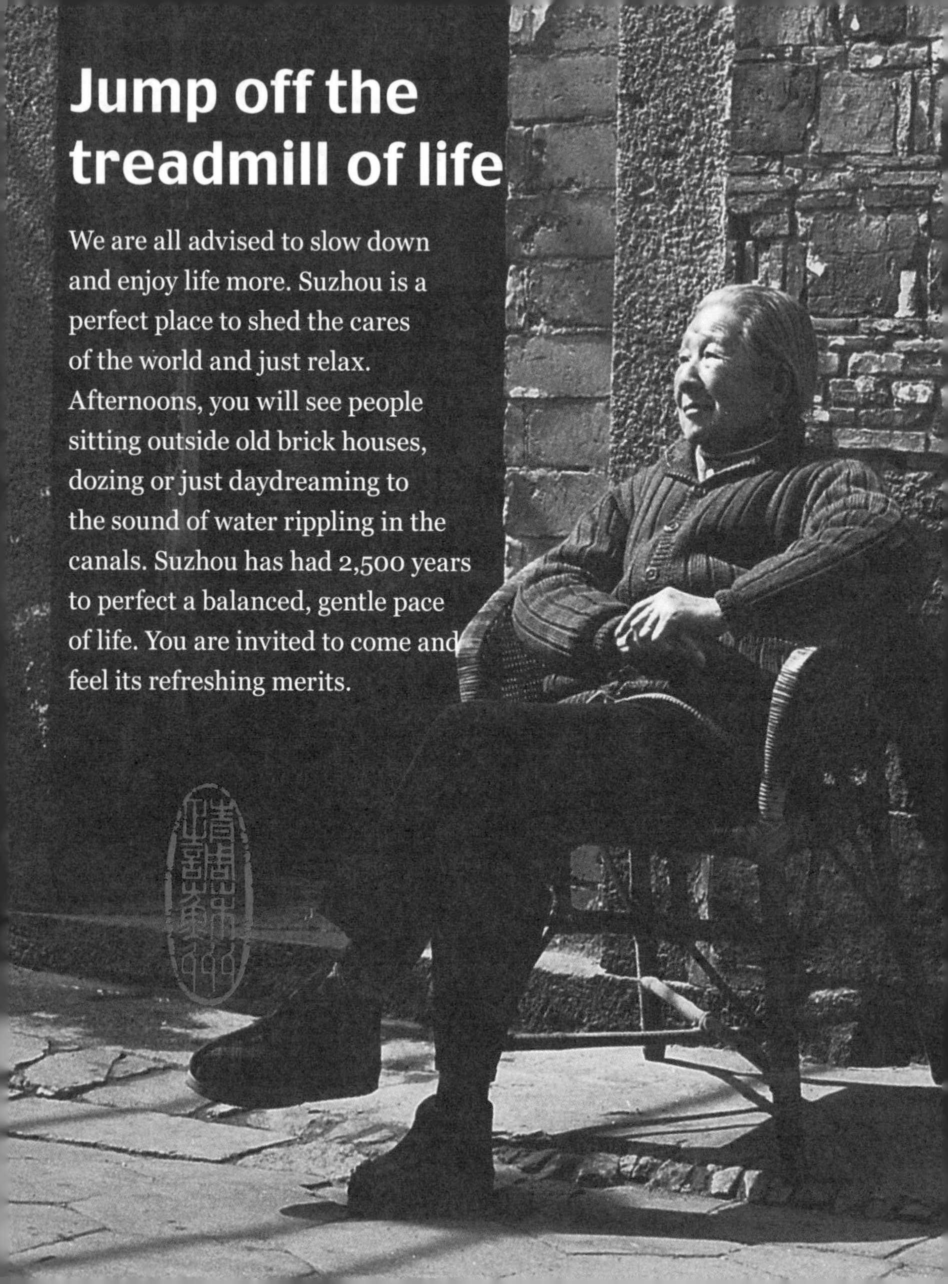

Jump off the treadmill of life

We are all advised to slow down and enjoy life more. Suzhou is a perfect place to shed the cares of the world and just relax. Afternoons, you will see people sitting outside old brick houses, dozing or just daydreaming to the sound of water rippling in the canals. Suzhou has had 2,500 years to perfect a balanced, gentle pace of life. You are invited to come and feel its refreshing merits.

VII

Inside the partly open door, imagination is given free rein. Every heart, whether lonely, happy or pining, will find solace here, as if floating through water on a spring day.

The old house, with its silence and the whispers of grandfathers past reprimanding naught children, make a heart leap. In the solitude of the moment, memories ebb and flow, and the everyday stresses of life seem to evaporate.

笑口且常開
財源滾滾來
好年好景好运气
多福多財多吉祥

In the morning, the hissing sound of a coal fire is music to the waking ears. On a bridge nearby, housewives with baskets of fresh vegetables stop to chat in their soft Suzhou accents.

The scene of washing clothes by the river evokes a sentimental wave of nostalgia that leads one to savor the roots of home.

A good time in the backstreet home, no iPad, just a real little cat to play with; a piece of leisure on the old bridge, and a thermos bottle to drink a cup of tea with. Food from the slow coal stove and grandma is more delicious than the best restaurants.

Cast aside the complexities of modern life. Buns and fried puffs for breakfast, a blue porcelain bowl on a kitchen counter or the drip of a faucet may remind you of life's simple pleasures.

Bridges are the great connectors between waterways and roads that have plied people and trade for centuries. Let me sit on a bridge like a fallen leaf, silently watching life pass by.

The old street is a stage for culture and folklore, such as the Da Lian Xiang dance, the lifting of the bride's veil and the walking across three bridges during the Lantern Festival. Double happiness and all other kinds of joy abound amid the exuberance of youth.

轧神仙
苏州人的狂欢节
老妈米线
Rice Flour Noodles
餐厅
清真
古城河 环古城游 团体 婚庆用船
神仙鞋都
龙虾

Brazilians have their sambas, and the people of Suzhou have their own special customs to stage a carnival. There are "tiger shoes" worn by some, and the beating of waist drums. Everyone hopes to encounter the fairy called Lv Dongbin, as tradition dictates.

Narrow alleyways become memory lanes, where you can hear the whispers of the past between stone walls. Legends and folktales still lurk in these long passageways if you stop long enough to hear them.

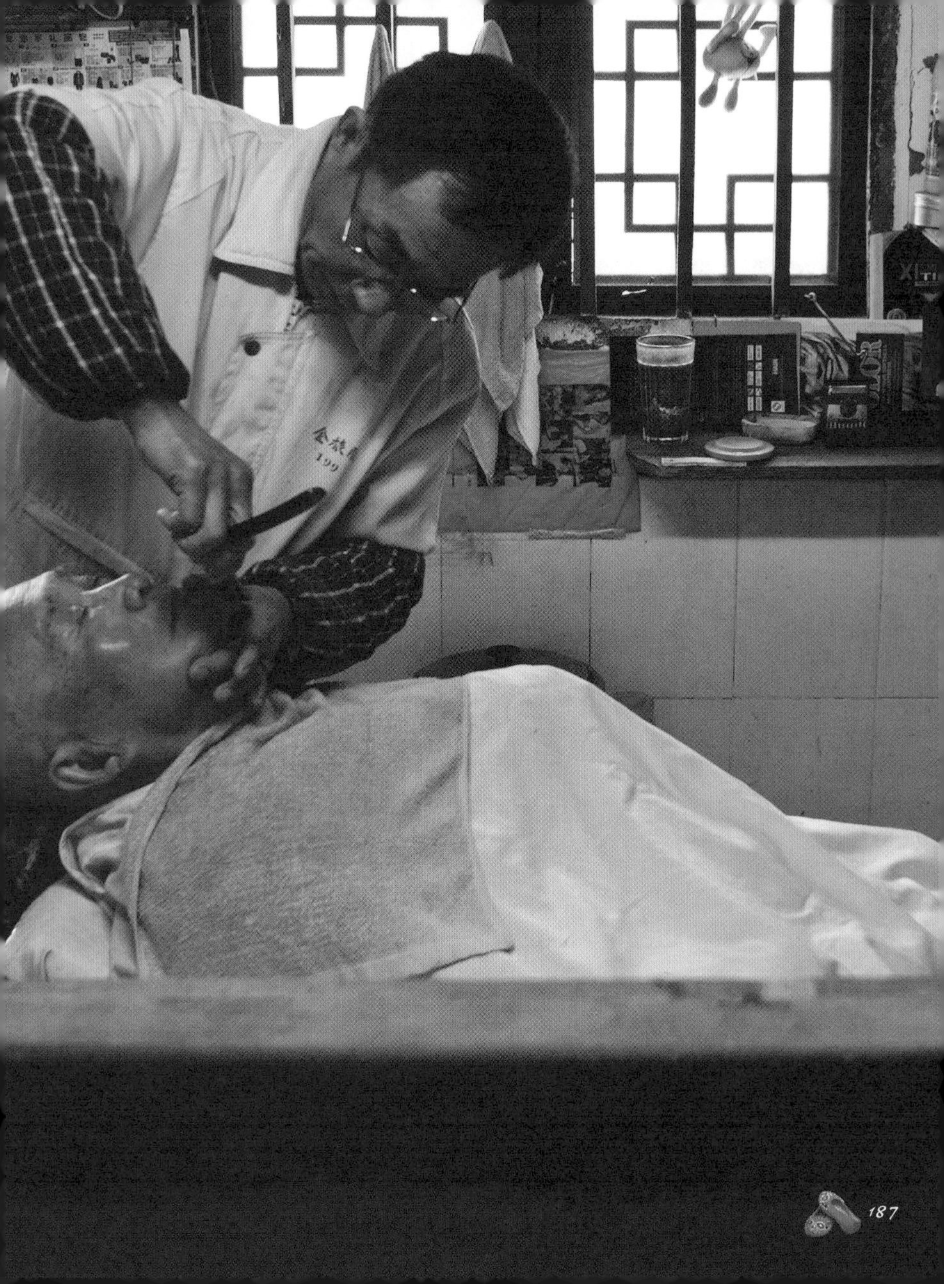

Green vegetables in old lady Hao's basket and the cheerful chirping of colorful birds in their cages evoke the famous Chinese poem that begins, "I don't know what season it is on this night."

As time flies, people start to wonder whether the bamboo basket bought by the old lady from Yejia Alley has ever been used to hold green vegetables covered with water drops, radish just plucked from the mud and arrowheads covered with big leaves. Just take leave from the city's hustle and bustle - and lose yourself in the magic of a moment.

VIII

Fashion code of Jinji Lake

We show our respect to Paul Andrew,
who has contributed two marvellous works in China:
National Center for the Performing Arts in Beijing
And Suzhou Culture and Arts Center, along the Jinji Lake.
While appreciating too much similar seasonal views,
You will no doubt be fascinated by the splendor of the Lake.
It belongs to the fads and fashion,
And to every particular taste.
Come on! Dance with moonlight,
And drink among the visual feast.

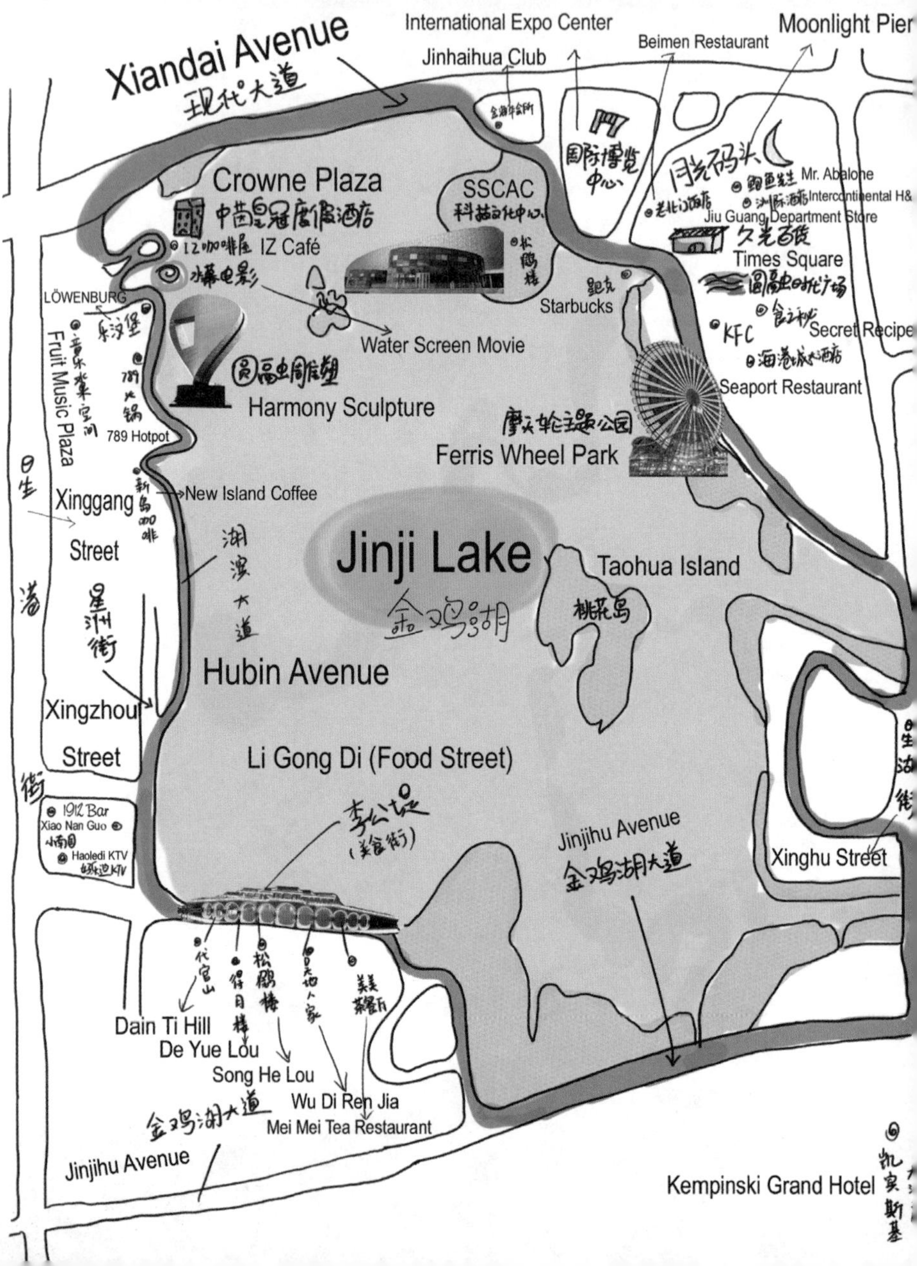
Xiandai Avenue
现代大道
International Expo Center
Jinhaihua Club
Beimen Restaurant
Moonlight Pier
Crowne Plaza
中茵皇冠假日酒店
SSCAC
科技文化中心
国际博览中心
月光码头
Mr. Abalone
Intercontinental H&
Jiu Guang Department Store
久光百货
Times Square
圆融时代广场
IZ Café
IZ咖啡屋
水幕电影
Water Screen Movie
Starbucks
LÖWENBURG
KFC
Secret Recipe
Seaport Restaurant
Fruit Music Plaza
789 Hotpot
圆融雕塑
Harmony Sculpture
摩天轮主题公园
Ferris Wheel Park
New Island Coffee
Xinggang Street
Jinji Lake
金鸡湖
Taohua Island
桃花岛
湖滨大道
Hubin Avenue
星洲街
Xingzhou Street
Li Gong Di (Food Street)
李公堤 (美食街)
1912 Bar
Xiao Nan Guo
Haoledi KTV
Jinjihu Avenue
金鸡湖大道
Xinghu Street
Dain Ti Hill
De Yue Lou
Song He Lou
Wu Di Ren Jia
Mei Mei Tea Restaurant
金鸡湖大道
Jinjihu Avenue
Kempinski Grand Hotel
凯宾斯基

金鸡湖

Jinji Lake

When writing a love story, you need the right elements: a gloomy night, foggy lights, a Ferris Wheel and a Lake that is so peaceful you could hear lover's whispers. Luckily, you will find it all beside the Jinji Lake.

书写一个爱情故事，你需要些恰当的元素。幽暗的夜晚，迷离的灯火，摩天轮和一池安静到可以聆听对方低语的湖水。幸运的是，金鸡湖畔这一切都有。

The other side of the double-sided embroidery

THE traditional double-side embroidery in Suzhou is really an amazing handicraft. The completely different patterns are perfectly merged on both sides of a fan.

Suzhou Industrial Park (SIP), located in the east of Suzhou, can be called the other side of the embroidery. The ancient city proper represents the traditional connotation of Suzhou, whereas the Industrial Park is the fashionable symbol of modern Suzhou. In fact, every visitor to Suzhou tends to forget that the city embraces thousands of years of history, but marvels at the fact that it's reputed as the second-largest industrial city in China.

The graceful melodies and the tranquil flowing waters in the ancient city of Suzhou, impress you with an extremely memorable view. While appreciating many similar seasonal views, you will no doubt be fascinated by the splendor of the lake. Under the misted moonlight, stroll along the side of Jinji Lake and leisurely go forward along the river bank of Li Gong Di; get on the Ferris Wheel and command a broad perspective of the sparkling Jinji Lake, in a daze for while; or visit the "Nest of Suzhou", Suzhou Art and Culture Center to enjoy a modern ballet, while imagining the performance with the dancers ...

It's quite easy to find a high-rise building that is comparable with any others in any cities of the world, yet remains fashionable. Thanks to Jinji Lake, the east of Suzhou has evolved

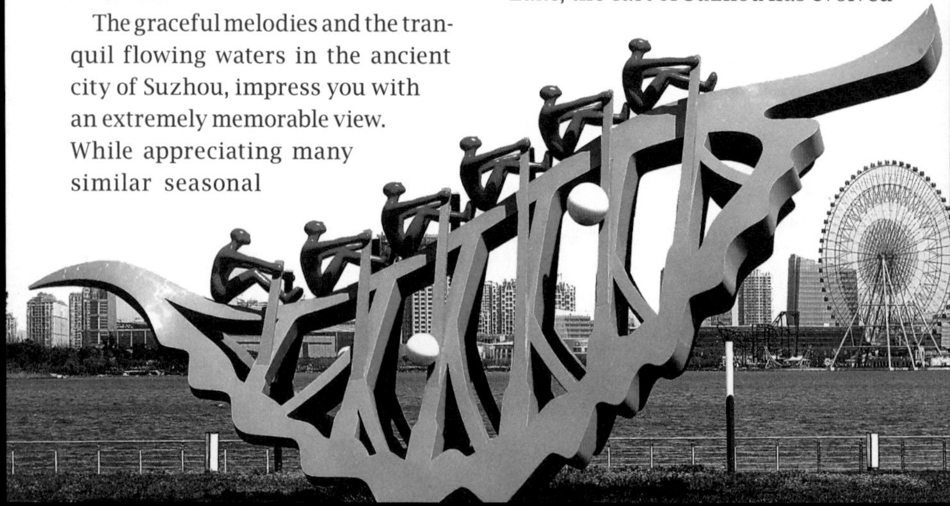

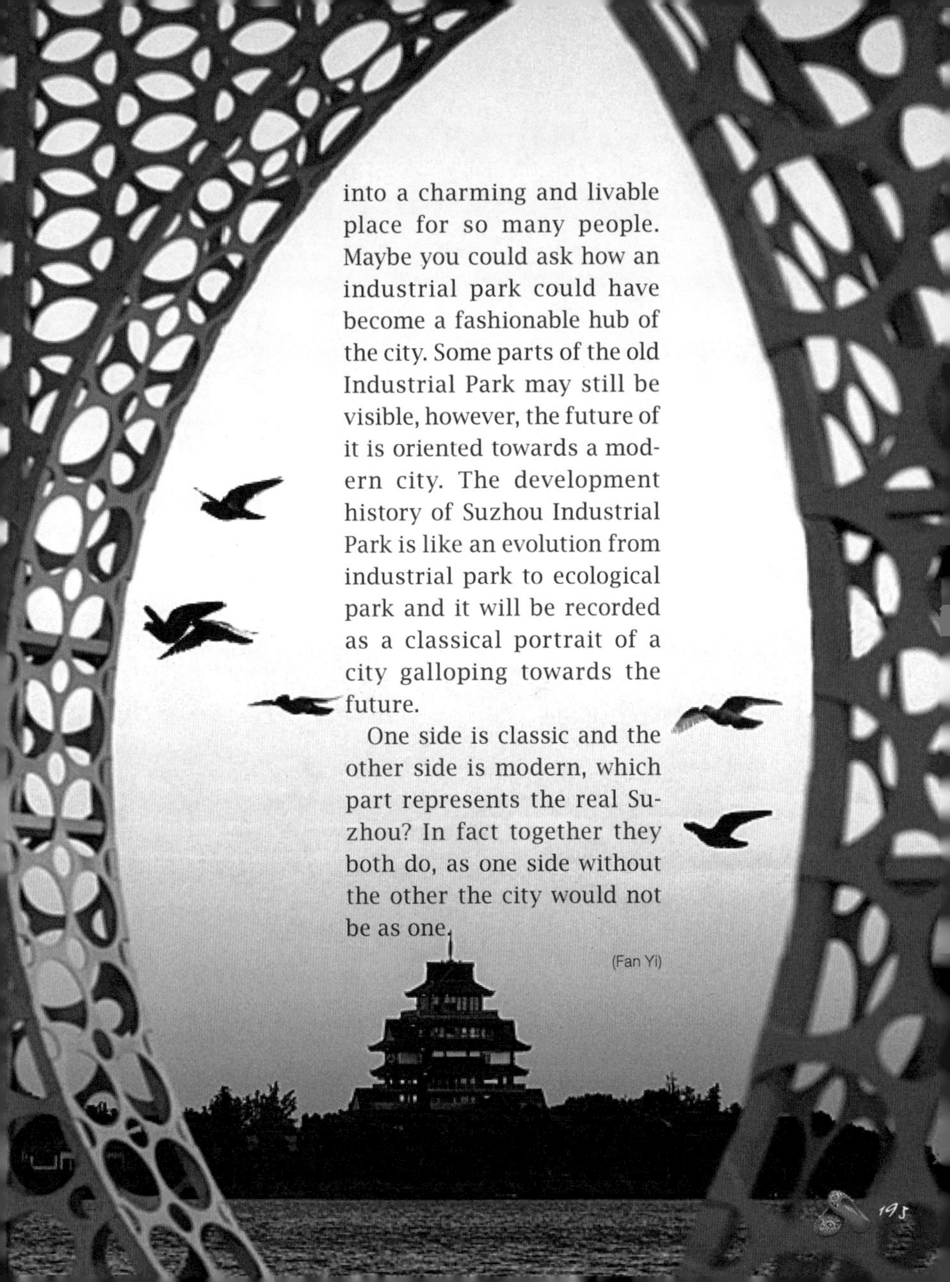

into a charming and livable place for so many people. Maybe you could ask how an industrial park could have become a fashionable hub of the city. Some parts of the old Industrial Park may still be visible, however, the future of it is oriented towards a modern city. The development history of Suzhou Industrial Park is like an evolution from industrial park to ecological park and it will be recorded as a classical portrait of a city galloping towards the future.

One side is classic and the other side is modern, which part represents the real Suzhou? In fact together they both do, as one side without the other the city would not be as one.

(Fan Yi)

Golden causeway encrusted with nightlife

A NATURAL freshwater body graced all year long by a light inland breeze, Jinji Lake was made into a hub of nightlife destinations, attractive promenades and world-class performance venues.

The most noticeable spot on Jinji Lake's trendy shores is Li Gong Di (李公堤), the lake's only causeway, for which a darting peninsula was built across its southern end. Li Gong Di extends over the mile long dyke, wielding restaurants, bars, live music venues and cafes.

Li Gong Di has everything the night visitor wishes to find: Western and world cuisine from every corner of the earth, nightclubs, quiet coffee houses and breathtaking views of the lakes' glittering shores. Not surprisingly, Li

Gong Di is also a wonder of modern architecture. Including natural features in its futuristic design, it builds on traditional Chinese imagery to create an environment everyone can feel comfortable in. Arched bridges, walkways, gardens and lawns sprawl like a flowing stream along the water, as if emanating from its depths.

Come to Li Gong Di, far from the stifling heat and busy crossroads of modern Suzhou, to find the best of China's international standards in urban design, entertainment and social settings.

(Alexis Lefranc)

A splendid and colorful center

I HAD heard so much hype about the Suzhou Culture and Arts Centre (苏州文化艺术中心) that I have to admit I was quite skeptical at first, fully expecting to be underwhelmed. Upon setting foot in the center, however, it soon dawned on me that it wasn't about competing with my Western-privileged history but rather about providing access to a panoply of enriching, entertaining, and educational experiences—new to some and familiar to others—for all visitors.

It is easy to see how the structure itself lives up to its promise to deliver "Life's Splendors In Full Color," as stated on its website. The interior proves no less impressive, both in terms of architecture and the kinds of programs it has to offer. The general feeling I got from my short stroll around the premises was one of polished composure but also of openness, as the space was obviously designed to invite and accommodate large audiences.

Another positive aspect of the center is its seemingly broad appeal. A brief survey of the movies showing as well as the current and upcoming

TIPS

Presenting bling-bling shows and movies, Suzhou Culture and Arts Centre is a desirable place for nightlife.

Add: No. 1, Guanfeng Street, SIP (close to Xiandai Avenue)

Public transport: Bus No. 2; 106; 108; 138; 156; 158; 206; 219; 258

live performances billed revealed that SSCAC makes efforts to cater to a wide range of audience interests, backgrounds, and age levels. Cinema listings included animated Chinese features, Western blockbusters and science documentaries. The 3D IMAX theatre ensures that all patrons can take their cinematic experience to ever more expansive dimensions. Live performance offerings included philharmonic orchestras from Western cities as well as Chinese ballets and Beijing operas.

Even the snack options show an attention to variety - standard Western movie-goer staples such as popcorn, soda, and candy stand alongside a soy milk tea bar, something more attuned to local taste buds.

(Duola Gong)

TIPS

Harmony Times Square (also known as Yuanrong Times Square) is located on the eastern side of Jinji Lake at SIP. Providing shopping, catering, entertainment, business, cultural and sightseeing services, it is a one-stop and comprehensive commercial center featured by large-scale and modern quality services.

Harmony Times Square attracts visitors from around the globe by its world's No. 1 screen. This giant 500-by-32-meter LED screen, constituted by 20 million lights emitting diodes and costing over 100 million yuan, has replaced the 400-meter one in Las Vegas as biggest in the world.

LED displays start at 6:30pm, 7:30pm and 8:30pm everyday.

Born to be famous

LOCATED on the eastern shore of Jinji Lake, and a short walk from Suzhou's giant Ferris Wheel, Times Square (时代广场) is a vast high-end retail hub.

Its main building is in effect a series of giant interconnected halls, partitioned in places for effect and broken up through necessity by escalators and walkways. With the first floor adhering to retail customers and selling perfumes and jewelry alongside clothing, the upper echelons of the center tend to be devoted to the latter good in the main. By contrast, the basement is a collection of restaurants and cosmetics shops, with a food market thrown in for good measure.

Crossing one of the nearby main roads on an elevated indoor walkway, one comes face to face with a floor devoted purely to children's entertainment. Play areas and toyshops cover the entire level, with clothing stores a few floors down. In addition to this, the smaller but just as busy additional shopping complex also caters to home decorations.

Outside restaurants and coffee shops are a notable addition to this locality. For the sake of extensiveness, an outdoors play area and indoor games center are also there. Again food and drink is the overriding feature, with the offerings covering just about all palate preferences, but traditional retail shops also predominate, and on the odd occasion television shoots have also been in the offering.

If one decides to walk towards the Ferris Wheel, it soon becomes apparent that this is a ride amongst many in a theme park. Walk a little further and you will find yourself among beautiful green walkways beside the river. Head in the opposite direction towards the cinema complex and just beyond the hotel, and an even more exclusive restaurant-filled waterfront emerges. Times Square quite clearly is as the name suggests a reflection of its age, but it is also one worth exploring.

(Gareth Morris)

Rainbow Walk

RAINBOWALK（湖滨新天地）is a series of buildings standing on the western shore of Jinji Lake and within shouting distance of a subway station. Housing primarily a collection of restaurants, in addition to a KTV and an education center, what makes this site impressive is that it faces directly out onto the exact spot on the lake where on weekends a firework and waterworks display takes place. In fact, Rainbow Walk occupies arguably the prime location from which to view this.

RainboWalk also provides an ideal start and finish point for anyone wishing to take a walk around Jinji Lake, whether heading south towards Li Gong Di or alternatively north towards Crowne Plaza, Moon Harbor and the SSCAC. This is because ample parking is provided, numerous bus stops reside

in the near vicinity, and food and drinks are aplenty, with quality offerings the norm.

When one also factors in the beautiful wooded copse that lies between the square and Crowne Plaza, and the stunning walk around the tip of RainboWalk, it is hard to imagine many better city-based lakeside locations.

Quite simply, this area is the perfect place to come on quieter days. It has the setting, is ideal for picnics, provides a great base for walks and, houses a number of quality establishments. The RainboWalk locality should certainly be a stop on any would-be travelers' itinerary.

(Gareth Morris)

TIPS

LÖWENBURG

A German restaurant with genuine German food and beer, not to mention the view from its windows.

Add: 1st Floor, RainboWalk, SIP

Tel: 0512-6762 8777

Recommendations:Signature offerings include German sausages, Eisbein (129 yuan each) and self-made beer (38 yuan for 0.3 liter, 90 yuan for 1 liter).

Fountain Square

Opening hours: Holidays and every Friday and Saturday, 8pm, lasting 30 minutes

Admission free

Venue: City Plaza, on the western shore of Jinji Lake

Transport: Bus No. 106, 307, SIP 2, Jinji Lake Tour Bus

Little Mexico, big taste

Modern SIP in Suzhou harbors many delights and Zapata's definitely ranks among them as far as good food is concerned. ZAPATA'S has all the usual Mexican dishes that we know and love.

Add: A1, RainboWalk, 158 Xinggang Street, SIP

Tel: 0512-6767 2780

Average cost: 100 yuan per person

Luxurious lakeside scenes at Kempinski

SAYING "cheers" by the lake - you drink, not in loneliness, but in delight. Never forget to toast yourself with a glass of wine or (Paulaner) beer.

Kempinski(凯宾斯基大酒店) is a German luxury hotel group. It has one hotel here in Suzhou. Unlike its classical European counterparts, the Suzhou hotel looks simple and unornamented, even a little strict - just like German engineers. Nevertheless, deep in its core, European romance and casualness remain.

Find a window seat and enjoy the bright sunshine reflecting on Jinji Lake - enjoying the freshness and tranquility, it might make you wonder when last such idleness has given you so much joy.

Unlike delicate wine glasses, Germans make beer mugs as bulky as their tanks so as to survive endless bangs against each other and thumps on the table. You need to grab the handle really tight to lift it and drink, and don't forget to dance to the band. Feel the coolness of the mug and feast your eyes on the crowd - what a sight!

Does it matter if you barely know each other? No! Just propose a toast, with the familiar sound of saxophones playing, to everybody around you - life is a journey, so celebrate with a beer.

(Fan Yi)

TIPS

Kempinski Hotel (Jinji Lake) Suzhou at No. 1 Guobin Road, SIP, with its exclusive driveway. Meeting its guests' high-end needs, provides romantic European ambiance as well as classy luxury, featuring German Paulaner Brewery and cigar lounge.

Kempinski rooms facing Jinji Lake: 2,100 yuan per night.

At Paulaner: stout and wheat beers are great. Enjoy them by the lake.

Tel: 0512-6289 7888

Prices (An additional tip of 15% is required):

Paulaner beer: 45 yuan for 0.3 liter, 58 yuan for 0.5 liter, 88 yuan for 1 liter.

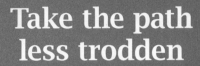

Take the path less trodden

PERHAPS one of Suzhou's best kept secrets, or most underappreciated beauty spots is Moon Harbor (月光码头). Located just beyond the Crowne Plaza apartment complex, this lakeside walk begins as soon as one leaves the bridge which heads towards Ling Long Wan and the Suzhou Arts and Culture Centre.

The sad truth though is that one could easily miss it because a pathway runs adjacent to the road disguising the wooden decking that follows the shoreline. However, making the effort to cross the grass that leads to this latter walkway is worth the effort.

With very few people actually taking the time to appreciate this area, you are likely to have it all to yourself – and with the moon and stars overhead there's no better place to spend a romantic evening.

In fairness, the actual

walk itself is relatively short. It runs only as far as the cinema and theater complex.

However, along the way one will see the best that nature and man can offer in tandem. Not only do the waters and sky offer peace and tranquility rarely found in modern day China by night, but you are also temporarily cut off from the world around by tree-lined grass verges helping to guard against roadside intrusions.

There really are very few places in Suzhou that have the capability to transport one away from the hustles and bustles of daily life as Moon Harbor can. Having lived in Suzhou for a number of years, this pier remains one of Jinji Lake's last natural sanctuaries where the human footprint has yet to fully stamp its mark over nature's delicate hand.

(Gareth Morris)

TIPS

Like a crescent elegantly moored upon the northeastern waters of Jinji Lake, Moon Harbor is stealing the show of the lake. Come and get caressed by romantic moonlight at this lakeside paradise.

Xiang Lian

A restaurant featuring Hunan cuisine, especially fish head.

Add: A5, Moon Harbor, SIP

Tel: 0512-6956 5777

Ganesh Indian Restaurant and Jazz Bar

Add: C3, Moon Harbor, SIP

Tel: 0512-6956 9808

Ophelie Bar

Add: C1, Moon Harbor, SIP

Tel: 0512-6936 8158

Spirit Bar

Add: 8, Moon Harbor, SIP

Tel: 0512-6509 8098

The One Restaurant

Add: B3, Moon Harbor, SIP

Tel: 0512-6936 0288

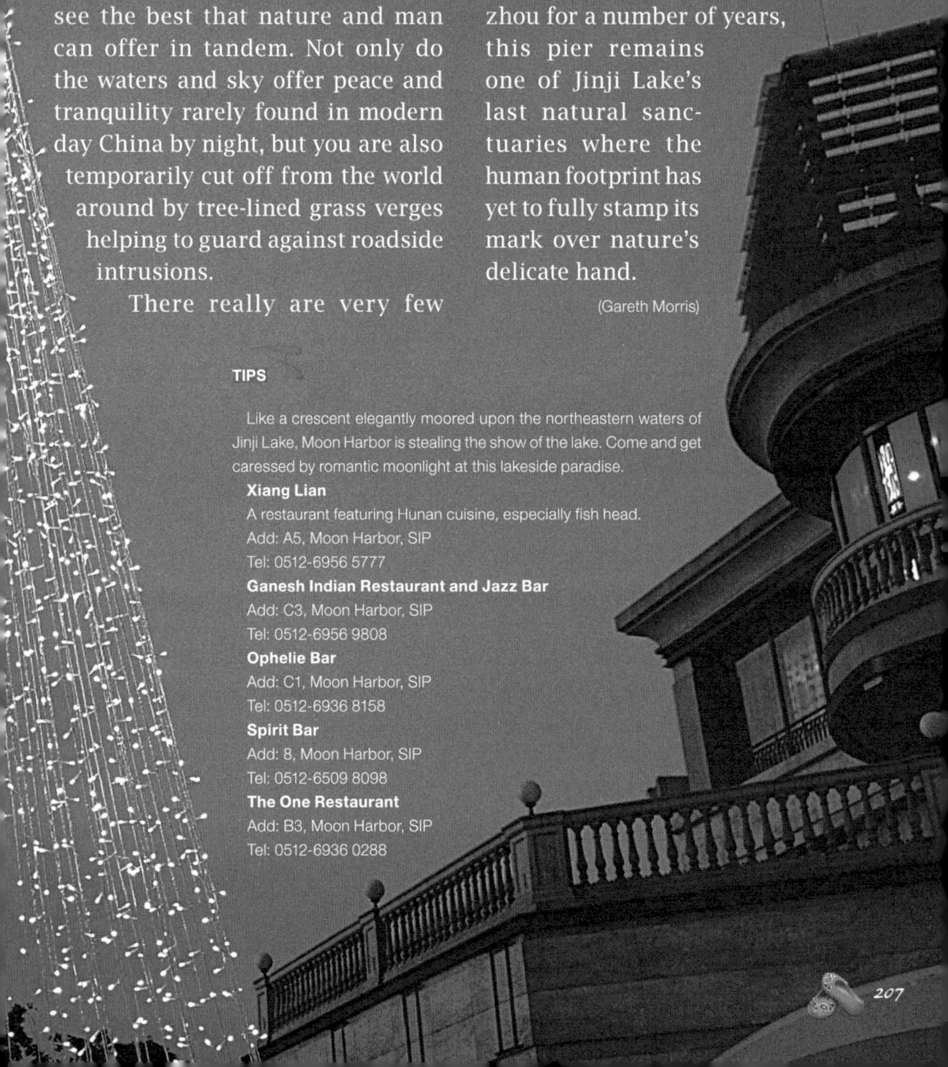

Heavenly treats on Earth

WITH its vast grasslands and shepherds, Xinjiang is a whole different world over 3,000 kilometers away. To most people in Suzhou, to visit the prairie means a long, exhausting and costly trip. But enjoying its cuisine is another thing.

Bei Jiang Restaurant (北疆饭店) serves a great deal of authentic Xinjiang food at fair prices. It has a good choice for group dinners and the sizes of the servings are rather big. It is a meat lovers' paradise as their specials are mostly lamb and beef. Chefs from the prairie have long mastered the skills of cooking red meat, and they also bring to Suzhou their peculiar spices for authenticity. Cumin seeds, a characteristic spice of the region, give the meat a unique flavor that guarantees an extraordinary taste from first bite.

You can always find a dish that will surprise you with its pleasant uniqueness. It can be stir-fried to bring out its original aroma, or roasted and served when still crispy on the outside yet juicy on the inside. It may be stewed with a hot chili sauce for added spice, or be fairly rich in taste after marinating in a carefully chosen combination of herbs. Some dishes might even impress you with gravy and veggies as a side dish, or, indeed, the handmade noodles and steamed thin pancakes that go with it.

Being faithful and authentic to their customs, the chefs of this restaurant do not garnish their dishes with any decorations. The food looks plain, simple, and offers you a most honest and earthly treat.

(Lu Rong)

TIPS

Bei Jiang Restaurant

428 Ganjiang East Road. Tel: 0512-6511 4888

In SIP: B1, Landmark Business Street, 108 Xinhan Street, SIP. Tel: 0512-6511 3888

In SND: 160 Tayuan Road, SND. Tel: 0512-6807 8333.

There is another Xinjiang-style restaurant worth visiting.

Xinjiang Zhaksy Restaurant

Add: 768 Shiquan Street

Tel: 0512-6529 1798

The renaissance of romance

WHERE skyscrapers graze the heavens and stand side by side with ancient temples and pagodas built 2,500 years ago, the Renaissance logo dazzles amid Suzhou's neon lights.

The serenity of the Renaissance Suzhou will fascinate you and ignite your imagination. After returning to your comfortable room, take off your shoes and pour a glass of complimentary local green tea. Return to the early days of your romance, while playing a chess game with your partner, or reading stories to each other. The selection of books in the hotel may offer just what you need to feed your reading appetite.

If you prefer to venture out, you will certainly find a lot to do locally in any season with the assistance of the Hotel's Navigator Team. Whatever type of romantic getaway in Suzhou you choose, there are always some kinds of adventures to enhance the romance. Drag yourselves away from your room, the best of the Central Park is on your doorstep and the grand Jinji Lake is five minutes

from here.

For those who love to remain active, there is the swimming pool; or perhaps you would prefer a game of badminton, or yoga on the lawn. Choose a place with shade under one of the many trees and just let yourself stroll in that book you've put off reading, tasting tea or coffee and imagine you are the hero.

Every time when you are here, you will possibly find something new and find indulgences there fit for an emperor, from the dazzling Brasserie and a chic Lounge.

At Renaissance, for whatever the reason you travel here, there is always something wonderfully new to be found – while the experience will always remain charming, romantic and luxurious.

(Lu Hehe)

TIPS

You can enjoy a beautiful view of Central Park, offering you a window into local life: Taichi, fan dancing, morning exercises.

Located in the business district, Renaissance Hotel in Suzhou CBD offers easy access to transportation, attractions, shopping, Suzhou International Expo and China-Singapore Suzhou Industrial Park.

Add: 229 Suhua Road, Suzhou Industrial Park (SIP)

Attractions on Li Gong Di, from end to end

Butterfly Restaurant

Where: 17, 19, 21 Li Gong Di Reservations: 0512-6295 3333

The Butterfly Restaurant is akin to a high-end club – suitable for business meetings, social gatherings and romantic dinners. Along with a sumptuous meal, patrons can enjoy premium wines and superfine cigars.

Special dishes: yellow shark fin soup, bird's nest lion head, Neptune shell.

Soochow Homestyle Hotel

Where: 29 Li Gong Di Reservations: 0512-6287 5888

Soochow Homestyle Hotel is the only restaurant in Suzhou themed around Kunqu Opera. It ambience is urban and elegant, with cuisine highlighting specialties from Suzhou and Wuxi.

Special dishes: hand peeled shrimp, squirrel-shaped mandarin fish, royal steak.

Hofbrau Royal Beer House

Where: 50, 52 Li Gong Di Reservations: 0512-6295 0988

Hofbrau Royal Beer House continues the heritage of the Hofbrauhaus in Germany, founded 1589 as the royal brewery of the Kingdom of Bavaria. This modern version is decorated in traditional German style and features beer brewed on the premises. The menu includes such German favorites as grilled pork legs and sausages. A Philippine band performs year round.

Peony Pavilion Innovative Cuisine Restaurant

Where: 7-11 Li Gong Di Reservations: 0512-6299 8777

The Peony Pavilion Innovative Cuisine Restaurant takes its name from the tender, lush Kunqu Opera called "Peony Pavilion." A 3.5-meter-high carved sandalwood door from the Ming and Qing dynasties sets the interior atmosphere of a canal town.

Special dishes: dream of plums, peony blossom, butterflies in love, purple mist from the east and jade juice with white bait.

Deyuelou Restaurant

Where: 8, 18, 22 Li Gong Di Reservations: 0512-6265 6999

Deyuelou Restaurant, which dates back to the reign of Emperor Jiajing of the Ming Dynasty (1368-1644), has been honored with an award as one of China's top 10 restaurants. The interior décor of classic Chinese simplicity has a timeless elegance.

Special dishes: squirrel-shaped mandarin fish, Deyue baby chicken, Xishi enjoying the moonlight, ham with honey sauce, Puli duck, tea-flavored shrimp, jujube paste cake and Suzhou-style snacks.

Tomato Kitchen

Where: 56 Li Gong Di   Reservations: 0512-6287 5966

The Tomato Kitchen has won restaurant awards for a menu that combines taste with healthy eating and fresh ingredients.

Special dishes: spaghetti, tiramisu, black forest cake, steak, tomato soup and beef pie.

Dain Ti Hill

Where: Building 15, 99 Li Gong Di   Reservations: 0512-6299 8980

Dain Ti Hill is a restaurant specializing in food from the Tang Dynasty (618-907). A tastefully decorated interior setting adds to the pleasure of a menu steeped in history.

Special dishes: Tang-style duck tongue, shredded chicken, teriyaki chicken wings, mushroom and baked tofu, and iced orange tea.

Wuguantang Vegetarian Restaurant

Where: Building 15, Li Gong Di Phase 3, SIP

Reservations: 0512-6873 3556

This vegetarian restaurant provides an elegant environment and an array of fine cuisine, with beautifully hand-written menus. The food is as healthy as it is tasty. Special dishes: mashed potato with red peppers, congee with shepherd's purse and sliced radish.

Shijia Restaurant

Where: Building 3, Li Gong Di Phase 3 (Jichang Road), SIP

Reservations: 0512-6679 7178

Shijia Restaurant was established in 1790 during the reign of Emperor Qianlong of the Qing Dynasty (1636-1912). It was originally named Xushunlou Restaurant and was located in Wuzhong District in Suzhou. Its Suzhou-style cuisine reflects more than 200 years of kitchen art. The food here is also known as "Shi's cuisine."

Special dishes: Shi's barb liver soup, stir-fried shrimp, smoked fish.

Basa Art Centre

Where: 401/501, building 12, 1 Li Gong Di

Basa Art Centre offers some of the best modern art in Suzhou. In addition to the exhibition of its works, it is also a venue for art-related seminars. The mission of the center is to encourage the artistic talent of young people.

Harley-Davidson

Where: 103/203, building 19, 1 Li Gong Di

Over the past century, the Harley-Davidson brand has become synonymous with dynamism, adventure and the passion for speed. Motorcycle fans from all over the world love the Milwaukee-based motorcycle brand.

The beauty of Taihu Lake, in the melodies

I know I have been touched,
The first time I see you,
I feel your gracefulness
And hear your laughter in the melodies.

Why you are so beautiful?
The moderate humidity
Matched with mild colors
And good taste,
Joined with our pleasant moods,
Present perfect lake scenes.

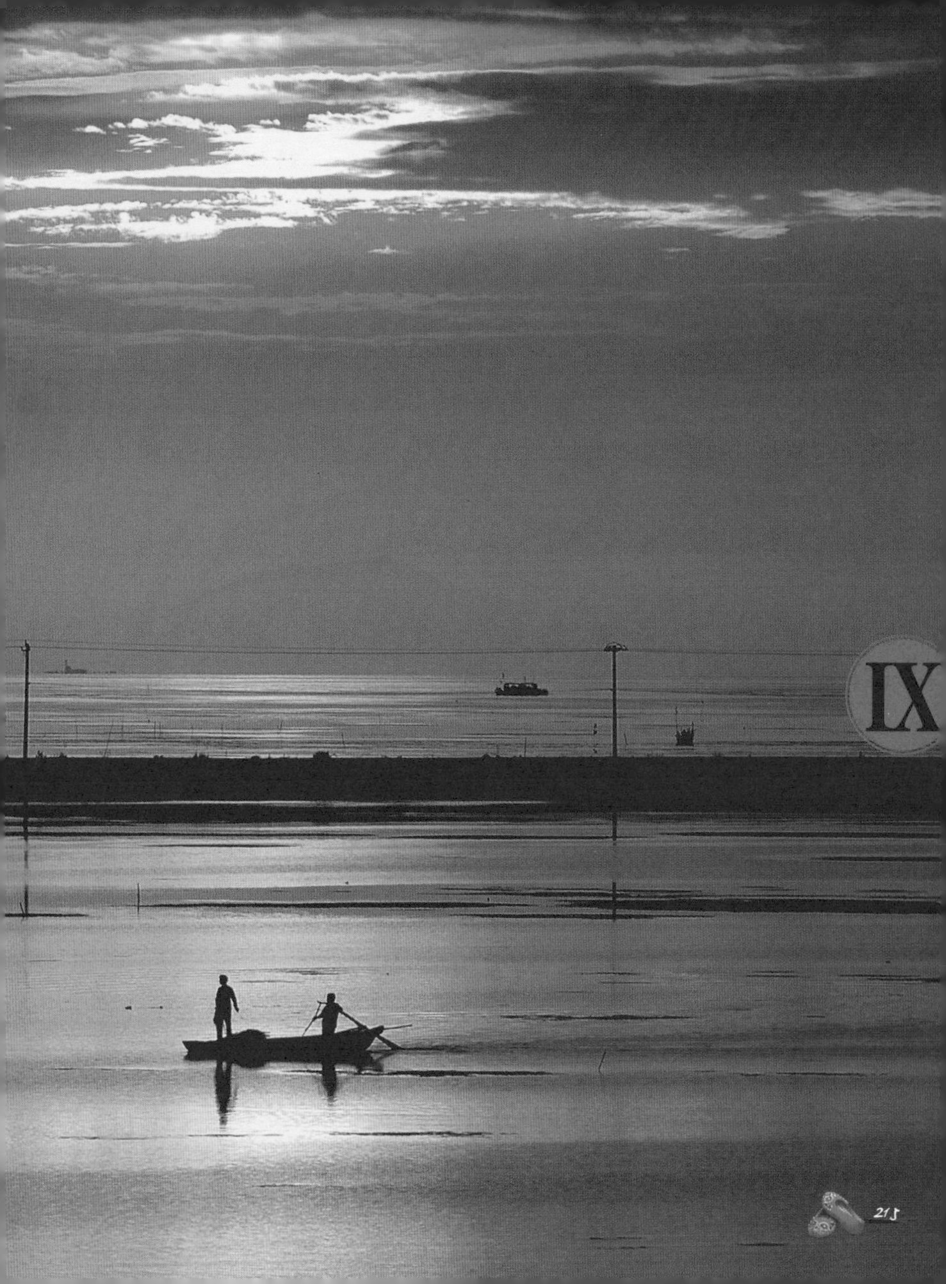

IX

铜观音寺
光福塔
Situ Temple
Taihu Lake Boat Cuisine
Xiang Xue Hai
香雪海
New Fourth Army Memorial Hall
新四军纪念馆
太湖船餐
司徒庙
太湖渔港
Taihu Lake Fishing Port
南山公园
环太湖大道
圣恩寺
Dongcun Ancient Village
Huantaihu Avenue
She
東村古村
后埠村
Houbu An
Tangli Ancient Village
植里古村
King Yu Temple
堂里古村
Zhili Ancient Village
古樟园
Ancient Ca
西山地质公园
禹王庙
缥缈峰
甪里古村
Piaomiao Peak
包山禅寺
Baoshan
Luli Ancient Village
東西蔡古村
林屋洞
Linwu
Arhat Temple
罗汉寺
Tang Xia Wan
消夏湾
逸园
Han Garden
西山宾馆
西山牛仔俱乐部
Xishan Hotel
Dongxicai Ancient Village
明月湾古村
Xishan Cowboy Club
石公山
Shigong Hill
Mingyuewan Ancient Village

lokitesvara Temple
goda
Cangshu
光福
藏书
Guangfu
木渎
Mudu
胥口 Xukou
ark
Linhu
Xishan
临湖
西山
e
Dongshan
东山
Round-the-mountain Road
Garden
环山公路
启园
Qi Garden
雨花胜境
Yuhua Scenic Area
太
莫厘峰
Moli Peak
东山大道
三山岛
胡
Sanshan Island
陆巷古村
Dongshan Avenue
Luxiang Ancient Village
雕花楼
Diao Hua Lou
(Carved Building)
轩辕宫
Xuanyuan Palace
Zijin Nunnery
u Lake
明善堂
Mingshan Hall
紫金庵

Fresh air and fresh food await at Taihu Lake

TAIHU Lake, the third-largest freshwater body in China, dominates the landscape near Suzhou and provides visitors a tranquil escape from urban bustle.

Known as Tai Hu in Chinese, the lake covers an area of 2,338 square kilometers – two-thirds of it within Suzhou's boundaries.

In addition to breathtaking scenery on its shores and 48 islets in its waters, the lake is famous for aquatic products, including the famous hairy crab, shrimp and whitebait.

The lake area is said to have the freshest air in Suzhou. Standing ashore, looking across the rippling waters, you gaze across a panorama of peace and solitude. Small wonder that so many city dwellers come here to unwind.

Driving yourself around the lake area is perhaps the most enjoyable way to see it. Autumn is the best

season. The roadsides are filled with golden reed flowers and the orchard leaves are turning color. This is nature's own palette.

Taihu Lake has long formed an essential part of local life in Suzhou, having a significant impact both on cuisine and on climate.

Two of the best scenic spots around the lake are Dongshan and Jinting. Both are actually two isolated islands, where old residences and pure folk customs are preserved from the past.

Dongshan Island, in particular, is known for its fertile soils that produce the famous Bi Luo Chun tea, loquats, red bayberries, dates and tangerines. Whatever the season, there's always something delicious to harvest.

But Taihu Lake is perhaps best known for its aquatic taste treats. Whitebait, white fish and white shrimp are among the most popular, earning them the name the "Three Whites of Taihu Lake."

Stopping to dine on local fish cooked in traditional styles is a perfect way to cap a perfect visit to the lake.

(Fei Lai)

A magical island steeped in legends

LEGEND has it that 2,500 years ago, Fuchai, the king of the Wu Kingdom and his concubine Xi Shi spent their summers at Xishan Island in Taihu Lake, basking in the glorious moonlight.

Visitors to this scenic island can enjoy the same evocative experience that brought royalty here so long ago.

A breathtaking sunset greets me as I follow in their footsteps at Ming Yue Wan (明月湾, Moon Bay) on the island.

Taihu Lake, China's third-largest freshwater body, sparkles with flickering diamonds under the last rays of the sun. A gentle breeze kisses the water and surrounding trees.

This is indeed a tranquil setting for meditation, dreaming and flights of imagination. A place for lovers.

Xishan (renamed as Jinting in 2007), is the largest island in the lake, connected to land by a large bridge. Before the span was constructed, the island was accessible by boat only, and its relative isolation allowed it to retain many of its

old customs and charms.

Residents make a living by growing flowers and fruits, especially oranges. There are no crowded streets, no big tourist sites, no feeling of urban bustle. Here everything is simple and quiet.

The narrow lanes, paved with flagstones, pass along brick houses that are coarse but strong. Dogs wander about, giving the streets a home-like atmosphere.

A huge camphor tree standing at the entrance of Xishan Village is believed to be 500 years old and said to possess magic powers that protect local residents.

After a dinner of fresh shrimp and lake fish, cooked according to time-honored local recipes, a ferry ride is a perfect way to cap the day and enjoy a moonlit evening.

(Fei Lai)

TIPS

1.One highlight of Moon Bay is the flagstone streets, containing more than 4,560 pieces of granite. They are called "chessboard" streets.

2.A moonlight dip may be nice for some, but bathing in the lake is best done under the sun during daytime.

3.The town has a street full of restaurants, where you can dine on the soft-shelled turtle, lake fish, crab, clams, chicken and duck.

Among the popular spots are Jinghu Restaurant (137 7608 9863); Moonlight Bay Farmer's Restaurant (139 6219 6419); and Huwei Restaurant (189 1550 2709).

4.Waxberry wine, dried shrimp and lake fish are among the best local specialties. Waxberry wine costs about 20 yuan a bottle. Dried shrimps sell for about 50 yuan a kilogram. Don't be afraid to bargain with the vendors.

5.Residents open their homes to visitors, and what a treat it is to spend the night in an authentic local home. The standard room rate is between 70 yuan and 80 yuan a night. Teacher Qin's Inn is one of the best. Reservations: 139 1558 8630.

Rocks look like animals, and food tastes divine

SANSHAN Island（三山岛）sits in the middle of Taihu Lake and can be accessed only by boat. That's part of its charm.

The island's name translates as "three peaks" after the scenic terrain.

Bubbling creeks and small bridges are set against a backdrop of natural rockery. Giant rock shapes suggest the 12 animals of the Chinese zodiac, but it's funny to use your own imagination and see what forms the rocks conjure up in the mind.

The mild lake climate gives the island a perfect environment for growing oranges, and during the season, they are sweet and luscious to taste. A variety of fruit is grown there. Orchards emit tantalizing scents along the strolling lanes on the island. When fruit is ripe, it's such a temptation to just stop and pluck one from an orchard by the path.

Local farmers are proud to say that

Sanshan Island is never short of flowers or fruit. In spring, the famous local Bi Luo Chun tea bushes carpet the fields in lush green as tea-pickers arrive for the harvest.

In summer, ripe red bayberries turn vistas scarlet, and in autumn, grapes and Chinese chestnuts are the pick of the season.

Rental bicycles are available, offering visitors a pleasant way to tour the island.

Sanshan Island has facilities for overnight camping, barbecues, fishing and outdoor sports, but you have to bring your equipment with you.

Be sure to try the famous local cuisine, which includes white fish, shrimp, silverfish, crab and soft-shell turtles.

(Fei Lai)

TIPS

Visitors can go to Sanshan Island by speedboat or ferry. The speedboat can carry up to 10 people at a time and charges 100 yuan for each tour.

There are more than 100 small restaurants on the island. It's best to make reservations if you want to eat at the rustic farmhouse restaurants, especially during the peak season in September and October. These restaurants also offer accommodation. It costs about 100 yuan per night, including dinner.

Wu Shi Family Restaurant
Tel: 139 6215 6589

Red Leave Mountain Villa
Tel: 133 0620 8050

Bridge beyond the Bridge
Tel: 135 1160 7150

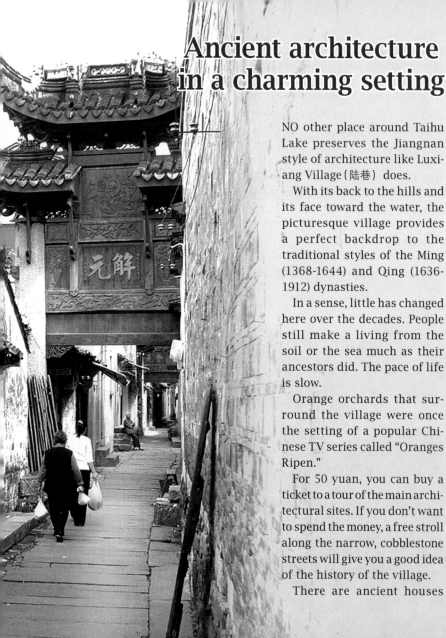

Ancient architecture in a charming setting

NO other place around Taihu Lake preserves the Jiangnan style of architecture like Luxiang Village (陆巷) does.

With its back to the hills and its face toward the water, the picturesque village provides a perfect backdrop to the traditional styles of the Ming (1368-1644) and Qing (1636-1912) dynasties.

In a sense, little has changed here over the decades. People still make a living from the soil or the sea much as their ancestors did. The pace of life is slow.

Orange orchards that surround the village were once the setting of a popular Chinese TV series called "Oranges Ripen."

For 50 yuan, you can buy a ticket to a tour of the main architectural sites. If you don't want to spend the money, a free stroll along the narrow, cobblestone streets will give you a good idea of the history of the village.

There are ancient houses

there built of brick, old shops with dim lighting, arches in the Ming style and a variety of halls commemorating ancestry.

Small wonder that some professionals have escaped the urban rat race to live here. One well-known expert in information technology came to the village, restored an old house where his ancestors once lived and resided in seclusion for five years before the media got on to his hideaway.

Close to the village, there is a scenic spot called Zijin Convent. It's a small temple, embedded in the mountains and off the beaten tourist track.

It was built during the Tang Dynasty (618-907) and restored during the Qing Dynasty. It is known for its vivid arhat artwork, done by the famous sculptor Lei Chao and his wife during the South Song Dynasty (1127-1279). The gestures of the figures are vividly etched. Some are thinking, some are napping, some are laughing and some are weeping.

Zijin Convent Teahouse is a great place to pause when you are in the vicinity. Locals say it is the best teahouse in the village, perhaps because of the charm of its rustic interior and old wooden tables.

Sitting by a window, with a cup of tea at hand, you can lose yourself listening to the wind ruffling through the pine trees nearby.

(Fei Lai)

TIPS

Luxiang Village is located in Dongshan Town by Taihu Lake.

Admission: 50 yuan (including admission to five scenic spots)

Opening hours: 8am-5pm

Transport: Take the Youxin Elevated Road and exit at Wuzhong Avenue. Drive along the avenue until you reach the bank of Taihu Lake. Turn left and drive to Dongshan along the Taihu Lake scenic avenue. Then take Huanshan Road to reach Luxiang.

Accommodation and dining: For higher-end service, try the Dongshan Hotel. Call 0512-6628 1888 or 0512-6628 2888 for information or reservations. For more traditional accommodation, try the Diao Hua Lou Hotel on 58 Zijin Road. Tel: 0512-6628 1001. For dining out, Gulong Restaurant and Moli Restaurant come highly recommended.

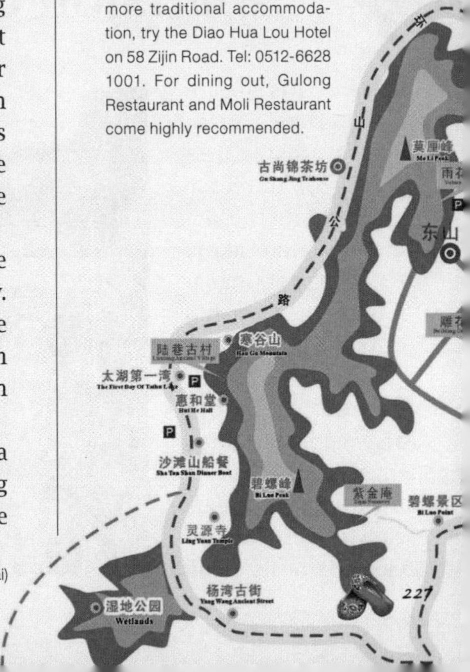

The breathtaking mansion of carvings

CARVING is an ancient art of China, and one of the best places to immerse yourself in the art around Taihu Lake is the village of Guangming in the township of Dongshan.

The Dongshan Carved Mansion, also known as Diao Hua Lou (雕花楼), is filled with marvelous carvings in auspicious patterns using

a variety of materials, including brick, glass and wood.

Its style and carvings taken from the Xiangshan school, the famous mansion started as a gift from businessman Jin Xizhi to his mother. Construction began in 1922 at a cost of more than 150,000 silver dollars. It took 250 craftsmen three years to complete

the project. The mansion from windows to door handles, from arches to pillars and ceilings, the carvings are a masterpiece for the eyes. There are peonies, chrysanthemums, phoenix, orchids, pomegranates and clouds signifying longevity etched for eternity.

Although the mansion appears to be two-story from the outside, it actually spreads over three levels. The top floor was used by the owner to stash secret treasures. It also contained a hidden escape passage.

The mansion is so magnificently preserved that more than 60 movies and TV series have been shot there.

(Fei Lai)

TIPS

Dongshan Carved Mansion

Admission: 60 yuan

Accommodation: The mansion also provides accommodation at just 350 yuan a night. There are 27 standard rooms available. Bigger, more luxurious villa suites are also available for up to 5,000 yuan.

Public transport: Bus No. 502, 62, and 500.

Best season: Each time of year has its own specialties: Bi Luo Chun tea in the spring; loquats and bayberries in summer; hairy crabs and chestnuts in the autumn.

Bi Luo Chun: The "real" green tea

ON many occasions, I have been asked by my Aussie friends:

"Why does the green tea you give us taste differently from what we usually get at a Chinese restaurant?"

I could not figure out why until I ordered a pot of green tea myself in a Chinese restaurant and realized the so-called "green tea" that they served was actually Jasmine Tea, which strictly speaking, does not belong to the green tea family.

I now make sure I provide some explanations before I give my friends some Bi Luo Chun（碧螺春） – the authentic green tea unique to my hometown Suzhou and one of the most famous teas in China.

Bi Luo Chun was given its name by an emperor from the Qing Dynasty (1636-1912). "Bi" describes the rich green color and "Luo" describes the spiral shape of the tealeaf. The word "Chun" means the season of spring, as this tea is best harvested in the springtime.

There is also a beautiful story behind the name of the tea. Once upon a time, a goddess-like young girl named "Bi Luo" fell in love with a brave young man. They both lived in a village in the Dongting Mountain at Taihu Lake. Everything was so peaceful until an evil dragon from the nearby lake came to destroy the village. The young man fought fiercely with

the evil dragon and eventually killed it. However, he was seriously injured in the battle and life was fading from his limbs. One day, Bi Luo went into the hills to search for herbs that might cure the young man, and found some newly grown tea trees on the battleground where he had spilled his blood. She thought those tea trees were special and carefully nurtured them until the tealeaves were ready to be harvested. Every day she boiled the tealeaves and gave it to her lover to drink.

The young man recovered gradually, thanks to Bi Luo's care and her green tea. But Bi Luo, eventually died at the bedside of her lover due to exhaustion. After her death, the young man named the tea "Bi Luo Chun", in memory of the girl whom he would always love.

That's why the tea needs to be treated with extra gentleness. Best infused in 70-degree hot water, the fragrance of the tea is like the smell of fresh air, with a slightly sweet aftertaste. It will certainly remind you of the love story behind it, or some love stories you have experienced yourself.

Therefore, in order to experience the authentic green tea, make sure you get the Bi Luo Chun from Suzhou, not from where you get your Chinese takeaway.

(Xinlu Cindy Huang)

TIPS

When to buy:

Bi Luo Chun tealeaves are usually harvested around April, but are available for purchase all year round. The best quality leaves are harvested before Tomb-Sweeping Day (April 5). Thus April will be an excellent time to come to Suzhou and taste this green tea.

Where to buy:

Several small towns in Wuzhong (a suburb of Suzhou) are the original areas where Bi Luo Chun is produced. Among those, Dongshan and Jinting are the most popular among tourists. Around April every year, both will offer day tours that allow you to observe the making of Bi Luo Chun.

Surrounding sceneries:

Apart from the famous green tea and small towns, the hill region is also worth having a look at. You can choose to go for a drive in your own car and stop along the way at each small town.

It's fun to catch your own dinner, "The sail is up. Let's go!"

I NEVER fancied myself a fisherwoman, but it's hard to resist the attraction of hiring a fishing boat in Yu Jia Huan, Guangfu Town and heading out onto Taihu Lake to try my luck.

The boat sets sail and the lake winds tousle my hair and give me a sense of complete freedom. Two veteran fishermen are on board to show me the ropes of freshwater fishing.

It's so easy to let one's imagination run wild and think about the fighting fish and white ocean sprays described by Hemingway or the adventure of being stranded in a strange land like Robinson Crusoe. Are there lake sirens or Loch Ness monsters here?

I am captain of my ship, but if I don't turn my attention to fishing, I will be a hungry one.

The crew performs their shipboard routines as their families have done for generations. They have sleeping quarters down below and cooking and dining facilities on deck. They know where the fishing is best. Indeed, our harvest today is a good one.

Taihu Lake is legendary in China. The lake and surrounding area were known in ancient times as the "land of rice and fish." The lake itself is famous for its bounty of white shrimp, whitebait and white fish - popularly called the "Three Whites."

These fish are best steamed, not braised, because of their delicate textures. The fishermen say it is very important to retain the original flavors of lake fish when cooking them.

We eat on board, which adds a nice seafaring touch to the meal.

Appetites sated, we head back to shore, ending what was for me a very exciting excursion.

(Fei Lai)

TIPS

Yu Jia Huan

Add: No. 1 Bridge , Hufu Road, Guangfu Town

Tel: 0512-6693 0238

If you want to hire a fishing boat, reservations are advised. The fee is 600 yuan, excluding meal. Local fishermen will serve you set meals of fish for either 600 yuan or 800 yuan.

The fishing boats come in different sizes. The biggest can hold up to 30 people and costs more. The more standard ones can carry up to 10 people.

The fresh fish available vary by season. White shrimp season is in May, and white fish in August. At the beginning of autumn, Taihu Lake saury is a special treat.

Red bayberries: Best eaten on-site

IN my mind, red bayberries and lychees have both been regal fruits throughout the ages.

Yang Guifei (highest-ranking imperial concubine), a famous beauty in ancient China and the concubine of Emperor Xuanzong during the Tang Dynasty (618-907), adored lychees. But the fruit is known for spoiling quickly. It starts fading immediately after being picked, and within three

days its taste, color and fragrance are gone. Luckily Yang, the great beauty, always got her fresh lychees and she was happy, although at the expense of several horses and men who had been worn out over the long distances from the southern part of the country to Chang'an where she was living at the time.

However, when compared with red bayberries, lychees can actually be stored for longer period. Even if the red bayberries were freshly picked in the morning, their flavor would change as early as in the afternoon. So, fortunately, it was lychees that the concubine loved. Otherwise the emperor would have had to move his capital to Suzhou to win his beauty's smile. Though Suzhou is nearer to Chang'an than Lingnan (the southern part of the country where lychees are grown) and at that time when horses were the major source of transport, the fruit would not keep over such a long journey. Enjoying the fruit just after having been picked is when red bayberries taste the best.

Even today, the Dongshan and Xishan (East and West Mountains) in Suzhou are still famous areas where red bayberries are grown. You should not miss the fruit if you come in late June. The best is to find a deep valley, pick the red bayberries from

Loquat

the trees and eat on site as much as you can. Beiwang, in the East Hill, has the greatest reputation among the locals. Grown in a deep valley, most of the red bayberry trees there grow on the hillside. Enjoying abundant sunshine, the berries are bestowed with great taste and a short maturity period. In Beiwang, trees several centuries old stand one next to each other, covering the hills and fields when the Summer Solstice arrives. Scattered among the deep green trees are the red bayberries, and once ripe they turn dark purple in color.

(Fan Yi)

TIPS

Besides the red bayberry, loquat is also a famous Suzhou fruit that you shouldn't miss.

Best times for tasting: May and June (when loquat and red bayberries are seen everywhere in Suzhou.)

Red bayberries taste great. But do not eat too much at a time, or you may have sore teeth the next day.

Price: red bayberry – 20 yuan per kilogram; loquat – over 40 yuan per kilogram.

An Oriental Venice without Gondolas

BEFORE coming to Suzhou, my family and I took a look at the city from the perspective of Google Earth. We had the option of going to three different countries to work but the view of all the lakes and canals of Suzhou made it an easy choice. All the guidebooks repeated the plug of Venice of the East.

When we got here we were not disappointed, but it struck us that except for industrial transport nobody was on the water. We brought our inflatable kayak and have since discovered a Suzhou that few people have seen. We have done most of the canals of the old city (the Suzhou city canals are well managed and are constantly being flushed by a complex water management system) and we still have lots to explore!

I was exploring a canal in Wuzhong suburb when I discovered the True Color Museum. They have a little harbor on the southern side and you can moor up and take in an art exhibition. I tied up in the canal in front of the Southern Cross

on Lindun Road and went in for a pint. You can easily pull up near the picnic tables of the Hofbrau House on Li Gong Di and have a bratwurst and a beer. It's also a good place to take the boat out of the water, roll it up and put it in the trunk of your car, in a taxi or on your bike.

Mercury Club and Marina on Taihu Lake is basically a place to entertain business guests but it does have boat slips, houseboat and runabout rentals. For me, I simply enjoy exploring Suzhou's waterways and will not stop my adventure until I have seen it all.

(Patrick Donahue)

TIPS

Suzhou Taihu Mercury Club & Marina

Add: 83 Lakeside Road, Suzhou Taihu National Vacation Zone, Suzhou.

Tel: 0512-6768 2288, 6651 5099

X

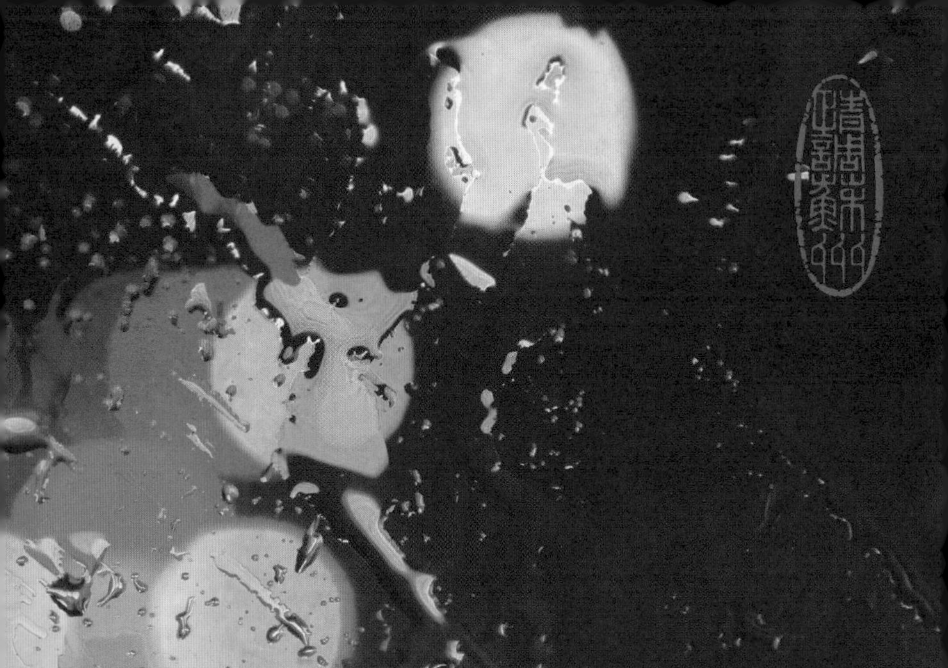

Starry, starry night

A starry evening in Suzhou is reason enough to explore the city by streetlight.
It's an enchanting world where women dress up and men put on their most charming smiles.
Romance in the air?
Well, who knows?
It might be your lucky night.

One night in Suzhou

ONE never fails to find Suzhou's charm at night in the city.

The local people are generally humble and reserved, just like their city. However, youngsters are gradually taking over Suzhou, or more specifically, Suzhou's night life. For those who spend their nights in sparkling light and sipping wine, and those who doze off in the daytime but come alive in the night, Suzhou can be a familiar fairyland.

On the other hand, Suzhou's unique culture also brings a difference to such bright

nights.

Tunes from folk instruments that you have never heard before, fill the city at night, and enlighten the newcomers' senses to this ancient city. Played by citizens also in alleys, they are an elegant way of communication between local people, as in former dynasties. The Kunqu Opera Museum also shows its charm in the evening.

Make sure you do not miss Jinji Lake in the east of Suzhou, where you can see the music fountain and the great LED screen nearby.

Another thing for sure is that no matter how late it is, mouthwatering midnight snacks can be found anywhere in the city – these local inexpensive wayside diners are also filled with enchanting Suzhou air.

(Fan Yi)

Block 1912: Endless entertainment

ASK any clubber over 20 how she's going to spend her birthday – "surely at 1912."

Ask any white-collar worker where to entertain his guests from the overseas headquarters – "1912 of course." He might also suggest Jenny's or Tunnel instead of the noisy Scarlet.

Or ask any Suzhou local snapper where to get the most edgy nighttime entertainment – "1912 of course!"

"Mecca for club goers" Block 1912 is, without doubt, the engine driving all the nightclubs forward.

For a special city as Suzhou, there's always a unique style of entertainment: celebrities, luxurious shops, major exhibitions ... none of which lack any excitement.

Suzhou's profound history since the Qing Dynasty (1636-1912) blends in with the modern vogue, and European buildings and neo-classic pavilions standing next to each other along Li Gong Di and around Jinji Lake, among which are first-class karaoke bars, bars and restaurants (mostly providing Cantonese cuisine).

1912's charisma has, since April 1, 2008, spread from Nanjing to Suzhou, and blossomed on this new fertile land of entertainment.

(Fan Yi)

TIPS

Bars/restaurants recommended:

1. SCARLET @A17, Block 1912, the largest and most popular nightclub in SIP, alluring countless fashion fans with its flaming SCARLET logo.

To be described with a little drama, Scarlet is no longer merely the center of fashionable society, but the headquarters of liberation – can you imagine how many bookworms have finally thrown away their glasses here and shake it up in this modern city?

2. JENNY'S BAR @A7, Block 1912, featuring imported drinks, popular among non-Chinese visitors.

Just as its name Suke in Chinese suggests, it welcomes guests (ke) visiting Suzhou. Featuring a country vibe with live bands playing light-hearted or classic gentle melodies, it is an ideal place to drink with playmates and drown your homesickness.

3. TUNNEL BAR @A7, Block 1912, with two eye-catching motorcycles at its gate. Most of its guests are foreign visitors and local white-collars.

Being the first motorcycle club in Suzhou and the base for motor fans, it is simply decorated with distinctive features. Featuring rock music, imported beers, outstanding cocktails and billiard tables, it is a perfect spot for parties.

4. INDIAN AT THE CROSS (South Pole) @ A9, Block 1912, serving Indian cuisine and European drinks.

Famous for its well-cooked Indian food, this restaurant stands as a unique scenic spot in Block 1912 with its elegant exterior look and large hall.

The nightlife unfolds like "Pulp Fiction"

I have come to live in a city on the other side of the world and yet I have somehow managed to find a bar that feels like home. Sharing a name with one of the coolest films in existence, "Pulp Fiction" is a bar situated on Shiquan Street in downtown Suzhou. In comparison with other options it is as good as any other place to have a drink, meet with friends and relax all at the same time. Importantly there is a comfortable "local" feeling; it caters for both expats and Chinese residents, replicates the look of a typical Western bar without feeling overdone and creates a sense of friendliness without being unnatural.

TIPS

Pulp Fiction
Add: 169 Shiquan Street
Tel: 0512-6520 8067

A large portion of success for Pulp Fiction seems to result from always giving visitors what they want; a wide range of options delivered by friendly people. A good pint? Check. Affordable prices? Check. Frequent special deals? Another check. They occasionally run theme nights that draw in extra visitors, but most nights the prices are low enough to satisfy the average pocket.

Sport is an important part of Pulp Fiction; memorabilia adorns the walls, TV often shows it and visitors even play it. You can watch football, F1, tennis, basketball and many other sports easily on the numerous screens dotted around the two floors of the bar. The classic pub games of pool and darts feature inside, but be sure to write your name on the board when the place is busy to ensure you get a turn – there are lots of people who like to play too!

(Craig Lindley)

TIPS

Before 9pm there are very few people in the bar. After 10pm it becomes busy. Especially on Fridays and Saturdays, the bar will almost be packed out at night. Live performances are offered everyday on a different scale. You will happily join the dancing and some people even jump onto the stage to show their dancing skills. The outside of the bar has tables and chairs for chatting, sobering up, or avoiding the clamor inside.

Inclub:

As the name of the club suggests, "fashionable." It has become a popular spot for trendsetters in Suzhou. Most of the visitors are regulars. Frequented late at night by: fashionable men and women, Westerners and celebrities.

Add: No. 818, Xuanmiao Square, Guanqian Pedestrian Street

Fees: Quoted by a friend online "most of the people there drink red wine, to show their expensive taste and the prices there are relatively high compared to other Suzhou's bars."

Surroundings: It's located on Guanqian Pedestrian Street and close to Ganjiang Road. You can also easily find nice restaurants for drinks and food. Muge KTV is at the front and Loquat No.1 Bar is close to it. There are a great number of other bars, coffee bars and clothes shops close by. Eat, drink, and be merry.

There are a great number of bars in Suzhou, big and small. Bars are relatively concentrated around the crossing of Renmin Road and Zhuhui Road, end of Xinshi Bridge, Changxu Road and Li Gong Di in Suzhou Industrial Park.

We recommend some of the more famous ones:

Boiling100°

Add: 1st Floor of Zhuhui Mansion, 208 Zhuhui Road, Canglang District

Playing stunning music, it is essentially a pub. It's packed almost everyday and you can hardly get in after 8.30pm at night. Remember to book early if you are interested.

K'BAR

Add: 859 Suzhou Panxu Road

The bar features vast space, several separated grand bars and splendid bar stools. Fashion parties are held here every week and the K'Bar is dedicated to parties for special occasions.

Phebe Club

Add: 1st Floor of Linkup Electronics Market, 688 Suzhou Zhuhui Road

It's one of the most fashionable bars in Suzhou, presenting unprecedented music and a fabulous stage. It is superb and draws a good crowd every day.

Huangting No. 2 Bar

Add: 838 Panxu Road

It's the first luxurious club in Suzhou under international management – you can feel and experience high standards.

SOS Storm Bar

Add: 826 Panxu Road

It's first in the new concept of entertainment in Suzhou, incorporating electrophonic effects, culture, visual arts, dancing art and other pioneering concepts and displays the new Disco KTV trend of an entertainment giant.

Joys Pub

Add: 798 Panxu Road

The splendor is patched with spots of melancholy, which is the feature of Jazz. The pub is a mixture of various styles, decadence of the industrial revolution, Baroque luxury and private appeal with a unique feeling of nobleness.

Dance to the music

OPENING the ancient wooden door of Harry's Bar, you see some patrons sitting face to face drinking, some are leaning lonely against the wall, some are chatting, some are singing and dancing, some are meditating and some are murmuring...

This could be the bar most frequented by foreigners in Suzhou. When you are bored of the boisterous bars, you can come here for a change in mood. It's cozy and almost all the patrons are familiar guests. Every night an Irishman jumps onto the stage and dances to the music. His dancing attracts many comments from the guests.

The band is fabulous. "Careless Whisper" unveils the night.

There are numerous videos of this band's performances on Youku.com. Members of the band cooperate extremely well, you can sing along with them or have an improvised dance on the stage. The guitar player is skillful, but very shy when talking to you. The drummer is cute, has a smile as pure as a baby's. The leading singer is perfect and song requesting is free. Simply write the song with the original singer's name on a napkin then give it to them, and they will sing it for you.

(Fan Yi)

TIPS

Harry's Bar

It's a bar restaurant frequented by foreigners in Suzhou, located in Qimen Road, close to the Suzhou Museum. The interior is decorated in Chinese style, classical and tranquil. Occasionally it will hold "Speed Dating" or similar activities. Besides the bar there is a dining room serving food. The food there is amazing, especially the curry. The boss is from Singapore and he offers authentic Southeast Asian cuisine. We recommend the Curry Chicken, and their fabulous soup; you can also enjoy performances of a Philippines band.

Generally speaking, the atmosphere there is pleasant, very suitable for chatting and you can appreciate the music and watch the sports game on TV. The bar is very popular and the beers there are moderately priced.

Average cost: 100 yuan per person

Add: 118 Qimen Road, Pingjiang District (close to Suzhou Museum)

Tel: 0512-6754 6411

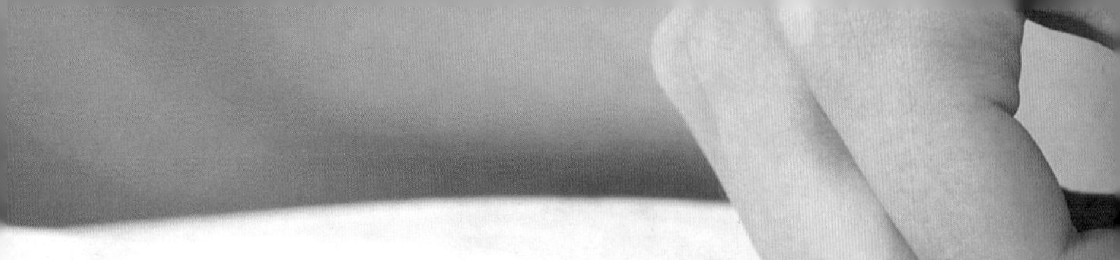

Foot massage: It's for everyone!

FOOT massage parlors are everywhere in Suzhou! You will see lighted signs with just a picture of a foot, and that could be a swanky massage place, or you might see a storefront lined with overstuffed chairs and ottomans. That's likely the neighborhood gathering spot, where people in the community stop in. Try them all!

Back home, a massage can be expensive, and only for the pampered few, but here in Suzhou the price is low enough that everybody can take advantage of this wonderful service. Suzhou people believe in taking good care of their feet!

It is frequently a group activity. You can take the whole family, or get the girls together before lunch. While your feet are being rubbed you can chat amiably with your friends, watch a little TV, and sip some tea.

The massage starts with a tub of piping hot water with good-smelling medicinal herbs, placed between the furniture, and you will sit on the ottoman. While your happy feet soak luxuriously, the masseuse will start on your neck and shoulders and head, rubbing away all of your cares. Then you lay back on the comfy chair with your feet on the ottoman, and let them work their magic on your calves, ankles and feet. Lots of lotion is used, but before you leave they wash your feet again so you can put your shoes back on. Walk or float out of there with a new attitude!

You will notice that Suzhou women have the cutest shoes in the world. The variety of patterns and colors, and mix of textures that Suzhou women wear on their feet is endlessly

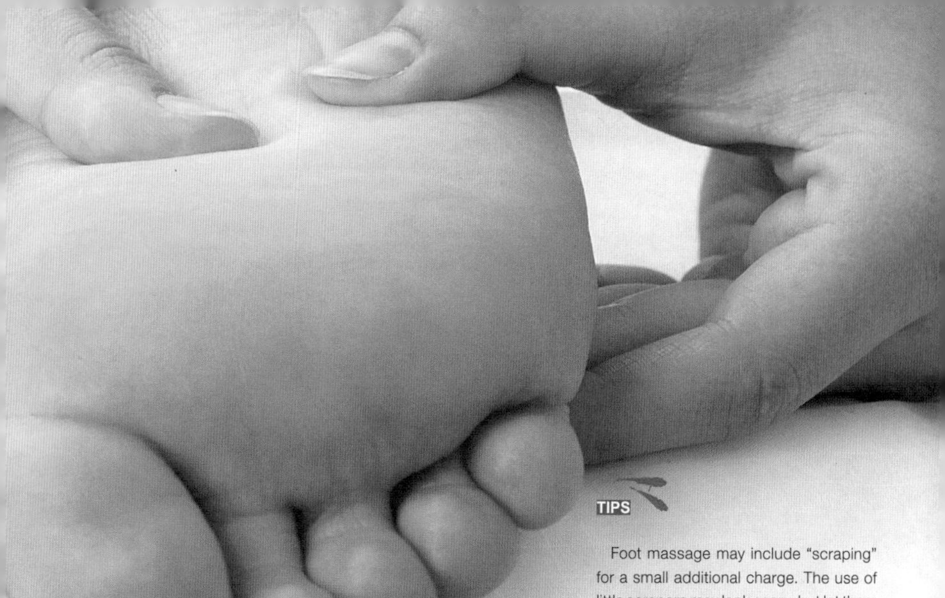

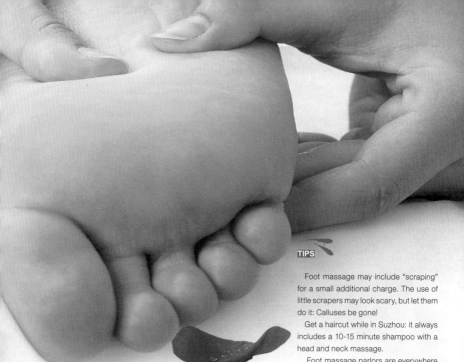

fascinating to observe, usually with fun and very sexy results, and most frequently with heels. Whether teaching young children, shopping for groceries, or visiting a hilly tourist site, Suzhou women will typically wear heels. So you see, it's a symbiotic relationship: after a day of trucking around in some punishing but fabulously fetching pink suede high heel boots that are trimmed with fur and have some sparkly silver-edged gems dangling from the ankles, a girl needs a foot massage!

(Susan Blauvelt)

TIPS

Foot massage may include "scraping" for a small additional charge. The use of little scrapers may look scary, but let them do it: Calluses be gone!

Get a haircut while in Suzhou: it always includes a 10-15 minute shampoo with a head and neck massage.

Foot massage parlors are everywhere and Qingmu Store is one of the best. Liangzi is good too, offering skillful physical therapy and health care services. Chongqing Fuqiao enjoys good reputation in China and it has branches in Suzhou too.

Qingmu Foot Massage: in Youngor Central Hotel, No. 63, Gong Xiang, 0512-6515 7198

Qingmu Foot Massage SND Branch: 2F, Golden River Mansion, 35 Shishan Road, 0512-6808 8889

Liangzi Foot Massage Shizi Street Branch: 457 Shizhi Street, 0512-6511 8537

Liangzi Foot Massage Shihuifang Branch: 108 Xinghan Street, SIP, 0512-6761 0121

Chongqing Fuqiao Health Care Store: 8 North Tongjing Road, 0512-6532 8838

Pamper your body: It's SPA time!

IF you are looking for a good spa place, I know a few places in Suzhou that are quite nice. My personal pick is the Lansol SPA. It is located in a nice antique building on a quiet street.

There, you can try their specially formulated herbal bath with rose petals, which will dissolve all your weariness. Followed by a full body Chinese massage with your own blend of essential oils.

My favorite masseuse is also the owner. The first time I visited the spa she noticed how tense my body was. In the dimly lit chamber, her soothing techniques helped to ease all my troubles and I could feel every inch of my skin getting more and more relaxed.

There is a hint of music echoing the room. A fine fragrance also floats in the air, so delicate that it's as if the room is filled with real flowers. In the end I fell asleep and had the sweetest dream ever.

Your body is your temple. Take an afternoon off and give yourself a treat, pamper your body with a nice spa. You will feel very relaxed and physically transformed.

(Lu Rong)

TIPS

Lansol SPA:

Add: 18 Jinfan Road

Tel: 0512-6522 6111

(Appointment is required)

Average price: 200 yuan per person per session

Dragonfly

Where you can experience oriental massage, nail SPA, tanning and waxing and all soul retreat sessions.

Add: 1st Floor East, Jiacheng Mansion, 128 Jinjihu Road, SIP

Tel: 0512-6763 9636

Lotus Nail SPA

Wonderful manicure and massage from head to toe.

Add: No. 516, Zhongyin Huilong Mansion, 8 Suhua Road, SIP

For appointments, please call 0512-6280 7896

Night snacks in Suzhou

WITH its reputation as a quiet city, Suzhou doesn't have the same degree of exciting nightlife as many other cities of comparable size. However, there is always something for a night owl to do, and one of the best ways to enjoy an evening out is to sample an array of tempting foods.

Shiquan Street

The street has often been referred to as artware or bar street. It offers an array of tempting late-night snacks, from barbecues to stir fries. Many of its restaurants, although small in size, boast distinctive menus.

Shi Lu Flavor Food Street

Here you can find regional snacks from across China, which provide a palette of diverse flavors.

Xiang Men Hou Zhuang (including the intersection of Jinjihu Road and Zhuangxianwan Road)

Here you can eat and shop. Alongside stalls selling delectable stir-fried goods are stands selling clothing and handbags.

Fenghuang Street

Strollers can eat their way from one end of the street to the other, taking a geographic culinary trip in the bargain. On the southern side are many traditional Cantonese dishes from China's south, while the northern half of the street features the famous home cooking at the Yangsi's Mother-in-Law restaurant.

Chongqing Morals Village Hot Pot
Add: Lindun Road Store (No. 198, Lingdun Road, Pingjiang District); Xujiang Road Store (No. 299, Xujiang Road, Canglang District)
Business hours: 24 hours

Boya Barbecue
Add: Under the Xiangmen Houzhuang Bridge
Business hours: from 6pm

Yaoji Soybean Milk
Add: No. 122, Xizhongshi, close to the ancient Changmen Gate
Business hours: from early morning until night. Soybean Milk is available at any time.

Chuanfu Bone Soup Restaurant
Add: No. 979, Sanxiang Road
Business hours: from noon to two or three o'clock in the morning.

Guaiguai Crawfish Restaurant (Summer), Xietianxiedi Sautéed Crab Restaurant (Winter)
Add: No. 55, Shiquan Street
Chef's choice: Guaiguai Crawfish (a type of freshwater crayfish that is only available in summer), Sautéed Crab in Hot Spicy Sauce (available in winter), Chicken Giblets, Cooked Duck with Beer, Poached Sliced Chicken

Honghuo Hunan-flavor Restaurant
Add: Xueshi Street, close to Jingde Road
Chef's choice: Two-flavor Steamed Fish Head, Shredded Cabbage in Oyster Sauce, Youxian Smoked Bean Curd, Fried White Pepper with Dry-cured Beef, Sour and Hot Chicken Giblets

---

Yuanyuan Northeast BBQ Restaurant
Add: Xinjiekou, East of Jinji Lake
Chef's choice: Shish Kebab, Chicken Wings

Shuixiang Wonton
Add: No. 754, Sanxiang Road (close to Tongjing Road), Shiquan Street, etc, around 10 stores in Suzhou
Chef's choice: Chinese Spinach and Pork Wonton

Yangsi Crawfish Restaurant (Fenghuang Store)
Add: Fenghuang Street (close to Ganjiang Road)
Chef's choice: Crawfish

Runji Restaurant
Add: Fenghuang Street Store, Trust-mart Store (in Trust-mart), Suzhou New District Store (in Commercial Street, SND)
Chef's choice: Roasted Goose, Clay pot Rice, Barbecued Pork, Beef Porridge

---

Overseas Dragon Fried Dumplings (Lindun Store, Fenghuang Store, 20-30 stores in Suzhou)
Chef's choice: Hot and Sour Soup, with Fried Dumplings

Yangyang Dumpling Restaurant

Add: No. 420, Shiquan Street

Chef's choice: Shredded Seafood Dumpling, Pickled Cucumber

Liyin Chao's Casserole Porridge

Add: Crossing of Shiquan Street and Fenghuang Street

Chef's choice: Casserole Shrimp Porridge, Pork Chop with Preserved Orange Peel

Xumen Northeast BBQ Restaurant

Add: No. 28, Laodong Road, Canglang District; opposite to Huating Mansion (close to Changxu Road)

Chef's choice: Barbecued Fish, Barbecued Squid, Barbecued Tendons

Haozhuang Restaurant

Add: No. 30, Yueyuan Street, Wuzhong District

Chef's choice: Barbecued Oyster, Oysters on Ice, Sliced Bass Fish with Green Onions

Wawajiao Griddled Food Restaurant

Add: No. 699, Shiquan Street; No. 11, Jiayufang

Chef's choice: Griddle Cooked Bullfrog

Haidilao Hot Pot Restaurant

Add: 7th Floor, Senso Place, No. 219, South Guangji Road

Business hours: 24 hours

XI

An earful of Suzhou

Close your eyes and the city takes on a whole new meaning.
Listen to the beautiful tones of the local dialect.
Hear traditional music.
Thrill to a bell chime.
Take time to let the ancient walls whisper their stories.

The magical world of Kunqu Opera

WHEN that twister lifted Dorothy's house, and swept her into the Land of Oz, the little Munchkins, bizarre hair-dos and clothes and all, welcomed her with squeaky, high-pitched voices. Thunderstruck, Dorothy whispered to her little dog, "Toto, I don't think we're in Kansas any more..."

Step into the magical world of Suzhou's most unique art form, and you will be similarly transported. Kunqu Opera is gorgeous and elegant, albeit "outlandish," and you will undoubtedly regard the performance as one of your greatest memories.

First, some traditions of the Kunqu Opera style of theater need to be understood:

Actors relate to the audience directly in a presentational style. When the character first makes an appearance, he will begin by telling

the audience who he is, and how he has come to this point in our story. Throughout the opera, the audience may be addressed at various times.

The set is minimal and usually consists of just a table and two chairs. We are meant to use our imagination when a character lies on the table to sleep, or the chair becomes a throne. A riding cop means the character is on a horse, and circling the stage implies a journey.

Stock characters are used to tell the stories, and are recognized by their make-up and costumes. They are primarily the old man, the young man, the young woman, and the jester, or clown (chou), who can be identified by the circle of white that is always in the middle of his face. The make-up is extremely vivid, with intense colors, and a fifth stock character (jing) goes even further with make-up.

Interestingly, the color symbolism in Eastern culture proves to be the opposite of the West: if he has mostly white make-up he is treacherous, but if his make-up base is black, he is trustworthy. A red face shows that he has great courage.

The young man is often a scholar who is on his way to the imperial examination. Along the road, he frequently meets a beautiful young woman, and then there are some problems to solve. Not surprisingly, back in the day, young scholars wrote all these operas!

Stylized speech and falsetto singing are very foreign to Western ears, but can be enjoyable anyway. It is fascinating to listen to the music performed on the traditional instruments by an orchestra that sits offstage. The bongs and clangs and percussion accompany the actors' speaking, and are designed to help us understand the characters' thoughts and feelings.

Kunqu is a visual feast as well. The make-up is stunning and the hair ornaments, enchanting. The costumes are lovely Ming Dynasty (1368-1644) era with overlong sleeves that the actors use to gesture, along with fans and other props. The actors have trained for many years to give these incredible performances that are not only vocally demanding but physically exacting, as well. It is fun to watch the attention to many details that gives the acting such grace. Some roles even include acrobatics!

You want to have the quintessential Suzhou experience? Kunqu Opera will enthrall and amaze you. Go for it!

(Susan Blauvelt)

TIPS

Get ready by visiting the Kunqu Opera Museum, which is free. Housed in a beautiful old Guild Hall, there are models of theaters and performance boats that plied the canals. Costumes and photos of actors prime you for seeing the real thing performed on Sunday afternoons on their classical stage. Pay 20 yuan to enjoy the performance.

Add: 14 Zhongzhangjia Lane, off Pingjiang Road.

Kun Qu (pronounced 'Kwoon Jew'; Qu means "opera") fans know the stories well. Arrive early and seek out an English-speaking native who can give you a basic plot outline. Knowing the story ahead of time just increases your enjoyment.

Performances are also given for special occasions at the Pingtan Training School theater, 1859 Binhe Road, SND, at 0512-6824 7915; and in the theater of the Suzhou Art Museum, 2075 Renmin Road. SSCAC (Suzhou Culture and Arts Centre), 1 Guanfeng Street, at 0512-6289 9899; brings in opera from other provinces as well. Qinlan Hall in Guanqian Pedestrian Street (behind Kaiming Theater) offers free performance every Wednesday and Thursday, mainly for students. Call these venues to ask if a show will be given during your stay in Suzhou.

Sometimes, English subtitles are supplied on an LED screen to the side of the stage. That's a lucky break if you get it, but don't let it stop you if there isn't. Kunqu is an experience that can be enjoyed enormously, even if you can't comprehend everything!

苏州评弹
Suzhou Pingtan

Singing in one of the most beautiful dialects, Suzhou Pingtan is perhaps not as spectacular as Western opera, but has a distinctive soft touch in it. To enjoy it, it is best to sit in a classic garden, with a cup of warm tea at hand, and let the sound of each word melt in your heart.

用一种最美的方言吟唱，苏州评弹并没有西方的歌剧那么恢宏，却有着独特的轻柔格调。要享受评弹，最好坐在古典的园林里，暖茶在手，让每一个字的声音融化到心里。

Hear and feel the melodies

A FAMOUS Chinese author once wrote an article about music. In it, she described Pingtan as "soft vocal music" and like a gentle bite on the skin by your lover. Maybe this sounds too exotic, but she certainly managed to capture Pingtan's softness in words. For you to appreciate what she meant, you need to experience it for yourself and feel the melody through your ears.

To talk about Pingtan, perhaps one should firstly explain that Suzhou has its own dialect. There are

over 100 different dialects spoken in China and each of them is quite different from the official language "Mandarin". It is said Suzhou's dialect is the softest and gentlest one of them all. That is why Pingtan is only sung in Suzhou dialect, to give prominence to the slow and delicate melody of the music.

Pingtan is often sung by only one or two people, and accompanied by the clear sound of Chinese lute (Pi Pa or San Xian). It comprises not just singing, but occasional comic dialogues as well. A complete Pingtan has a long list of acts, as its story is usually adopted from some of China's famous historic novels. As TV was not generally available to most Chinese people in the 1950s, Suzhou people would go to their favorite opera theater and listen to dramas instead. This tradition has not been so much passed on, but the significance of Pingtan in our culture has been preserved.

Nowadays, Pingtan has become a popular tourist attraction. Some performances are even held on the tourist boats. Listening to the music while drifting around Suzhou's old water canals, certainly will give you an opera experience that is unique to Suzhou.

(Xinlu Cindy Huang)

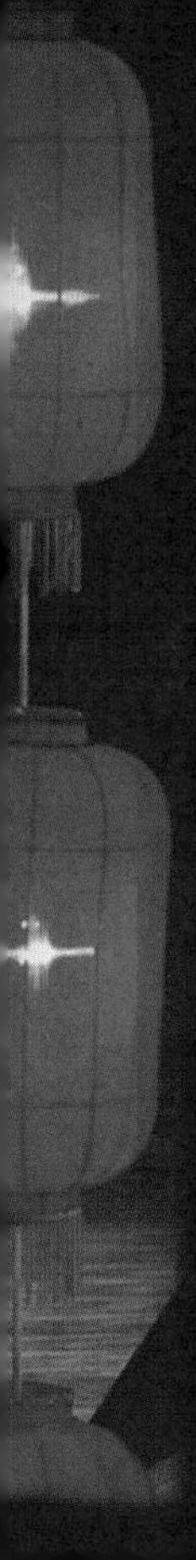

TIPS

Plum and Bamboo Storytelling Garden

Add: No. 30 Taipingfang, Shi Road

Opening hours: 1:30pm-3:30pm

Transport: Tour Bus No. 1 and 5, Bus No. 3, 6 and 401

Tel: 0512-6533 1854

Price: 15 yuan per person (including tea)

Guangyu Storytelling Hall

Add: No. 8 Di Yi Tian Men, Guanqian Street

Opening hours: 1:30pm-3:30pm

Transport: Bus No. 2, 4, 23, 28, 29, 54, 55 and 401

Tel: 0512-6524 3011

Price: 25 yuan per person (including tea)

Pinfang Teahouse

Add: No. 24-25 Xijiaomen, Guanqian Street

Opening hours: 1:30pm-3:30pm

Transport: Bus No. 2, 4, 23, 28, 29, 54, 55 and 401

Tel: 0512-6728 8816

Price: 18 yuan per person (including tea)

History unfurls its stories in neighboring towns

No one can fully appreciate Suzhou without visiting the small towns that surround the city. In the absence of urban bustle, these towns provide a quiet view of life as it once was. Old buildings and houses exude charm and tell stories of the past. These are great places to lose yourself in the sea of time.

XII

A water town perfect for a walking tour

ONE of the joys of travel is the serendipity of stumbling onto gems off the beaten track.

For that special experience, head for Tongli (同里), a water town surrounded by five lakes and 18 streams and criss-crossed by bridges - each with its own folklore.

The township is located on the eastern shore of Taihu Lake, an easy bus trip from Suzhou just 18 kilometers away.

This town dates back at least 1,300 years and was home to painters, poets, scholars and eminent government officials during its long history. Each of the famous residents contributed something lasting to the history of Tongli, and many streets still bear the names of their auspicious titles.

At one time, it was called fu tu, which literally means "richness," and it was accessible only by boat. For a time, visitors to the town were charged money to enter, but the practice caused outrage and was dropped, and the town was renamed Tongli, which means "friendship," to repair its image.

An array of bridges makes this water town an ideal walking town. There are almost 50 stone bridges of all styles joining the islands created by the streams and lakes. The bridges have poetic names, such as Taiping (peace and tranquillity) Bridge and Jili (luck) Bridge.

Taiping Bridge was built during the Qing Dynasty (1636-1912). Jili is an arch bridge inscribed with ancient couplets describing the scenic views from the span.

Tongli is a sleepy town perfect for daydreaming and letting your thoughts wander. There's a 300-meter shopping street where it's possible to find many traditional products and specialty local foods.

The town's glorious history of famous

residents has left many elegant old mansions worth a visit. In fact, the town is often hailed as a "museum of ancient architecture."

One of the most spectacular is the mansion of Ren Lansheng, a retired official. He built his Tui Si garden in the mid 1880s. A tree planted there by the owner still survives as a metaphor for life. The garden, as its name in translates, is a place of "retreat and reflection." The house itself has a tearoom for VIP guests and a charming wood interior with intricate carvings.

(Caterina Bernardini)

Yang Mingyi

Tongli

Opening hours: 7:30am-9:30pm

Tickets: 100 yuan (extra 20 yuan for the Sex Culture Museum)

Transport: Buses available at Suzhou's South Bus Station and North Bus Station.

Where to go:

Chuanxin Lane: Chuanxin Lane in the old town of Tongli is 300 meters long and 0.8 meters wide. It was built with stone slabs, which make melodic sounds when stepping on them. That's why the lane is also called Xiangban Lane, meaning "resounding slabs" in Chinese.

Retreat and Reflection Garden(退思园): Retreat and Reflection Garden is the most famous garden in Tongli. It was built during the reign of Emperor Guangxu (1875-1908). Some people say the garden has a kind of beauty that lingers in your mind. Surprises are hidden behind two small gates that lead to a forecourt and a backyard.

Luo Xing Zhou: This small island east of Tongli is a sanctuary for Buddhism, Taoism and Confucianism. It is several minutes from the old town by boat. "Listen to the rain on Luo Xing Zhou" was a joy for the Chinese literati in the old days.

Mingqing Street: This ancient street is lined with antiques and embroidery shops. Don't forget to try Jiu Niang Bing and Wa Di Su, both local sweet snacks, there. If you want to take some home, buy them from Lin's Store or Gu Xiang Cun or Hao Chi Lai. Their products taste good and are reasonably priced.

What to eat:

Grandma's tea: Grandma's Tea is

something you shouldn't miss when visiting Tongli. The Grandma Li's Tea House is highly recommended. Sitting in the traditional-style house, you will be served tea and entertained by live music performed by the tea house owner. Besides tea, a variety of local delicacies is served as well, such as three-colored shrimp shortcakes and steamed lotus root. Grandma's tea costs 80 yuan/pot and 300 yuan in a 15-bag package.

Where to stay:

Zheng Fu Cao Tang is a chain hotel with branches in Tongli and Zhouzhuang.

Tongli: 138 New Mingqing Street

Tel: 0512-6332 0576.

Zhouzhuang: 90 Zhongshi Street

Tel: 0512-5721 9333

Get drunk,
you don't need to drink at all!
美酒佳釀名四方
酒
園林宅第誉江南
酒

Zhouzhuang

Well-known for its picturesque settings of a canal town, Zhouzhuang (周庄) is among the first group of heritage towns certified by the Chinese government. The town has many bridges over a labyrinth of canals flanked by old houses. A score of stone bridges were constructed in the Ming and Qing dynasties, including the Double Bridges and Fu'an Bridge. Due to protection from water on all sides, most of the town's old houses and bridges survived the ravages of wars. The main attractions include the Double Bridges, Zhang's Residence, Shen's Residence and Milou Restaurant.

Opening hours: 7:30-21:00

Tickets: 100 yuan (7:30-20:00), 80 yuan (16:00-21:00)

Transport: Buses available at Suzhou South Bus Station and North Bus Station.

Tel: 0512-5721 1655

What to eat:

Wansan's Pig Knuckle: Well-cooked in brown soy sauce, the pig knuckle literally melts in your mouth. The skin is quaveringly soft and the meat tastes delicious with a hint of sweetness.

The Shenting Restaurant is the best place to savor the Wansan Pig Knuckle as it is the original kitchen where this delicacy was invented. Tel: 0512-5721 2176.

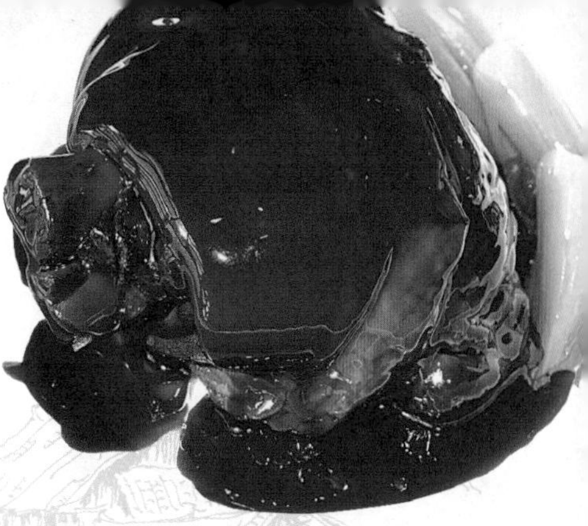

What to see:

Zhouzhuang in Four Seasons is a stage performance that represents the charms of the canal town in different seasons. The show is staged on floating platform against the backdrop of a bridge and waterside houses. Its music is typical of the region south of the Yangtze River. The spectacular performance will send you on a trip back in time and let you relive the glorious days of this ancient town and its idyllic life.

Tickets: 150 yuan, 280 yuan for VIP seats

Performing time: 7-8pm daily

Venue: Water stage, Jiang Nan Ren Jia

Tel: 0512-5720 5622

Carried away in a boat to your dreamland

Luzhi

"Small bridge over flowing stream, harmonious household standing beside the river", are typical pictures of Luzhi (甪直), the renowned water town. The one square kilometer ancient town used to have "seventy two and a half" stone bridges from Song, Yuan, Ming and Qing dynasties and now 41 bridges are still existing and the town is then reputed as "Chinese ancient bridge museum".

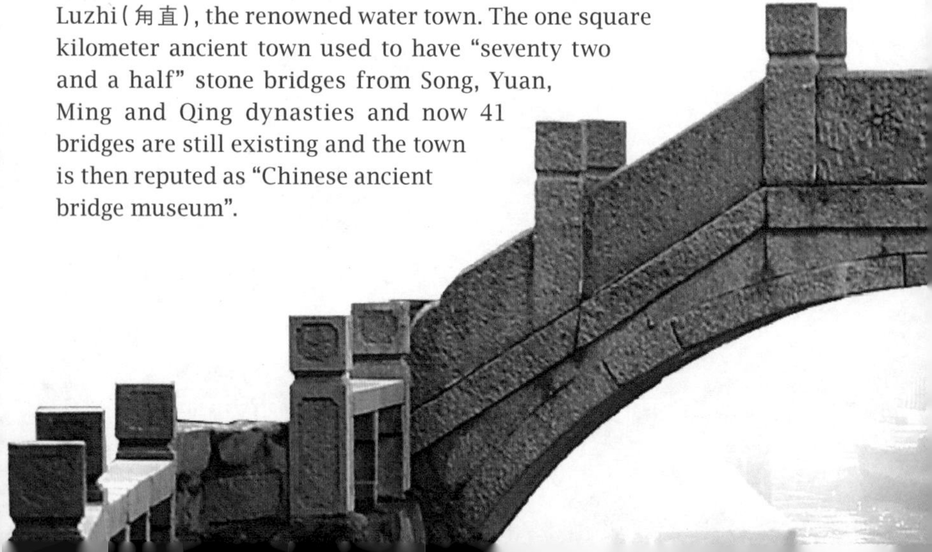

Through ticket in the scenic area is 60 yuan and rumor goes that it may possibly rise to 78 yuan. When travel to Luzhi, a paddle boat is a must-try, otherwise you will be there in vain. It costs 60 yuan to try the boat, which could hold 4 people.

Xihui Restaurant is a local and famous one in the town and the decoration presents reminiscent sense. Its telephone number is 0512-6501 0397. If you visit Luzhi in winter, try to taste the most famous Duck Soup.

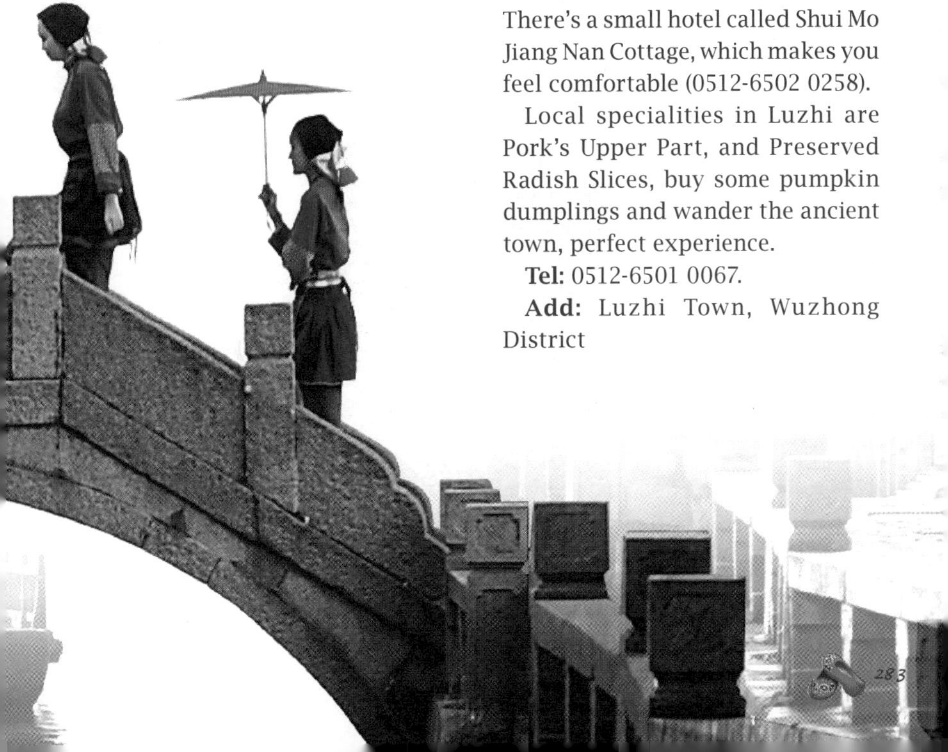

Besides, Wansheng Restaurant , which Ye Shengtao's famous article was based on, is also nice, and the whole article is carved on a wall. There are many old farm tools on display and its telephone number is 0512-6501 1187. Jiang Nan Cun Restaurant has distinctive features too; its number is 0512-6602 3678, mainly serving local dishes.

If you want to stay overnight, Yang Ming Mountain Villa is fairly good (reservation number 0512-6601 1117). Jun Yue Hotel is close to the ancient town (0512-6602 3188). There's a small hotel called Shui Mo Jiang Nan Cottage, which makes you feel comfortable (0512-6502 0258).

Local specialities in Luzhi are Pork's Upper Part, and Preserved Radish Slices, buy some pumpkin dumplings and wander the ancient town, perfect experience.

Tel: 0512-6501 0067.

Add: Luzhi Town, Wuzhong District

Qiandeng

Ticket: 60 yuan/person (including entrance to all the scenic spots)

Hotel industry in Qiandeng (千灯) is not very prosperous and we recommend you to stay in Green Tree Hotel or Motel 168. Yurong International Hotel is a little better; the retail price for its standard room is 238 yuan/day.

It's nice to take meals in Mingdu Restaurant and Jingu Farmhouse, with an average cost of 40 yuan per person.

The specialities in Qiandeng are Sole-shaped Pastry, Smoked String Beans, Euryale Cake and Dragon Whiskers Noodles.

Tel: 0512-5747 2152

Add: 15km, south of Kunshan

Jinxi

Jinxi (锦溪) is located in the southwest of Kunshan City and it's said that there are "36 bridges and 72 kilns" in that town. Jinxi is famed as "Home of Chinese Folk Museums" and the Sole-shaped Pastry and Chaudfroid there have special taste.

Tickets: 50 yuan/person

Tel: 0512-5794 0661

Add: in the southwest of Kunshan City, eight kilometers away from ancient town Zhouzhuang

There is no window here without a view.

Mudu

Mudu (木渎) is located in the east of Suzhou and on the bank of Taihu Lake. It's a renowned ancient town in Yangtze River Delta and shares the same age as Suzhou City.

Tel: 0512-6656 1218

Add: Foothill of Lingyan Hill

Tickets: A through ticket of Mudu, 60 yuan (including Yanjia Garden 30 yuan, Hong Ying Shan Fang 30 yuan, Ancient Pine Garden 20 yuan, Runner-up Scholar's Residence 10 yuan), Lingyan Peony Garden 20 yuan, Lingyan Scenic Spot 20 yuan and Pleasure Boat 10 yuan/person.

Accommodation: there are a great number of hotels in Mudu and its surrounding area, two 5-star hotels, four 4-star hotels and nearly 10 3-star and 2-star hotels, vacation villages and sanitarium, and a few chain budget hotels with the price ranging from 100 yuan to 800 yuan.

Violet Residence: a hotel decorated under the styles of Ming and Qing Dynasties; all the beds, tables and chairs are made of mahogany, displaying extreme sense of luxury. The telephone number there is 0512-6679 5905.

China Garden Hotel and Tianping

Grand Hotel are both 4-star hotels and located in Jinshang Road. Their telephone numbers are 0512-6625 6666 and 0512-6626 8888.

If you are interested in more substantial price, you can choose the budget hotels, for instance, Home Inns, Hanting Inns & Hotels, GreenTree Inns, which are open to the public.

Cuisines: food in Mudu are distinctive in four seasons: wild vegetable and Bi Luo Chun in spring; white fish, white shrimp and silver fish in summer; Barb Liver Soup and hairy crab in early autumn and Cangshu mutton in deep autumn and winter.

The most famous restaurant with traditional brand in Mudu is Shi Jia Restaurant and the most delicious food is Barb Liver Soup; in addition, the Shi's Red Cooked Pork Rib is famous too. The telephone number of Shi Jia Restaurant is 0512-6626 1351.

Longsheng Restaurant at the entrance of the ancient town enjoys traffic convenience and its telephone number is 0512-6651 7778.

We will not enumerate the restaurants one by one, just want to say that the famous restaurants in Mudu are generally in Jinshan Road.

We also highly recommend Cangshu mutton. Go west from the ancient town and extends to Cangshu Cuisine Street, dozens of mutton stores there sell delicious and characteristic whole lamb feast.

Take me home, late night snow!

From Suzhou, with love

Apart from memories, there are a multitude of more tangible reminders you can take home from a trip to Suzhou.

Snapshots of canals and stone brick bridges.

Artfully designed packages of special local teas.

The gentle fragrance of sandalwood sculpture.

The soft touch of Suzhou silk.

Don't forget souvenirs!

They may one day bring you back to Suzhou.

XIII

苏州丝绸
Suzhou Silk

There was a secret. A secret that is brighter than any jewel, softer than the newborn's skin, gentler than the lover's kiss. It was a luxury that worth the Byzantine emperor have someone come to steal. This secret is "Suzhou Silk", that has blended into the soul of this town from the very beginning.

有如此一个秘密。一个比珠宝要闪亮，比新生儿肌肤要柔软，比爱人的亲吻要轻柔的秘密。一件值得拜占庭帝国派人来偷取的奢侈品。这个秘密就是苏州丝绸，而它自始至终是和这个城市的灵魂交融在一起的。

As womanly as it gets

LADIES, if I told you that you can get a beautifully finished silk dress, tailor-made to suit your curves, all for under 200 U.S. dollars, how would you react?

Well, it is true, and you have a choice of patterns or just plain silk.

It is not a piece of Chanel or Versace, but Qipao, or Chinese sheath dress, is more special than any designer's dresses. It originated from the dresses worn by women in the Qing Dynasty (1636-1912) and its modernized version then topped the fashion trend in the 1920s.

Nowadays, although the dress has been significantly shortened in length (to show beautiful legs of course), it has kept most of its original design charm and is a symbol of China. Most Chinese movie stars will wear a beautiful Qipao when they are invited to international events.

So what's so unique about Qipao? The original style of Qipao was actually a piece of traditional women's clothing of the "Man" people (one of China's minority ethnic groups). It had a

veryloosedesigntocoverawoman's curves. Later in the 1920s, Qipao was made to emphasize a woman's figure. This change of design was at the time considered as a huge step in improvement of women's rights and identities in the history of China. "Man" women needed to wear trousers underneath Qipao, until the 1920s and 1930s when women wore them as a one-piece dress.

Qipao is made from different types of materials. Since Suzhou has China's finest silk, it is the first choice for Suzhou women. The color of Qipao varies but the most popular color is always red. Some are as rich as roses while others are as subtle as water lilies. Today's Qipao is still not revealing, but will show enough to spark a man's imagination.

If you have time, make sure you get your Qipao tailor made. Otherwise, choose a size that suits you the best from a great range of ready-to-wear dresses. You will be amazed how this dress will not only make you look elegant, but also bring out the womanliest side of you.

(Xinlu Cindy Huang)

TIPS

Where to buy:

Rui Fu Xiang Shilu Shop

Add: 29 Shilu Road

Tel: 0512-6531 6008

Rui Fu Xiang Guanqian Shop

Add: 246 Guanqian Street

Tel: 0512-6727 0989

This shop sells probably the most famous brand of Suzhou's Qipao and silk. They can certainly guarantee the quality, but make sure to look at the price tag first as some might be expensive.

Xin Yuan Qipao Shop

Add: 122 Pingjiang Road

This is a very exquisite shop that sells tailor-made Qipao.

Business hours: 10am-7pm

Long Feng Clothing

Add: 70 Gong Xiang Alley

Most students that are studying Pingtan, or Suzhou Opera (which requires the singer to wear a Qipao when performing) have their outfits made in this shop. It will often take 7-10 days to make the dress and the price is about 400-500 yuan each.

Tel: 0512-6512 9896

Jin Xiang Drapery

Add: 2 Di Yi Tian Men, Gong Xiang Alley

Also takes tailor-made orders, average price 400-450 yuan.

Kang Kang Clothing

Add: 6 Di Yi Tian Men, Glong Xiang Alley

Tailor-made Qipao costs between 350-500 yuan a piece, depends on which type of material you choose.

Wo He Yun Er in Shiquan Street

A clothing shop that sells exotic dresses, which mainly come from different ethnic groups. Prices vary from 300 yuan to 800 yuan.

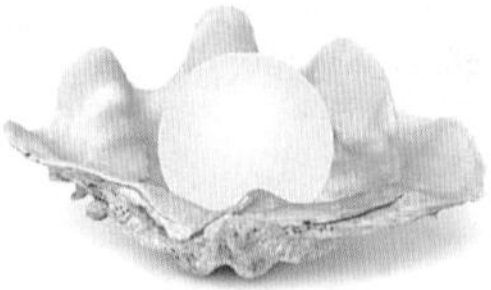

Feed your pearl obsession

"HEY, do not forget to bring me pearls and pearl powder, or I will thump you." After reading this message, I really did not know how to reply to my cousin. Five strings of pearls and 20 packages of pearl powder! I was just wondering if these were for herself or for her to sell?

I've gotten used to doing things for my older female cousin, who is only 12 days older than me, but I could not understand her this time.

She has become obsessed with pearls since I took her to Weitang some time ago. Why do Suzhou's pearls attact her so much?

Well, never mind. I will do this favor for her as usual. Before I left Suzhou on a trip, I went to Weitang again. But it was so awkward for me as a man to go in and buy pearl necklaces and pearl powder.

Weitang is the hometown of Suzhou pearls – and they are all real! Pearls and prices vary depending on their quality. They can be as cheap as 100 to 200 yuan or can be very expensive as well. The value of a pearl is based on several factors. These factors are: the type of pearl, the thickness of its nacre, its luster, cleanliness, the texture of its surface, its shape, its color and its size. Because pearls are naturaly cultivated in living creatures, their quality vary significantly.

I found a stall in the lobby and asked the stallholder to show me some fine quality pearl necklaces. The stallholder was very nice and patient, and showed me a lot of different ones. Finally, I got the pearl necklaces and pearl powder for a reasonable price.

(Shen Dan)

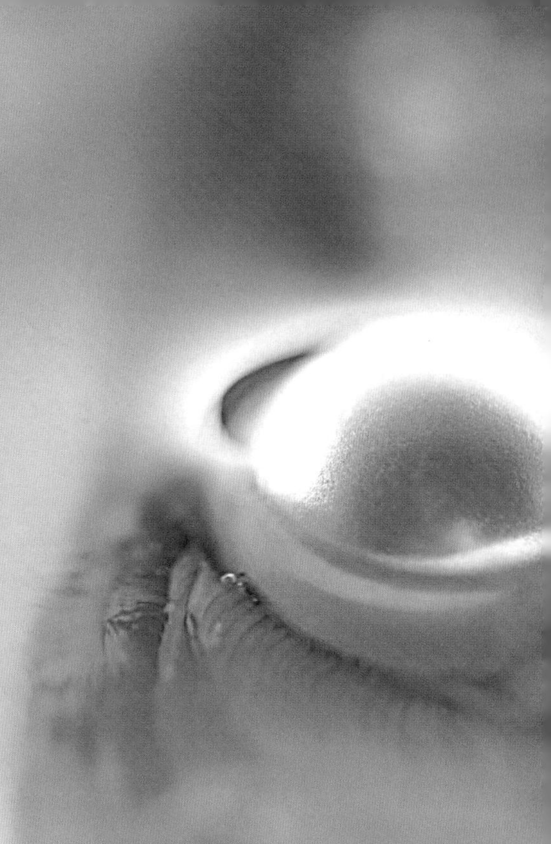

TIPS

Wei Tang pearl is a type of fresh water pearl that is unique to Suzhou. It is really worth buying as a gift.

How to choose:

Size is not the only measurement. The roundness, luster, texture and shape also determine the price. It is not likely that you will become a pearl master in such a short time, but follow your instincts and do comparisions between shops.

How to haggle:

Make sure that at first your offer is as low as possible as you can always offer more if you need to.

Where to buy:

Pearl and Gemstone Market in Weitang (a suburb of Suzhou)

Add: 88 Pearl Lake Road, Weitang, Xiangcheng

Suzhou International Jewelry Center

Add: 123 Pearl Lake Road, Weitang, Xiangcheng

Public transport: Bus No. 83, 84, 711, 712 and 812

Free shuttle bus: you can catch them at Yuan Zhong Yuan Hotel bus stop (147 Wuzhong East Road), buses leaving at 8:30am, 12pm and 2:30pm (traveling time around one hour).

Pictures for New Year's happiness

FOR me it was love at first sight. It is a picture of a chubby Chinese woman with round happy face had a big smile. Her gaily-patterned robe used the same four bright colors throughout and she held a scroll with four characters on it. Loose translation: Family Harmony.

This is a well-loved example of Taohuawu-New Year pictures. Chinese people used to have a tradition of buying these pictures and putting them on their doors and windows at the beginning of the New Year. Removing the old pictures and putting up some new ones was symbolic, and the charming designs and bright colors were an irresistibly festive touch as well. The message on each picture was an auspicious wish that would surely bring good luck and fortune to the family in the coming year.

They are woodblock prints, a folk art form that had its glory days in the Qing Dynasty (1636-1912).

Suzhou's Taohuawu style of making these New Year pictures has been acknowledged by many as the best in China.

These Taohuawu pictures have a special fascination that is unmatched by any other art form. My other favorites depict mothers enjoying time with their children, and women playing musical instruments or working on embroidery. Some pictures portray Chinese legends and gods, and some designs can be quite complicated, like city scenes or kung fu fights.

Four hundred years later, and these charming pictures are still made the same way. However, they are no longer tacked up onto the door for a year; people are collecting them!

(Susan Blauvelt)

TIPS

You can go to the small Taohuawu Museum that is also a working studio. It's inside a private garden, called Pu Garden, quite lovely, and you can sit there on the terrace and have tea and snacks. The address is 8 Jiaochangqiao Road.

It is near the North Temple Pagoda, on an ally called Xi Da Ying Men. The museum is in a house to the right, a bit hidden behind some rock sculptures. No sign indicates the treasures that await you, but two woodcarvers are there, keeping the Taohuawu art form alive and the beautiful prints are for sale.

A few blocks away at 158 Taohuawu Street, is the Gu Zhijun Studio of Engraving Arts, and Gu is also an artist faithful to the time-honored tradition of hand-cut print-making.

Lady Gu Erniang and her inkstones

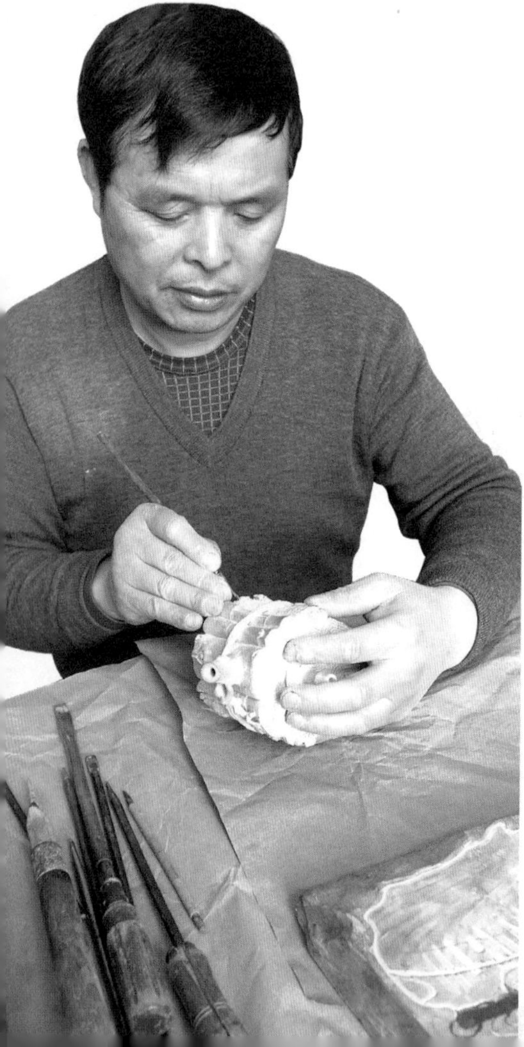

YOU may not have heard of inkstones, but I am sure you have heard of Chinese calligraphy. Together with brushes, paper and inksticks, they are called the Four Treasures of Study and used for writing Chinese calligraphy and also for traditional Chinese painting.

In ancient times, Chinese ink was solidified into inksticks. The inkstick is rubbed over the flat surface of the inkstone with some water to produce ink. Every family in ancient times would have had an inkstone in their household. Gradually, inkstones became more than just a tool, but an artwork produced by brilliant Chinese craftsmen.

Suzhou's Lady Gu Erniang was one of the most famous inkstone craftspeople some 300 to 400 years ago. She inherited her father-in-law's workshop

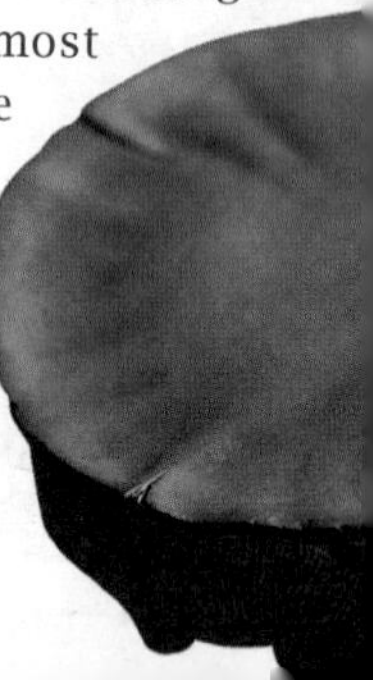

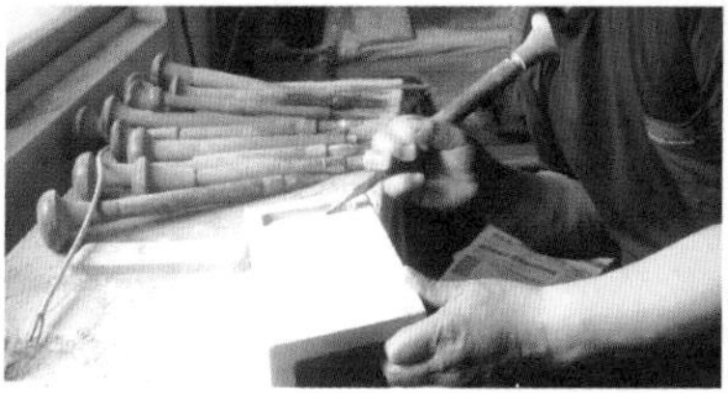

after her husband's death and soon became renowned for her ability to carve and produce beautiful inkstones.

Meanwhile, a famous scholar who had recently retired bought hundreds of Rui Stones (the best material to make an inkstone) and was desperately trying to find Lady Gu Erniang. He traveled thousands of miles looking for her and eventually found her. After some discussions with the lady, he was impressed with her skills of carving inkstone: "The best inkstone is where it displays a softness and warmth after being produced out of a cold, hard stone."

Lady Gu Erniang was also very particular about what stone material she used. Rui Stone and a local stone from Lingyan Hill were her favorite. The exquisiteness of her work and her philosophy of making inkstones are still widely appreciated among the modern inkstone craftsmen in Suzhou.

(Xinlu Cindy Huang)

TIPS

There are many shops that sell inkstones in Cangshu Town and Mudu Town in the Wuzhong suburbs. Some of the famous shops are: Huishi Gallery run by the great craftsman Cai Jinxing (2338 Qiongling Road, Cangshu, Mudu Town, Tel: 0512-6624 2472). Other great craftsmen are Cai Yundi (158 Taohuawu Main Road), and Zhang Wenbiao's Inkstone Research Institute (150/2 Sufu Highway, Cangshu Town, Tel: 0512-6624 2756), etc.

If you are in town, inkstones can be found in some of the stationary shops that sell the Four Treasures of Study, you may find them on Pingjiang Road, Pishi Street, Shantang Street and Minzhi Road.

Buying an inkstone: You don't need to use an inkstone to appreciate its beauty. The price varies from several hundred yuan to tens of thousands of yuan. The craftsmanship and the material determine the quality of an inkstone. Good inkstones often have simple but detailed designs and a dark, rich color. The Rui inkstone is considered to be the most precious and also the dearest, while local Chenni Stone ones are often a lot cheaper. Before your purchase, always make sure to haggle!

Fan away the flames of summer

SUZHOU has been making hand fans since the Song Dynasty (960-1279), nearly 800 years ago. Originally people used leaves and feathers that they mounted on a handle to make fans. This was the origin of fans. They used them to cool themselves, drive away insects, block sunlight, and fan fires in furnaces for making ceramics. The ingenious craftsmen of Suzhou in the Song Dynasty made smaller, portable versions of hand fans by using bamboo, silk and paper. Because hand fans are elegant and eye-catching, the nobles started using them so frequently that they became symbols of status, royalty and power shortly after. That was when the traditional Chinese fan was born. Artists then used hand fans as a medium to express their creativity by painting and writing poems on them.

A typical Su Fan (Su as the name given to all types of fans that are unique from Suzhou), as they call it, now has to go through over 30 processes in its creation. The material, the

shape, the painting and calligraphy, the stamps, the engraved poetry, the carving and the inlays all contribute in deciding the value of a single fan.

In general, girls from Suzhou love to use hand fans made from sandalwood. Just think of their petite hands waving as the tassels swing along – and the sandalwood scent starts to enshroud you and her.

When shopping for a Su Fan, keep in mind that hand fans now symbolize many things like good education, accomplishment, high social status, beauty, happiness, and the femininity of Suzhou women.

(Chen Zidao)

TIPS

Su Fan is a summary of sandalwood, folding, silk palace and paper paddle fans, with prices ranging from hundreds to several thousands of yuan.

Where to buy: Xibei Street harbors such stores as Wenjin Fan shop, Chenchen Fan shop and the sandalwood fan plant as well as the Wangjian fan studio.

Sandalwood Fan Plant:
Add: 90 Xibei Street
Tel: 0512-6751 9987
(Prices start at 1,000 yuan)

Wenjin Fan Shop:
Add: 91 Xibei Street
Tel: 0512-6753 2770
(Prices range from a couple of hundred to a few thousand yuan)

Wangjian Studio:
Add: 17 Shitang Alley Xibei Street
Tel: 139 1405 3412
(Designer fans)

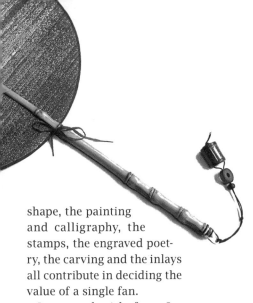

After centuries Ming furniture retains appeal

WOODEN furniture has always been Chinese people's favorite. Among the different types of wooden furniture, the Ming Dynasty (1368-1644) style is considered the most exquisite. A Suzhou-made Ming era bed can be dismantled into 5,000 pieces and reassembled without any bolts or nails.

Whenever I have a chance to see time and again the priceless pieces of original Ming style furniture, I just can't help but wonder: is this hard wood bed really so comfortable? The revelation came after eavesdropping on a story: that in fact it is extremely comfortable.

In 1985, leading Hong Kong connoisseur and collector Grace Wu Bruce met with the late national curator Shixiang Wong. The then fledgling connoisseur made her debut in the business by taking home a piece of fragrant rosewood Ming furniture, a rare choice for the 1980s Hong Kong antique market. She continued to purchase tables, chairs and chests of that category.

In 1990, Shixiang Wong published the English version of his book "On Ming Furniture." Soon afterwards, Ming furniture became popular on the market. Grace Wu Bruce turned from collecting to dealing

and earned the title "Fragrant Rosewood Queen."

As the price of fragrant rosewood and sandalwood soared, Grace Wu Bruce started making a fortune. Transactions of Ming furniture happen around the world, but the best pieces are mostly made in Suzhou.

If you are traveling through Suzhou, you may take the time to view, and perhaps purchase some items of Ming furniture, because they are beautiful items.

(Chen Zidao)

TIPS

Suzhou-made furniture is simple, sturdy and stylish without nails.

Items made from either rosewood, sandalwood or redwood, are still a little expensive and prices are still rising.

Places to shop include Pishi Street market; Arts Museum on Xibei Street and the famous Suzhou Redwood Carving Plant. Guangfu in Wuzhong District also has a number of production plants. Famed ones include Shen En Fang and Zi Tan Ge.

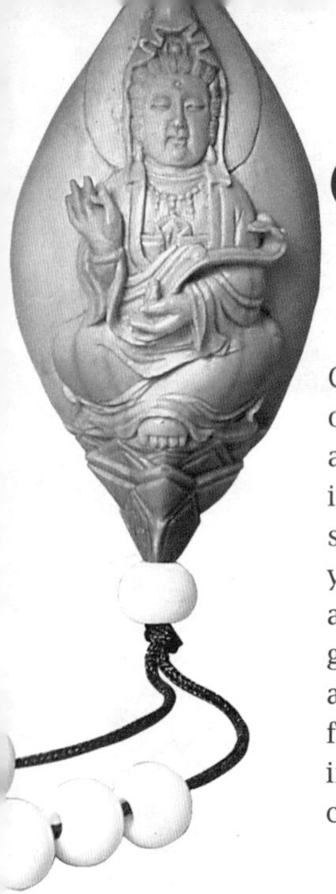

Olive nuts grow into art in craftsmen's hands

CAN you believe that a small olive nut can be carved into a boat, with 24 people on it with vivid facial expressions? I can confidently tell you, it's real. In Xiangshan and Guangfu of Suzhou, a great number of carving artists are capable of transforming a humble olive nut into exquisite art, which is called Olive Nut Carving.

Zhoushan Village, a mountain village in Xiangshan, is a reputable olive nut carving site and almost every household there can carve. It is the cradle for numerous master carvers.

Though the olive nut is not big, olive nut carving has standards on the size of each olive nut - they should be either big or small and the moderate size is usually ignored. Olive nut carving as an art form used to belong to ethnic minorities, but now more and more people are joining in. The olive nut carving from Zhoushan has taken root and become increasingly popular in Beijing and Shanghai where they are keenly sought after.

(Fan Yi)

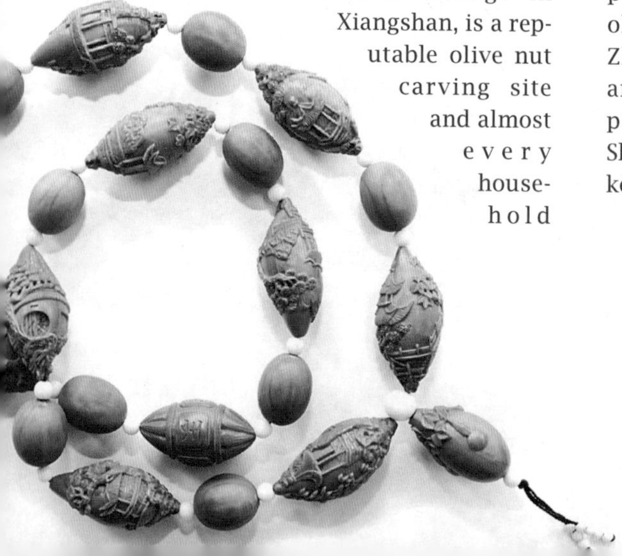

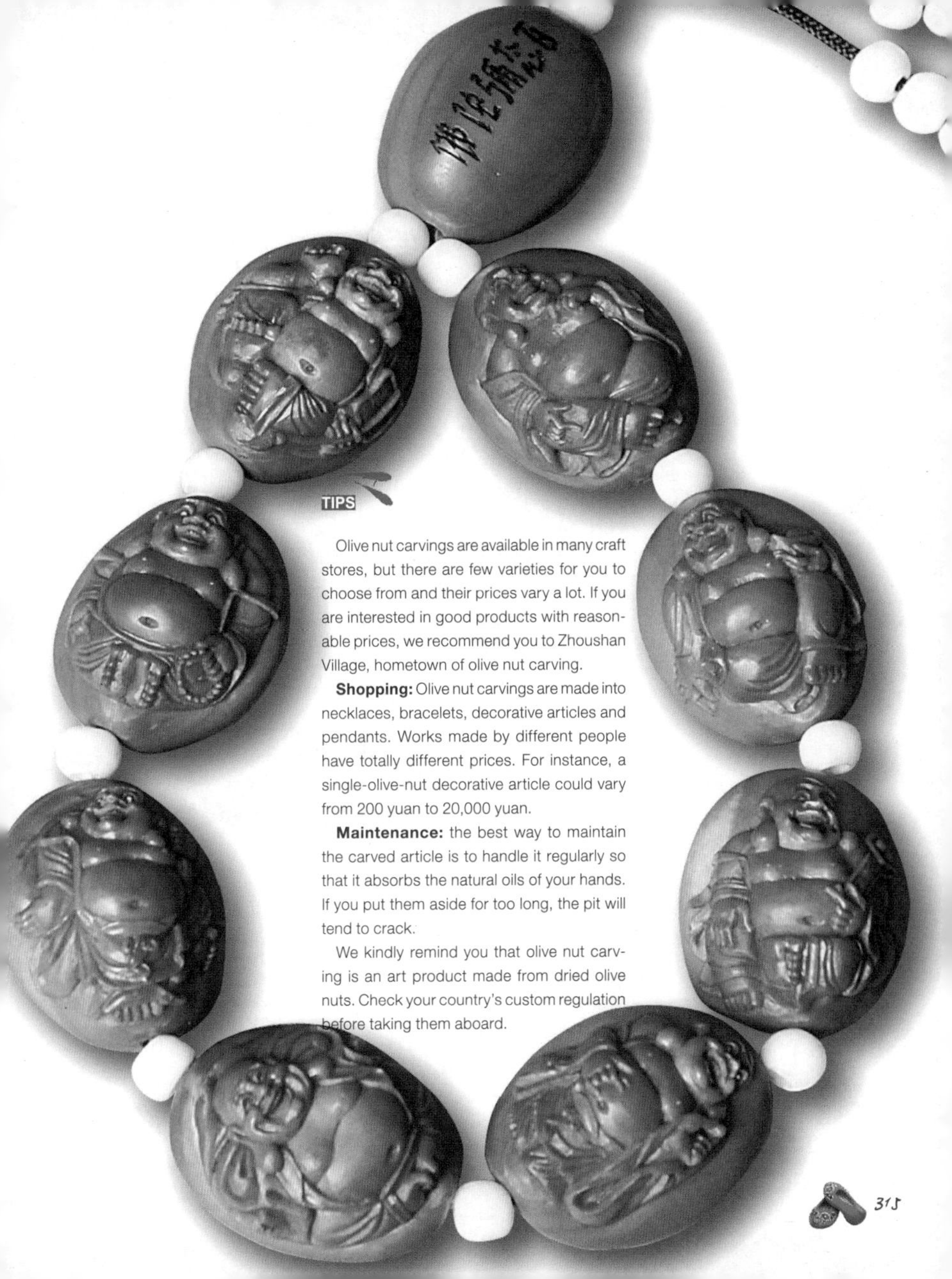

TIPS

Olive nut carvings are available in many craft stores, but there are few varieties for you to choose from and their prices vary a lot. If you are interested in good products with reasonable prices, we recommend you to Zhoushan Village, hometown of olive nut carving.

Shopping: Olive nut carvings are made into necklaces, bracelets, decorative articles and pendants. Works made by different people have totally different prices. For instance, a single-olive-nut decorative article could vary from 200 yuan to 20,000 yuan.

Maintenance: the best way to maintain the carved article is to handle it regularly so that it absorbs the natural oils of your hands. If you put them aside for too long, the pit will tend to crack.

We kindly remind you that olive nut carving is an art product made from dried olive nuts. Check your country's custom regulation before taking them aboard.

Where jade is a woman's best friend

WHEN I first left my hometown Suzhou to go to Australia, I never prepared for spending the next eight years of my life on foreign soil, away from my family. The only piece of jewelry I took with me was a jade bracelet, which was given to me by my mother.

I never took the jade bracelet off my wrist. Occasionally I was asked in Australia what the bracelet was made from. Western people consider jade as a symbol of China. For the Chinese it is a treasure, as diamonds are forever to Western people.

When you are in Suzhou, you will notice how much the locals adore jade. It is said that the aura from jade can repel evil spirits. The aura is invisible during the day but can be seen at night. A person who wears jade will be blessed with a safe and sound life.

Like the cut of a diamond, a good piece of jade also needs good craftsmanship. One of the most famous jade craftsmen in history was called Lu Zigang and he was from Suzhou. There are many stories about his excellent jade carving techniques. One was about him receiving an order from the emperor himself, who asked him to carve a hundred horses from a piece of jade. The only problem was that the jade was about the size of a matchbox.

Such seemingly an impossible mission only took Lu Zigang three days to complete. He carved ranges upon ranges of hills and a city gate among them. As for the horses, he carved only three of them, one running towards the gate, one passing

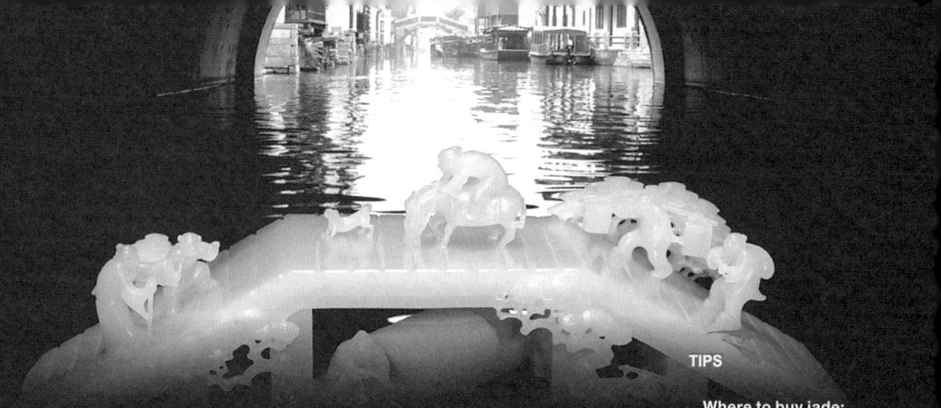

the gate and one merging into the hills. Had the other 97 horses gone into the hills? Or were they inside the city?

Lu Zigang certainly knew the beauty of imagination and used it very well.

The stories of Lu Zigang have become an urban legend in Suzhou. What remains is people's love for jade. Not long ago, I woke up one day and discovered my jade bracelet had broken into two halves. It immediately felt like I had lost a dear friend. Then my mum told me that jade will break on its own when something terrible was about to happen to the owner. The shattering of the jade is its final sacrifice to protect the owner.

I still keep the broken jade bracelet under my pillow and believe it still protects me from evil spirits. For me, jade is a girl's best friend.

(Xinlu Cindy Huang)

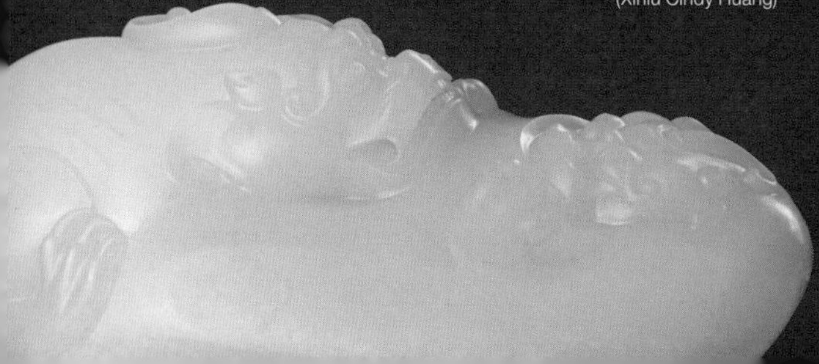

TIPS

Where to buy jade:

1. Xiangwang Alley
2. In Guanqian Pedestrian Street shopping area: Yue Hai Square, Lao Feng Xiang (Jewelry Shop), Guanqian Art and Cultural Market, Xinfu Jade Market, etc.
3. Yuanlin Road
4. Qimen Road, Baita Road, Shiquan Street, Ximei Alley. Jade shops are scatted all over Suzhou.

Where to buy raw jade stone:

1. Raw jade stones are spread out on the ground for sale in Xiangwang Alley everyday.
2. Saturday and Sunday Market in Confucius Temple

How to pick good jade:

Looking for whiteness, moistness, texture and craftsmanship. Most of all, find one that you like the most and is also affordable.

Live in Suzhou

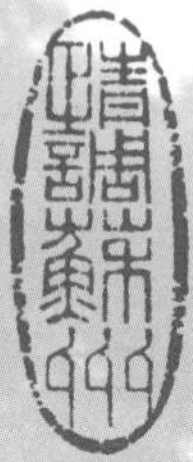

A visit turning into a lifetime,
People visit Suzhou and realize the opportunities.
They decide to stay a little longer.
The opportunities start to grow.
They develop friendships with the locals,
Going home gets forgotten.
Before you know it, Suzhou is home.

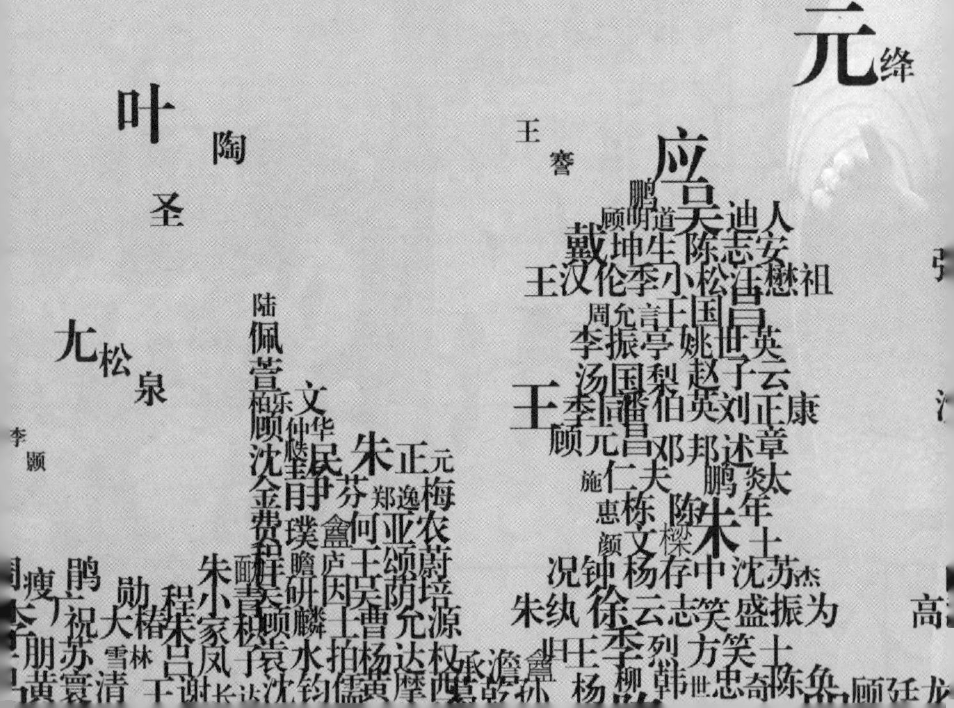

XIV
孙权
项羽
阖闾
干将
吴宽
严讷
李士群
夫差
张籍
薛传钢
伍子胥像
顾启华
章惇
林则徐

Name: Turner Sparks
Nationality: USA
Title: CEO of Mister Softee Ice Cream China
Living in Suzhou for more than seven years

Bringing soft serve to Suzhou streets

I HAVEN'T always wanted to be the "ice cream truck guy," although it does seem like something a child would pick for his future profession.

"When I grow up, I'm going to drive an ice cream truck and eat chocolate cones all day."

My dream job as a child was to be the spokesman for Thrifty Car Rental, but that was only because I thought that with this job I could travel anywhere in the world for free. The first part of that dream never materialized, but when I graduated university in 2004 and found out that I could get paid to teach English in China, and the second half of that dream became a reality.

That is how I ended up in Suzhou.

English teaching lasted for about

a year and by late 2005 I was ready to do something else, but I wasn't ready to leave Suzhou. I called an old friend from my university days and proposed a crazy idea.

"Hey Alex, remember that company called Mister Softee that your family has owned in America for 50 years?"

"Yeah?" Alex Conway said, unsure of what was coming next and confused by the stupidity of the question.

"Why don't we introduce some of their ice cream trucks to Suzhou?"

"OK," he said, without thinking it through.

"Awesome," I said, without thinking anything through.

"Wait," Alex said. "We should probably make sure it's OK with my Dad first."

Alex and I brought in a third partner and together we spent the next 12 months trying to prepare for a task that had never previously been attempted by a foreign company in China. We were going to set up an American style ice cream truck on the streets of Suzhou.

We toured factories where they made the cones, we held taste tests to tailor our flavors to the Chinese market (people loved the kiwi ice cream and hated anything butterscotch) and we met with government officials to convince them that the purpose of our business was not to run over children with our brightly colored trucks.

Eventually the government relented, the menu came together and our first ice cream truck hit the streets of Suzhou on October 1, 2007. Since that time we have sold millions of ice cream products including cones, sundaes, shakes, milk tea floats and anything else we can dream up.

Our fleet of trucks cover territories all over Jiangsu Province and, through franchising, we are on our way to reaching our goal of having trucks in cities throughout China.

Name: James McGough
Nationality: Ireland
Career: Business Consultant/Musician
Live in Suzhou for more than seven years

Finding a little piece of Ireland in China

I DESCRIBE myself as "adaptable." I have lived in many countries including Ireland, Australia, New Zealand, the USA and Vanuatu, and in many cities, "four years here and four years there." Suzhou is the one city where I have spent the longest time so far and I have no plans to leave.

Suzhou is an amazing city of contrasts; ancient and advanced, energetic and calm. Suzhou is also a city of great style where its local people value their culture, their music and a quiet life of relaxation and chatting with their friends.

In my free time I ride an electronic bicycle around the city. I especially like the old town area of Pingjiang Road running alongside one of Suzhou's many canals with craft shops, tea houses, restaurants and cafes. Another special area for me is Baitadong Road where they have converted several old pre-reform factory buildings into loft-style nightlife venues.

I'm very familiar with the nightlife in Suzhou, especially as I have set up two bands in the city with musicians coming from England, Scotland, the USA and Ireland. All of my music colleagues work in regular jobs during the week and play music on evenings and weekends; we have all met in Suzhou.

They often perform three or four times each week in Suzhou and neighboring cities like Wuxi and Shanghai. They play a variety of music genres. The original "Dash Band" was formed in 2008 to play American country music, blues and rock music, while the most recently formed "Boxty Rebellion" came together in 2010 and plays traditional Celtic and Irish punk music. I'm especially pleased to see the Chinese audience stamping their feet to Irish music!

These days, much of my Suzhou's nightlife is centered around the modern east side of Suzhou on the shores of Jinji Lake. In addition to my residence being on Jinji Lake, most of our music venues are also around the lake.

Places like Li Gong Di have a wide range of restaurants and live music bars. Rainbow Walk on the Hu Xi side of the lake also has many restaurants and bars with great lake views. The more recent Moonlight Pier area on the Hu Dong side of the lake is home to the Suzhou Science Culture & Art Center, a large theater and cinema complex surrounded by lakeside walks, restaurants, cafes, bars and the Times Square shopping street.

I feel at home in Suzhou; from my perspective the cultures of Ireland and China have some strong similarities. Chinese people care for their friends, enjoy chatting with each other, enjoy going out, having a drink and singing songs just like we do in Ireland.

Name: Kim Mahaffy
Nationality: Australian
Title: General Manager for Renais-
sance Suzhou Hotel
Live in Suzhou for more than six
years

Kunqu Opera? Yes, I can!

I HAVE lived in Suzhou for six years now and I can say my life has completely changed just as the landscape has changed since my arrival in 2005.

I have found in Suzhou a community of caring and family-minded people – ready to laugh, share their meals, help you find directions or in particular share proud stories of their long and colorful history.

Over my time here I have found it

difficult to learn the language, since my role is to create an International Hotel experience – everyone wants to talk to me in English. I have attempted in vain many times to take lessons but when I am not working I want to be exploring my new country so my Mandarin revolves around eating, shopping and traveling.

Suzhou is such an amazing blend of ancient and modern China, I love to be in a high-rise shopping mall sipping a Starbucks in the morning and to take an afternoon stroll down the quaint Pingjiang Road enjoying stewed milk bean curd, sipping licorice tea, and watching one of the numerous brides and grooms taking wedding shots.

Of all the amazing experiences I have enjoyed since moving to Suzhou, the one that stands out most is my transformation to a Kunqu Opera star. After an early start (7am), I was getting loads of oily make-up to make my face porcelain white, while peony-colored eye shadow and dark liner made my eyes dramatically beautiful.

A hairstyle created with glue and a traditional wig made sure no one, not even my own mother, could tell who this face belonged to.

I dressed in the robes and flowing pants and then my lessons began with Ms Zhou, a real Kunqu Opera star. She patiently showed me the way to place my feet, my head, my hands, my eyes – how to enchant the audience. These finishing touches helped transform me, a five-foot-seven Australian girl into a traditional Kunqu Opera star.

I know one day I will leave this beautiful place but I know I have so many wonderful memories of Suzhou and it will always hold a special place in my heart.

Daniel likes Suzhou!

My name is Daniel. lam 5 years old, my mother is from Spain and my father is Italian. I lived in Suzhou since my birth. So, lam one third Spanish one Italian and one third "suzhou ren" I enjoy living at Suzhou, the most I like is spring and autumn time when I go out with my bike to the park. There are many parks at Suzhou. Close to my home there is a lake with lots flowers. every season the lake looks different, it is very beautiful. My parents say that we cannot find something similar in our countries. I like to see the grandpas dancing at the night, doing taichi and especially when they play with the swords. meanwhile I can practice skating

I am student at the last year in the International kindergarden at Suzhou Foreign Language School. I have a lot of friends at the school. I go to the school very happy every day. I am full of energy all the time !! I am learning a lot at the school. Mum says my drawings are improving also maths and english are getting better. I like being with people. I like to talk every time, everywhere. it doesn't matter which language I use: Spanish. Italian. English or Chinese... I like Suzhou. I like my school!

Itineraries

Take a one-day tour and unlock the beauty of Suzhou

Route 1:

Morning: Lion Forest Garden – Humble Administrator's Garden – Suzhou Museum

Lunch: Guanqian Pedestrian Street

Afternoon: Panmen Gate Scenic Spot – Canglang Pavilion – Pingjiang Road

Dinner: Pingjiang Road (wherever you like)

After dinner: Enjoy Suzhou Pingtan Opera or Kunqu Opera

Route 2:

(On weekends, we recommend Route 2)

Morning: Confucian Temple (Brick Carving Museum) – Canglang Pavilion – Master-of-Nets Garden

Lunch: Shiquan Street

Afternoon: Panmen Scenic Spot – Humble Administrator's Garden (or Suzhou Museum, Lion Forest Garden) – Pingjiang Road

Dinner: Pingjiang Road

In Shiquan Stree

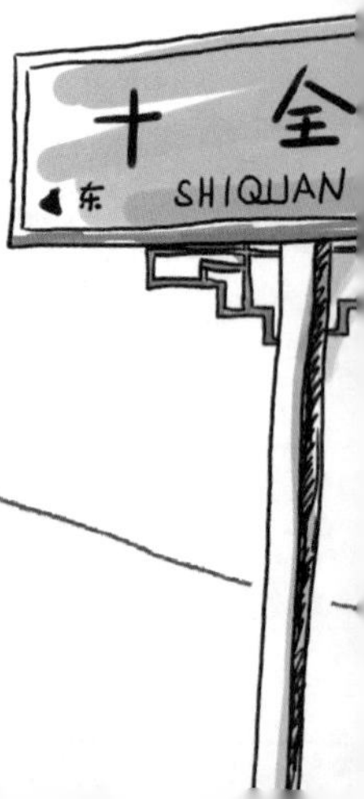

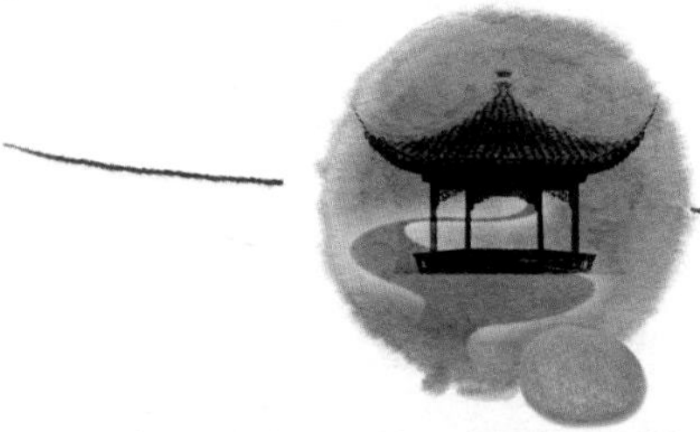

Master-of-Nets Garden 网师园

Tiger Hill

Shantang Street

Route 3:

Morning: Shantang Street (on foot or by boat)

Lunch: Shantang Street

Afternoon: Mountain Villa with Embracing Beauty – Humble Administrator's Garden – Ancient Xumen Gate (Wannian Bridge)

Dinner: Shiquan Street

After dinner: Night tour in Master-of-Nets Garden

Mountain Villa with Embracing Beauty

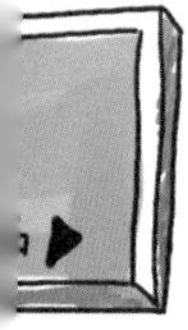

Wannian Bridge

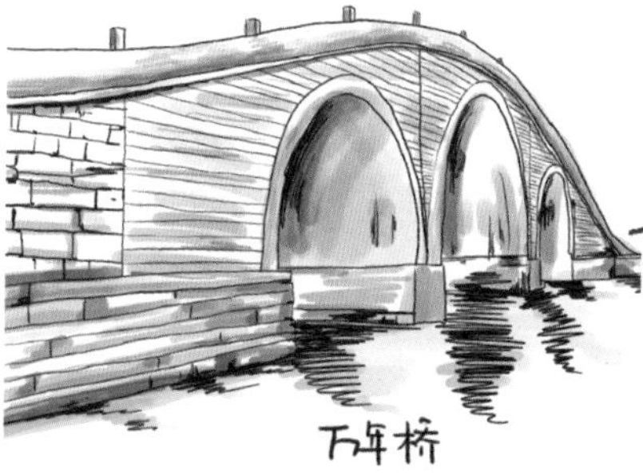

Humble Administrator's Garden

Two-day tours

Route 1:

First day:

Morning: Tiger Hill – West Garden Temple – Lingering Garden

Lunch: Shantang Street

Afternoon: Panmen Gate Scenic Spot – Canglang Pavilion – Confucian Temple – Shiquan Street (You will be greeted by several charming lanes, Sheng Jia Dai is one of them. If time permits, you can also stroll around Soochow University)

Dinner: Shiquan Street, tour in Master-of-Nets Garden (or the city moat cruise). Then kill some time in a bar on Changxu Road and stay over in Shiquan Street

Second day:

Ancient Street of Fengmen Gate (early morning) – Mountain Villa with Embracing Beauty – Humble Administrator's Garden – Suzhou Museum – Lion Forest Garden

Lunch: Pingjiang Road

Afternoon: Pingjiang Road – Couple's Garden Retreat

Night: Dinner at Li Gong Di (or Rainbow Walk), tour Jinji Lake and stay in Suzhou Industrial Park

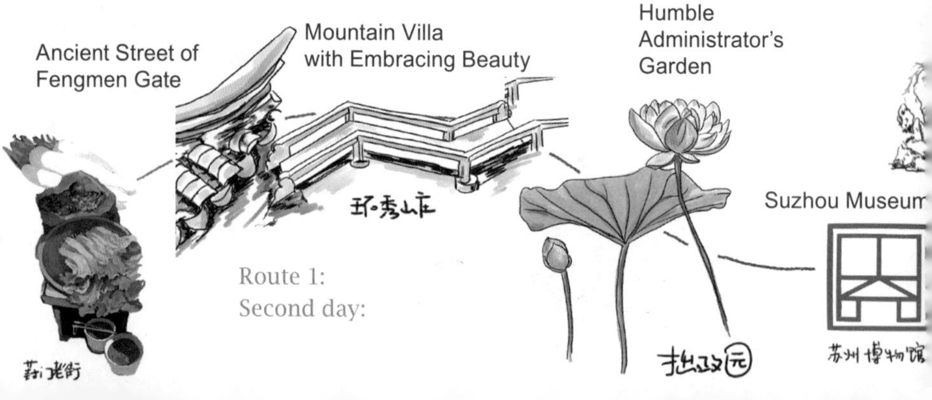

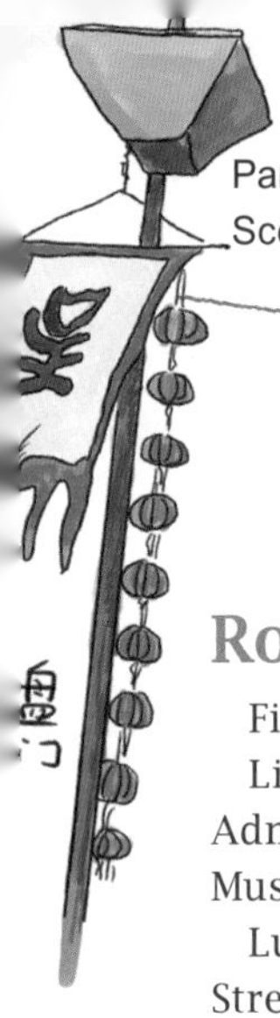

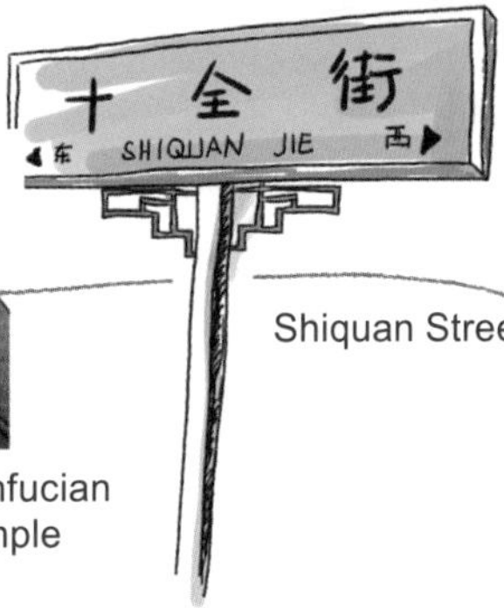

Route 2:

First day:

Lion Forest Garden – Humble Administrator's Garden – Suzhou Museum

Lunch: Guanqian Pedestrian Street

Mountain Villa with Embracing Beauty – Canglang Pavilion – Panmen Gate Scenic Spot – Night cruise on city moat

Stay in hotel on Pingjiang Road

Second day:

Bird and Flower Market, taste Suzhou noodles as breakfast

Morning: Tiger Hill

Then leave for the ancient water town Zhouzhuang or Tongli

Route 3:

First day:

Tiger Hill – Shantang Street (lunch here)

Afternoon: Taihu Lake (Sanshan Island or Moonlight Bay), stay in local inn, taste fresh fish and shrimps and Bi Luo Chun tea

Second day:

Enjoy Taihu Lake sceneries, then go back to Guanqian Pedestrian Street for lunch

Mountain Villa with Embracing Beauty – Suzhou Museum – Lion Forest Garden – Humble Administrator's Garden

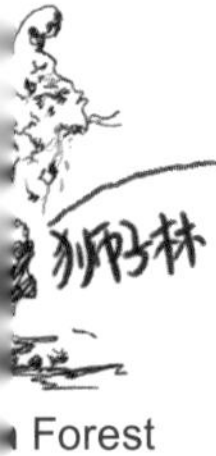

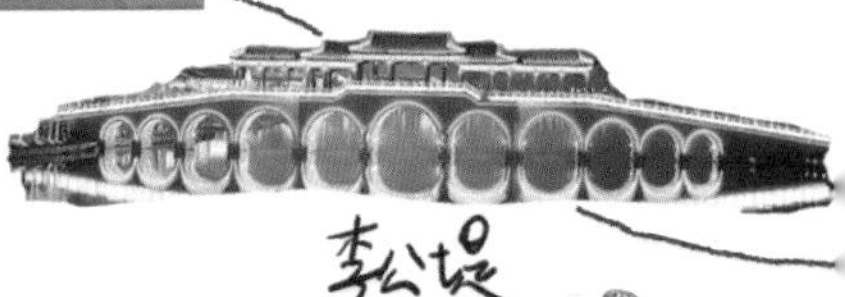

Three-day tours

Route 1:

First day:

Morning, Tiger Hill - West Garden Temple - Lingering Garden

Lunch: Shantang Street

Afternoon, Panmen Gate Scenic Spot - Canglang Pavilion - Confucian Temple - Shiquan Street

Dinner: Shiquan Street

Tour the Master-of-Nets Garden at night (or city moat cruise).

Kill time in the bars of Changxu Road and stay in Shiquan Street

Second day:

Morning, Ancient Street of Fengmen Gate - Humble Administrator's Garden - Suzhou Museum - Lion Forest Garden -- Mountain Villa with Embracing Beauty

Lunch: Pingjiang Road

Afternoon: Pingjiang Road - Couple's Garden Retreat

Night: Dinner at Li Gong Di (or RainboWalk), tour Jinji Lake and stay in Suzhou Industrial Park

Third day:

Morning: Weitang Pearl City

Then leave for Jinxi Town before lunch (or any ancient towns in Suzhou)

Route 2:

First day: Tiger Hill - Shantang Street

Lunch: Shantang Street

Afternoon: Taihu Lake (Sanshan Island or Moonlight Bay), stay in local inn, taste fresh fish and shrimps and Bi Luo Chun tea

Second day: Enjoy the sceneries of Taihu Lake - Baodai Bridge

Mountain Villa with Embracing Beauty - Suzhou Museum - Lion Forest Garden - Humble Administrator's Garden (suggest visiting at a late time, with less visitors) - Guanqian Pedestrian Street

Night: Stay in Pingjiang Road,

appreciate Kunqu Opera and Pingtan

Or stay in Shiquan Street, tour the night Master-of-Nets Garden, kill time in Changxu Road

Third day:

Fengmen Hengjie Street (early morning) - Panmen Scenic Spot - Lion Forest Garden - Confucian Temple

Noon: Leave for Zhouzhuang (or Tongli)

Route 3:

First day:

Morning: Tiger Hill - Lingering Garden - Hanshan Temple (Or West Garden Temple)

Afternoon: Taihu Lake (Sanshan Island or Moonlight Bay), stay in local inn, taste fresh fish and shrimps and Bi Luo Chun tea

Second day:

Morning: Ancient town Luzhi

Afternoon: Weitang Pearl City

Night: dinner at Li Gong Di (or RainboWalk), tour Jinji Lake and stay in Suzhou Industrial Park

Third day:

Morning: Fengmen Hengjie Street (early morning) - Panmen Scenic Spot - Canglang Pavilion - Confucian Temple

Afternoon: Mountain Villa with Embracing Beauty - Humble Administrator's Garden - Pingjiang Road

Our five-star hotels

Pan Pacific Suzhou Hotel	0512-6510 3388	259 Xinshi Road, Suzhou
Garden Hotel	0512-6778 6778	99 Daichengqiao Road, Suzhou
Suzhou Aster Hotel	0512-6829 1888	156 Sanxiang Road, Suzhou
Shangri-La Hotel	0512-6808 0168	168 Tayuan Road, Suzhou New District
New City Garden Hotel	0512-6825 0228	1 Shishan Road, Suzhou New District
Crowne Plaza Suzhou Hotel	0512-6761 6688	168 Xinggang Street, Suzhou Industrial Park
Suzhou Jinji Lake Grand Hotel	0512-6288 7878	168 Guobin Road, Suzhou Industrial Park, Suzhou
Palace Lán Resort & Spa Suzhou	0512-6298 8888	Yangcheng Lake Travel Resort, Suzhou Industrial Park
Kempinski Hotel Suzhou	0512-6289 7888	1 Guobin Road, Suzhou Industrial Park
Traders Hotel	0512-5868 7788	42 Renmin Middle Road, Zhangjiagang City, Suzhou
Xin Yuan Holiday Hotel	0512-5881 8888	8 Chenyang Road, Zhangjiagang City, Suzhou

Huafang Jinling International Hotel	0512-5881 1888	388 Changan Middle Road, Zhangjiagang City, Suzhou
Changshu International Hotel	0512-5210 1888	288 Huanghe Road, Changshu City, Suzhou
Changshu Tianming Grand Hotel	0512-5287 7777	12 Haiyu North Road, Changshu City, Suzhou
Crowne Plaza Hotel Changshu	0512-5272 9999	6 Kaiyuan Avenue, Changshu City, Suzhou
Yushan Jinjiang Hotel	0512-5211 8888	8 Beimendajie, Changshu City, Suzhou
Swissotel Kunshan Hotel	0512-5788 5788	387 Qianjin Middle Road, Kunshan Development Zone, Suzhou
YiZui Crown Hotel	0512-5733 8888	216 Qianjin Middle Road, Kunshan Development Zone, Suzhou
Garden Hotel	0512-5353 1888	59 Renmin North Road, Taicang City, Suzhou
Jinjiang International Hotel Taicang	0512-5358 0000	89 Shanghai East Road, Taicang City, Suzhou
Tongli Lakeview Hotel	0512-6333 7888	8 Jiulihu Road, Tongli Town, Wujiang City, Suzhou
Noble Resort Suzhou	0512-6651 5999	18 Changsha Island, Taihu National Tourism Resort District, Suzhou
Dyna Sun Hotel	0512-6392 8888	88 Wenyuan Road, Wujiang City, Suzhou
Kingrace Hotel Changshu	0512-5218 8888	73 Ximendajie, Changshu City, Suzhou
Merryland Traders Hotel Changshu	0512-5298 8888	176 Zhujiang Road, Changshu, Suzhou

Youth hostels

Suzhou Water Town Youth Hostel
Add: No. 27, Dashitou Lane, Renmin Road, Suzhou
Tel: 0512-6521 8885

Suzhou Ming Han Tang International Youth Hostel
Add: 81 Guangji Road, Suzhou
Tel: 0512-6583 3331

Suzhou Joya Youth Hostel
Add: Daxinqiao Lane 21-1, Pingjiang District, Suzhou
Tel: 0512-6770 9649

Hostelling International-Suzhou
Add: 178 Xiangwang Road, Suzhou
Tel: 0512-6510 9418

Other economy hotels

Home Inns

Humble Administrator's Garden Store
Add: No. 20, Bashang Lane, Yuanlin Road (opposite to Lion Grove Garden)
Tel: 0512-6728 8808

Shantangjie Store
Add: No. 127, Xizhongshi, Pingjiang District
Tel: 0512-8220 5888

Hanting Inns & Hotels

Yinmaqiao Store
Add: 525 Shizi Street, Canglang Street
Tel: 0512-8777 9918

Guanqian II Store
Add: No. 218, Yangyu Lane, Pingjiang District
Tel: 0512-6581 1222

Useful telephone numbers

IF you're looking for tourism information or happen to face some emergencies, please do not hesitate to dial the following numbers to meet your requirements.

Name of the Authority	Tel. (Area Code: +86 512)
Service Line of City Post	65111555
Tourist information	65203131
Suzhou Garden Ticket Administration Center	65731671
Tourist Complaint Hotline	65223377
Dial-a-Cab	67776777
Cab Compliant Hotline	96196
Suzhou Bus Station Hotline	65776577
Railway Station Inquiry Service	12306
Train Ticket Telephone Sales	95105105
Bus Inquiry Service	96196
Airport Bus Service	65231774 (Pudong); 13771818097(Wuxi)
Highway Inquiry Service	96777
Citizen Service Hotline	12345
Bank of China (Suzhou Branch)	65113558
Consumer Complaint Hotline	12315
Suzhou Post Services	11185
Weather Forecast	96121
First-aid	120
Police	110
Traffic Accident	122
Suzhou Children's Hospital	65223820
No. 1 Hospital Affiliated to Soochow University	65223637

Where to go, you should have known

Air Travel

Despite being an important tourist destination, Suzhou does not have its own international airport at present. It is best to use the airports of nearby Shanghai. Shanghai Hongqiao International Airport (SHA) and Pudong International Airport (PVG) are frequently used by domestic and international visitors.

Hongqiao Airport (SHA) is 86 kilometers (about 53 miles) away from Suzhou. Upon arrival, passengers can walk to the connected Shanghai Hongqiao Railway Station, and then take a 30-minute bullet train to Suzhou. The nearby Hongqiao West Traffic Center also operates coaches to Suzhou.

Pudong International Airport (PVG) is located 120 kilometers (about 75 miles) away from Suzhou. There are scheduled airport buses running to Suzhou, and vice versa.

Buses from PVG to Suzhou:

Add: The parking lots at the 2nd floor of PVG's terminal building.

Buses from Suzhou to PVG:

Add: 115, Ganjiang Xi Road

Duration: 3 hours

Tickets: 84 yuan

Regular buses are available from Sunan Shuofang International Airportto Suzhou and the departure interval is around 55 minutes. Address of Suzhou Urban Terminal for Sunan Shuofang International Airport, where you can check in and enjoy free bus service to the airport: (100 Daoqian Street, Suzhou Convention Center)

Train

Suzhou Railway Station

Location: Pingjiang District

Reconstructed in 2011, Suzhou Railway Station is the main gate for passengers to and from this city by rail. Through the Shanghai-Nanjing High-Speed Railway, there are bullet trains from Suzhou to Shanghai, Kunshan, Wuxi, Zhenjiang and Nanjing. On the other hand, from this station, passengers can take fast trains to Chengdu, Xi'an, Yinchuan, Zhengzhou, Xi'ning, Guangzhou, Fuzhou, Yantai among many destinations. The train tickets for this station are printed as Su Zhou.

From Nanjing – (105 yuan) The new G-Series trains will get you to Suzhou in one hour.

From Shanghai – (41 yuan) Trains depart from the Shanghai central station and Shanghai Hongqiao station (40 yuan) getting there in about 25-30 minutes.

Buses that connect to Suzhou Railway Station: Express service No. 2, Normal service No. 1, 6, 7, 8, 10, 33, 38, 40, 44, 50, 69, 79, 80, 81, 83, 102, 103, 166, 178, 202, 317, 502, 518,522, 529; Tour Bus No. 1, 3, 4, 5

Suzhou North Railway Station

Location: Xiangcheng District

This station serves bullet trains running on the Beijing-

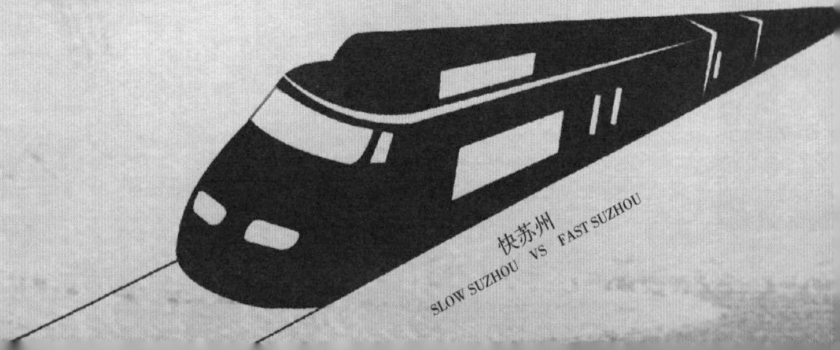

Shanghai High-Speed Railway. Departing from Suzhou, passengers can get to Beijing in five hours. The train tickets are printed as Su Zhou Bei.

Buses that connect to Suzhou North Railway Station: Express service No. 8 and Normal services No. 77, 80, 711, 811 and 819

Suzhou New District Railway Station

Location: Hushuguan Town, New District

This station operates 11 scheduled bullet trains on the Shanghai-Nanjing High-Speed Railway every day. The train tickets are printed as Su Zhou Xin Qu.

Buses that connect to Suzhou New District Railway Station: Normal service No. 306, 326, 329, 335 and 815

Suzhou Industrial Park Railway Station

Location: Suzhou Industrial Park

Everyday, this station serves for 46 bullet trains of the Shanghai-Nanjing High-Speed Railway. The train tickets are printed as Su Zhou Yuan Qu.

Buses that connect to Suzhou Industrial Park Railway Station: Normal service No. 115, 116, 119, 166, 258, and 262

Ticket Offices in the city: 908 Ganjiang Road; 1606 Renmin Road; 558 Sanxiang Road; 166, Xiangwang Road (close to Shiquan Street); 199 South Guangji Road.

Long-distance Bus

Suzhou is known as the "Southeast Gate" to Shanghai and Zhejiang Province because of its well-developed highway network. Three long-distance bus stations are in use in Suzhou nowadays. The Suzhou North Bus Station has the most bus routes to Anhui, Hubei, Fujian, Shandong, Jiangxi, and Zhejiang provinces. Buses also depart for Shanghai from the North Bus Station once every 20 minutes. The ticket price varies from 26 yuan to 30 yuan.

Buses that connect to North Bus Station: Express service No. 2, Normal service No. 10, 26, 55,79, 101

South Bus Station: Located at the corner of Nanhuan Eastern Roadand Yingchun Road. Buses going to Anhui, Hubei, Shandong, Jiangxi, and Zhejiang provinces plus Shanghai are available here.

Buses that connect to South Bus Station: Express service No. 6, Normal service No. 3, 10, 39, 43, 60 and 931

West Station:

Located on Jinshan Road, Suzhou New District. Buses to Anhui and Zhejiang provinces and Shanghai depart from here.

Buses that connect to West Station: Normal service No. 42, 51, 67, 302, 303, 304, 322, 324

Bus

Taking a bus in Suzhou is relatively easy if you have a basic grasp of Chinese, or horribly bewildering if you don't. Buses cover the whole city, run at 10-20 minutes intervals from 5am-11pm on most routes and are a cheap way of getting around. Unfortunately all bus information boards and on-board announcements are in Chinese only, however bus route information can also be found on Google Maps.

Bus fares will be displayed on the bus schedule as well as on a digital display above the driver's seat. Exact change is required, so keep plenty of 1 yuan coins handy. Buses displaying a green or blue "snow-flake" symbol next to the

route number have air-conditioning and an extra 1 yuan surcharge is paid on top of the regular fare.

There are five handy tour route buses numbered Y1-5 - all serve the railway station and connect most of the tourist sites within the city proper, so if you are unfamiliar with the city, they are a good way to familiarize yourself.

Buses are often crowded, and it's good custom to offer your seat to elderly, disabled or mothers with children.

If you are in town for a while, it's advisable to get a Suzhou-Tong card (available from several outlets around town) - it's a prepaid smart-card that gives you 40% discount on bus fares.

Taxis

Suzhou's silver-and-teal VW Santana taxis are a very reasonably priced way of getting around and are easily available outside of rush hour. Fares start at 10 yuan for the first 3 kilometers. Always get a receipt from the taxi driver at the end of the ride, so you may call the taxi company if you have left anything behind.

Few, if any, taxi drivers speak English or any other foreign languages, so be sure to get your hotel's business card, and have the names and addresses of your destinations written in Chinese to show your taxi driver.

Car Renting

If you want to drive a car on your own:

The car rental company would usually require the clients to submit their original passport and driver's license approved by authorities in China to be copied and their credit card for preauthorized debit.

If you not only require a car, but also a driver from the rental company:

The car rental company would generally require the client to submit a written letter of attorney in which certain qualifications are requested, for instance, driver's competence in spoken English, good communication skills and gratifying services among others and the company will help find several qualified drivers for the client to choose from.

Some rental companies and phone numbers:

Datong Car Rental Company: 0512-6752 5566

CARPLUS Auto Leasing Corporation: 0512-6767 1666

Suzhou Jinhua Enterprise Service Ltd: 0512-6807 3417

Dayang Car Rental Company: 0512-6515 3028

Lianhuajiaxun Car Rental Company: 0512-6260 0358

Youhe Car Rental Company: 0512-6862 8830

Bicycle

Cycling is an interesting way to explore Suzhou.

How to rent a public bicycle?

Foreign tourists from 16 years to 65 years old can apply for a visitor card for public bicycles with their passports. Pay a 300-yuan deposit and 20 yuan for pre-consumption when applying for the card. Deposits will be refunded when the visitor card is returned. Remember to submit the passport, rental card and the rental receipt when returning the card.

The first hour of using a public bicycle is free after which extra fees will be charged on an hourly basis (time less than one hour will still be calculated as one hour). The top fee per day is 10 yuan.

Application sites

1. 1724 Renmin Road (in Jintaiyang Health Care Shop)
2. 461 Zhuhui Road (in Xinzhu Hotel)

Tel: 400 071 1882

Metro

The Suzhou Metro is under construction and will open in 2012.

Talk

The local Suzhou dialect belongs to the Wu family of Chinese dialects, and is not mutually intelligible with standard Mandarin. As Suzhou is the traditional cradle of Wu culture, the Suzhou dialect is taken to be the prestige dialect of Wu Chinese. As such, Suzhou is the place to start for people who want to learn to speak Wu Chinese. However, as with elsewhere in China, most people are bilingual in the local dialect and Mandarin, and you should have no problem speaking Mandarin unless you are talking to the elderly.

English is not widely spoken, though staff at major hotels will likely be able to speak some basic English. Be sure to have the names of your destinations written in Chinese, so that taxi drivers can take you to where you want to go.

Stay Safe

Suzhou is a safe place on the whole, but there are a few things to watch out for.

On crowded buses around the bus station and the train station, take good care of your belongings.

Be aware that the charge for rickshaws is negotiable: usually the starting fare is 10 yuan. With the best intentions, we do not suggest you to go to the scenic sites recommended by rickshaws.

Remember that in China it's LEGAL for car drivers to make a right turn against a red light - so we kindly inform you to be careful and keep an eye out in both directions when crossing the streets, to avoid the cars, particularly the trucks, which usually drive too fast at the intersection.

WiFi Cafes

New Island Cafe has many locations throughout Suzhou and China offering free WiFi.

Starbucks and Costa Coffee have several branches in Suzhou, both offering free WiFi.

Climate

Suzhou, located on the eastern coast of China, lies within the humid subtropical climate zone and is characterized by a monsoon climate. The city enjoys abundant sunlight, a long frost-free period, and high temperatures accompanied by ideal rains.

The average annual temperature in Suzhou is 15.9 degrees Celsius, but July reaches an average high of 28.2 degrees and January a low of 3.6 degrees. The year's precipitation in Suzhou amounts to around 1,110.6 mm, with about 128 rainy days. During June every year, it rains the heaviest and longest.

Four Seasons in Suzhou:

Spring (March-May): with an average temperature of 14.2 degrees however the temperature doesn't maintain itself during the entire length of spring. April can have temperatures under zero.

Summer (June-August): the hottest season of the year with an average temperature of 26.6 degrees. June is the rain season; July is the hottest month and can reach a maximum temperature of 35 degrees.

Autumn (September-November): with an average temperature of 17.6 degrees, the season starts with days of over 30 degrees and cools as September arrives.

Winter (December-February): The coldest weather is felt during late January (as low as -8 degrees), but winter's average temperature is of 4.4 degrees. In recent years, winter has not shown itself to be as cold.

For more information, visit www.livingsu.com

快苏州

SLOW SUZHOU VS FAST SUZHOU

Xia Xia Nei

(Acknowledgements)

THE mighty Great Wall was not built in just one day, nor was it built by just one person.

If you have not already noticed, as Chinese, we very much value Collectivism in our culture and we believe there is nothing we cannot achieve by combining individuals' strengths into something as remarkable as the Great Wall.

When we decided to put together a book about Suzhou in English, we had doubts and hesitations. We were afraid that our Chinglish would not be able to describe the allure of Suzhou.

Fortunately for us, we have found some most valuable companions along this journey. Some of them are Westerners who have made Suzhou their home. Some were born in Suzhou and now live on other continents. However, they all have one thing in common - they have never stopped loving this city and would like to let the world know how unique and beautiful Suzhou really is.

Well, let the music start. We have a long list of people we would like to extend our appreciation to.

First of all, we would like to thank our foreign friends: Michael Paul Frank (USA), Mochizuki Hisashi (Japan), Steven Bernath (Australia), Suzanne Hill (Australia), Michael van Zyl (South Africa) and Robert Fraser (USA). Your brilliant photos or your insights on how to adequately and artistically compose English, made it possible for us to present to our readers a book that is easy to read and hard to forget.

We also need to thank our Chinese brothers and sisters who have captured the beauty of Suzhou through their cameras: Wang Wenlan, Liu Lei, Wang Miao, Li Ge, He Yanguang, Xie Hailong, Yu Zhixin, Zhang Feng, Hu Jinxi, Yan Daojing, Han Congyao, Tang Sheng, Bao Liwen,Gong Jun, Zhang YanLong, Yu Dabo, Wu Wanyi, Lin Junwu, Ruan Qiang, Qin Haifeng, Wang Hao, Gu Changchun, Yang Xiaozheng, Shen Han, Zhu Hong, Hu Rongfu, Hu Jiangqiao, Que Mingfen, Wang Haiyan, Yao Yongqiang, Xu Zhiqiang, Yang Haishi, Yu

Xiang, Qi Zhenlin, Pu Jianming and Jiang Shiyin.

We would like to give special thanks to Yu Feng and Chen Gao, two experts from the Foreign Affairs Office of Suzhou Municipal Government, Wang Ming, designer of the book cover, Cai Tinghui, a carving master, and Bo Wenxi (8 years old) from Suzhou Jinchang Foreign Language Experimental School, who is the illustrator for the article "Daniel likes Suzhou". Last but not least, we would like to thank Yang Ximeng and the team from Shanghai Daily for their outstanding work.

We have to stop here as the music is fading away (why do "thank you" speeches always have such short time limits?), but we will not forget anyone who has helped with his or her wonderful input.

Suzhou thanks you all, dearest friends, with our most sincere appreciation.

To all our readers

To publish a book about Suzhou in English has been a great challenge for us. We started composing the articles in December 2011 and the final drafts were sent to print in March 2012. For a city that has so much history and so many stories, four months were really not quite enough. However, we eagerly want to present to you Suzhou as never presented before. We are looking forward to your feedback so we might present it better in the next edition. Please send your feedback and comments to:

theallureofsuzhou@163.com

Or visit our official website: www.isuzhou.me

First Edition 2012

图书在版编目（CIP）数据
情调苏州：英文 / 陈嵘、黄漪沦等编著；陆禾禾等译.
— 北京：外文出版社，2012
ISBN 978-7-119-07552-5
Ⅰ.①情… Ⅱ.①陈… ②黄… ③陆… Ⅲ.①旅游指南—苏州市—英文 Ⅳ.① K928.953.3
中国版本图书馆 CIP 数据核字 (2012) 第 038394 号

主　　编：陈嵘　黄漪沦
翻　　译：陆禾禾 等
责任编辑：兰佩瑾
装帧设计：盛诚　小茹　达子
责任照排：小惠

情调苏州
出版：外文出版社有限责任公司
（中国北京西城区百万庄大街24号）
邮政编码：100037
网址：http://www.flp.com.cn
印刷：苏州报业传媒集团有限公司
苏报印务分公司
发行：新华书店
开本：889mm × 1194mm　1/32
版次：2013年10月第1版 第3次印刷
书号：ISBN 978-7-119-07552-5
定价：58.00元（英文）

Published by Foreign Languages Press Co. Ltd
24 Baiwanzhuang Road, Beijing 100037, China
http://www.flp.com.cn　E-mail: flp@cipg.org.cn
Printed in the People's Republic of China

謝

[ziaV\]

謝

[ziaVr]

è le
饿了 – Hungry

kě le
渴了 – Thirsty

hǎo lèi
好累 – Too tired

jiā bīng
加冰 – More ice

wǒ de mā ya
我的妈呀 – Oh My God

piào liang
漂亮 – Pretty

zhēn bang
真棒 – Great

wǒ ài nǐ
我爱你 – I love you

qīn ài de
亲爱的 – Dear

dòu nǐ wán
逗你玩 – Just kidding

bú jiàn bú sàn
不见不散 – See you next time

When greeting someone, call a woman "美女" (Pronunciation: měi nǚ; Meaning: pretty woman) or call a man "帅哥" (Pronunciation: shuài gē ; Meaning: handsome guy) . You will then strike a good impression.

When you want to invite a lady to dinner, you should say "我买单" (Pronunciation: wǒ mǎi dān; Meaning: Dinner is on me)

If you simply want to strike up a conversation, you can say "今天天气不错" (Pronunciation: jīn tiān tiān qì bú cuò; Meaning: Nice day today)

When you are buying souvenirs, no matter how much they ask for, always say to them "太贵了" (Pronunciation: tài guì le; Meaning: Too expensive) and then haggle.